Economy and State

Economy and Society series

Nina Bandelj & Elizabeth Sowers, *Economy and State*
Bruce G. Carruthers & Laura Ariovich, *Money and Credit*
Miguel A. Centeno & Joseph N. Cohen, *Global Capitalism*

Economy and State

A Sociological Perspective

Nina Bandelj
and
Elizabeth Sowers

polity

First published in 2010 by Polity Press

Polity Press
65 Bridge Street
Cambridge CB2 1UR, UK

Polity Press
350 Main Street
Malden, MA 02148, USA

ISBN-13: 978-0-7456-4454-7
ISBN-13: 978-0-7456-4455-4 (pb)

A catalogue record for this book is available from the British Library.

Typeset in 11 on 13 pt Sabon
by Servis Filmsetting Ltd, Stockport, Cheshire
Printed and bound by MPG Books Group, UK

For further information on Polity, visit our website: www.politybooks.com

Contents

Detailed Contents

Detailed Contents

List of Illustrations

List of Illustrations

1

Introduction

On November 4, 2008, the people of the United States of America made history by electing Barack Hussein Obama the country's forty-fourth president, the country's first black chief executive. Three months into his presidency, to aid the crisis-wrought American – and global – economy, Mr Obama's government put in place a stimulus bill of nearly $800 billion, mortgage relief, a huge capital injection into the banking system by the Federal Reserve to lower interest rates and expand credit, and a public–private program for buying up toxic assets. Should President Obama do all this? More generally, to what extent should governments be involved in economic affairs? After all, one of the most familiar economic tropes is that of a "free-market" – free of government intervention.

The connection between the state and the economy has been a perennial issue of social theory and policy, though not always with equal verve. A very basic comparison of the number of news articles on this topic in different time periods is illuminating. For instance, there were about 500 articles mentioning economy and state published in *USA Today* over the twelve months of 2006, or approximately forty per month, compared with the almost 140 articles on that topic that appeared in each of the first three months of 2009. The content varies remarkably as well, from "Inflation reports rev up stocks; Fed's latest stance gains credibility" (August 17, 2006, p. 1B) to "Another big drop: Dow down 508; Fed efforts, rate hint fail to stem massive losses" (October 8,

2008, p. 1B). Why such differences in quantity and content? We suggest that this is because the relationship between economy and state is not of *one kind*, whereby, in the *laissez-faire* spirit, the goal is to strive to maintain as little governmental intervention in economic affairs as possible. Instead, we argue that economy and state intertwine and forge *multiple kinds* of relationships with varied consequences. Our aim is to elucidate the different ways in which state action influences economy, and therefore all of us, in our roles as students, employees, employers, entrepreneurs, homemakers, retirees, consumers, and tax payers. Why does this generation have more trouble finding jobs than did their parents? Are taxes too high? Who is really right about the economy, the Republicans or the Democrats? Should governments do something to reduce social inequality? Why are some nations more prosperous than others? These issues all relate to the role of the state in economy, and we hope to address them in this book.

We adopt a broadly comparative approach and aim to integrate our knowledge of capitalist, socialist, and postsocialist economies, discuss the experiences of the developed as well as the developing world, and tackle the challenges brought by the most recent wave of economic globalization. Across these diverse topics, we pay special attention to how different social forces influence policy decision-making about economic affairs, which, in turn, influences the economy.

This is a short book and we don't claim to exhaust scholarly research on the topic (and you are probably thankful to us for not using up more pages than we do). Specifically, we want to acknowledge three limitations. First, we will place our inquiry primarily in the work of economic sociologists, although references will be made to more general sociological literature and comparisons drawn to work in political science and economics on economy–state nexus. Second, we will focus on the interplay between economy and *modern* nation-states, going back to the past no more than a couple of hundred years. Third, our point of departure is the functioning and organization of the economy rather than state. Hence, we discuss the state governance of two central economic objects (i.e. property and money), two crucial economic subjects (i.e. labor and firms), and two consequential macro-economic processes (i.e. economic development and economic internationalization/globalization). This also provides the rationale for the chapter organization that follows this introduction, where we lay out the theoretical perspectives on economy–state relations. However, before turning to theory, we want to define more precisely what we mean by "economy" and what we mean by "state."

What is Economy?

The word **economy*** has its origin in ancient Greek, where *oikos* ("eco") meant a Greek household and *nomos* ("nomy") meant act, law, or principle. As years passed and the political organization of communities unfolded, "the principles of maintaining a household" became associated with the complex of the activities involving production, distribution, exchange, and consumption of goods and services, which is how we define economy. Although an economy doesn't have to be particularly large (we also speak of local and regional economies), we will use the term to refer mostly to a national economy of a particular country, such as that of the United States, and use the term international or global economy when we refer to the economic activities that encompass multiple countries or even the whole world.

Why should we care about economy? For one, it is an enormous sphere of social life, quantitatively and qualitatively. The Gross Domestic Product (GDP) in the US was over 14 *trillion* dollars in 2008 (Bureau of Economic Analysis 2009). For any one average full-time worker in the US, this means about fifty weeks of working from 9 a.m. to 5 p.m., with relatively little in the way of vacation. Workers in all other Western countries spend less time at work, primarily because they take more holiday and vacation days, ranging between 4 and 5 weeks, which are prescribed by the

---

* Terms in bold throughout the text appear in the glossary at the end of this book.

state in a statutory minimum policy (Dreier 2007). The US has no such policy; thus people work more, but not as much as those in Hong Kong, Bangladesh, Singapore, or Thailand, who average an additional 200 to 300 of work hours per year.

While time at work seems to be linked most directly to economy, most activities outside work are as well. How about shopping, eating out, going to the movies or concerts, getting your car fixed or your clothes cleaned, banking, investing in the stock market, or fixing up homes? Even on vacation, from booking flights and hotels, to getting that cocktail on the beach, to tipping the guy who carries your suitcases to the taxi on the way back, it's all about economy.

Further, "the economy" does not include only paid activities in the formal sector. Non-paid work, work in the informal sector, and illegal work are all part of a nation's economy even if it is harder to evaluate their contribution to GDP. While we will occasionally provide examples of the economy and state connection as it pertains to non-paid work or the informal and illegal economies, most of our discussion will be centered on the production, distribution, exchange, and consumption of goods and services on the legal market. Hence, it seems appropriate that we briefly discuss these other aspects of economy here.

Economic sociologists writing about care work have acknowledged that many activities that contribute importantly to the production of goods and services are not paid, such as household work or the care of children and elderly within families (Trabut and Weber 2009). Others have emphasized that pay for some activities does not adequately reflect the effort required, such as domestic work done by immigrants hired informally or work by inmates in prison. States certainly play a role in these non-paid, non-market activities. For instance, it is the courts, a part of the state apparatus, which tend to exclude prison work from the legal category of employment because they classify it as belonging to the penal rather than the economic sphere. These formal classifications have important life consequences: only employment relationships are subject to labor protection such as the minimum wage, so the legal definition of prison work as non-economic prevents inmates from challenging wages that can be less than $1 per hour (Zatz 2009).

Moreover, informal economic activities are intrinsically linked to the actions of state because, as Portes and Haller (2005) emphasize, the **informal economy** exists only because of the regulations enacted to create the formal economy. The expansion of the state's capacity to intervene in economic affairs increases the opportunities for informal economic action (Lomnitz 1988). There would be no tax evasion schemes if not for the system of taxation. Thus, it is precisely the state regulation of the economy that gives rise to the opportunities to engage in informal economic activity. It could be said, then, that the informal economy exists not outside of the formal economy, but rather because of it.

There are also many activities that are considered illegal but are part of the economy because they involve production, distribution, and consumption of – albeit illicit – goods and services. The value of illegal trade is substantial. According to the *Human Development Report* (UNDP 1999: 103), "The illegal drug trade in 1995 was estimated at $400 billion, about 8% of world trade, more than the share of iron and steel or of motor vehicles, and roughly the same as textiles (7.5%) and gas and oil (8.6%)." A crucial point related to the economy–state discussion is the fact that whether an activity is considered illicit as opposed to licit is a result of legal regulation, not because of the intrinsically damaging nature of drugs and gambling as opposed to alcohol and stock market investing, for instance. You could go to the Netherlands and order a joint in a coffee shop in Amsterdam in the way you would coffee in Arlington, Virginia. Or you can gamble as you please in Las Vegas but would be arrested for this in Los Angeles. Thus, it is clear that the role of the federal and state government is central for what we define as the **illegal economy**. More generally, one of the foundational roles of the state in economy is the regulation of what can or cannot be produced as a commodity and traded on the (formal) market.

Finally, we want to say something about how we usually measure and evaluate the state of a nation's economy. Common measurements include GDP, GDP growth, national debt, interest rates, unemployment, inflation, consumer spending, exchange rates, and balance of trade. Based on some of these indicators, scholars and practitioners classify countries as "developed" and "developing" states or as "advanced industrial nations" and "least developed countries." The classification of individual countries in any of these categories is quite controversial. As the United Nation's convention declares: "The designations 'developed' and 'developing' are intended for statistical convenience and do not necessarily express a judgment about the stage reached by a particular country or area in the development process" (United Nations 2010).

Precisely because of the widespread use of these categories in the collection and analysis of statistical data, the status and recognition of a country as "more or less developed" is perpetuated. To be clear, countries differ significantly in terms of their economic wealth, as measured by GDP per capita (see map 1.1). Chapter 6 on economic development discusses how countries lagging behind the rich ones are trying to catch up in terms of their economic growth. Still, simply considering the economic growth of a particular country is an imperfect measure of a country's overall economic strength and of its citizens' economic well-being. Other indicators include income, earnings, and wealth inequality, which measure the economic distance between different segments of the population. Poverty levels give a sense of what proportion of the population cannot afford to buy basic goods and services. Levels of unemployment show the condition of the labor market. Inflation captures the stability or fluctuation of prices. Consumers' purchasing power indicates the value of money as measured by the quantity and quality of products and services it can buy. Trade balance shows the ratio between exports from and imports to a single country, and national debt is the amount of money owed to other governments or to the international financial organizations who lent it. Exchange rates indicate how much a nation's currency is worth compared with that of other nations. Amid the wealth of economic indicators (no pun intended), we should realize that not one of them is absolutely more important than the other. As we argue throughout the book, desired economic goals – be they GDP growth, full employment, low inflation, or low inequality – are politically and socially defined.

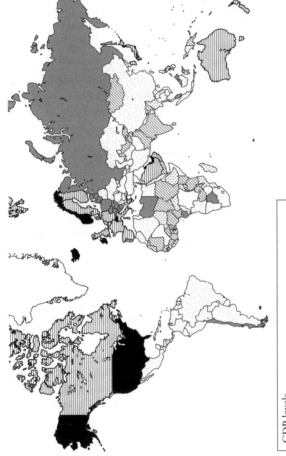

GDP levels

▦ $935 or less	▥ $20,001 – $35,000
▨ $936 – $3,705	■ $35,001 or more
▧ $3,706 – $11,455	☐ No data
▓ $11,456 – $20,000	

Source: World Development Indicators, 2005.

Map 1.1 Size of world economies, GDP per capita in PPP

What is State?

A classical sociologist, Max Weber (1958: 78), defined a state as "a human community that (successfully) claims the monopoly of the legitimate use of physical force within a given territory." Basically, this means that a state is an entity with sovereign authority over a specific territory, not subject to any higher authority. Although the era of transnational globalization has increased the prominence of supra-state organs such as the United Nations, as of now, these associations have no real authority and rely on each individual member state to enforce compliance with its resolutions and impose sanctions on those states that fail to comply.

The fact that states are sovereign authorities also implies that bodies such as the state bureaucracy, courts, police, and military exercise jurisdiction and force in order to maintain internal order and prevent foreign aggression. Following Weber's distinctions between different kinds of authority, the authority of a modern state is of a rational-legal kind, meaning that it is based on impersonal rules – so-called bureaucratic structures – which constrain the power of elites. In modern Western states, elites cannot simply take action without conferring with civil society through a use of what Michael Mann (1984) calls despotic power, such as that possessed by Byzantine emperors or other oppressive "masters of the house" (which is where the word *despot* originates). Rather, as Mann differentiates, modern states rely mostly on infrastructural power: they can coordinate society's activities but still remain an instrument of civil force. They do not rely on power over society but power "through society," entailing a cooperative relationship between citizens and government. We will reference some cases where contemporary autocratic rulers use despotic power, but will focus on the infrastructural state capacities as they pertain to the economic sphere of social life. We are interested in how states penetrate the economic sphere, such as by taxing, spending, and organizing economic relations.

However, a world made up of sovereign nation-states characterized by the ability to act with infrastructural power has not always been the case. In the past, there were many different kinds of political units, from small dukedoms and principalities (such as the Principality of Wales, which existed in the northern and western parts of Wales between the thirteenth and sixteenth centuries) to large empires, such as the Roman, Ottoman, Chinese, or Austro-Hungarian Empire. Imperial powers such as France and Britain ruled colonies in Africa, North America, Asia, and Oceania. After World War II, the Union of Soviet Socialist Republics (USSR) controlled sixteen of its union republics as well as its satellite states Poland, Czechoslovakia, and Hungary, ruled by their communist parties. The rapid decolonization of the twentieth century led more than 130 colonies or dependencies to become independent states. In 1989 most of the Soviet satellite states removed communist leaders and declared political sovereignty from the Soviet Union, and in 1991 this last great empire disintegrated into fifteen states. Today the world is composed almost entirely of sovereign nation-states. Figure 1.1 reflects the growth of the number of the world's independent states over the past century by listing the official United Nations members for the period between 1945 and 2005.

We are concerned not only with what states are, the authority they have, or what kinds of states have existed in the world, but also with how we study and think about them. Apropos of scholarly research, the nation-state as a unit of analysis was not the point of much discussion by Western social scientists after World War II. Scholars attribute this to the fact that fascism was so closely associated with nationalism and statism as to give the state-centered phenomena a bad name. Rather, the postwar order in Western countries was organized around liberal ideas, and this also set the intellectual agenda (Hall 2003). Beginning in the 1970s, however, in light of the Vietnam War draft, the civil rights movement, the expanding welfare state, and the government management of the economy in the late 1960s and early 1970s, scholarship on the state and state-related questions experienced a comeback, or, as the title of an influential publication announced, the state was "brought back in" (Evans, Rueschemeyer, and Skocpol 1985).

Still, beginning in the late 1980s, a whole new set of circumstances arose that supposedly undermined the power of

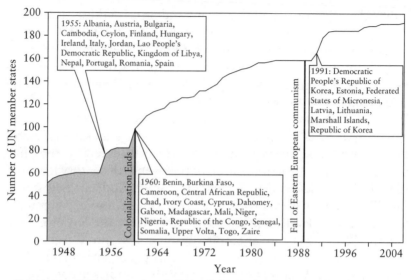

The figure contains the following labels:

1955: Albania, Austria, Bulgaria, Cambodia, Ceylon, Finland, Hungary, Ireland, Italy, Jordan, Lao People's Democratic Republic, Kingdom of Libya, Nepal, Portugal, Romania, Spain

1991: Democratic People's Republic of Korea, Estonia, Federated States of Micronesia, Latvia, Lithuania, Marshall Islands, Republic of Korea

1960: Benin, Burkina Faso, Cameroon, Central African Republic, Chad, Ivory Coast, Cyprus, Dahomey, Gabon, Madagascar, Mali, Niger, Nigeria, Republic of the Congo, Senegal, Somalia, Upper Volta, Togo, Zaire

Colonialization Ends

Fall of Eastern European communism

Number of UN member states — Year

*Initial Members (1945): Argentina, Australia, Belgium, Bolivia, Brazil, Byelorussian Soviet Socialist Republic, Canada, Chile, China, Colombia, Costa Rica, Cuba, Czechoslovakia, Denmark, Dominican Republic, Ecuador, Egypt, El Salvador, Ethiopia, France, Greece, Guatemala, Haiti, Honduras, India, Iran, Iraq, Lebanon, Liberia, Luxembourg, Mexico, Netherlands, New Zealand, Nicaragua, Norway, Panama, Paraguay, Peru, Philippines, Poland, Saudi Arabia, South Africa, Syrian Arab Republic, Turkey, Ukraine, Union of Soviet Socialist Republics, United Kingdom of Great Britain and Northern Ireland, United States of America, Uruguay, Venezuela, Yugoslavia

Source: United Nations (2009).

Figure 1.1 Membership in the United Nations over time

state-centered views. The collapse of state socialism delegitimized central control of the state in the economy. The signing of the Maastricht Treaty by the European Community states brought about what we now know as the European Union and led to the creation of the euro as a common supra-national currency. Emphasis by international financial institutions on freeing the financial markets across countries and the surge in global foreign investment flows boosted the power of transnational corporations to the detriment of nation-states. Or so it seemed.

The self-assertion of several new independent states following the collapse of communism made clear that nation- and state-building are very much alive and are sometimes so powerful that they result in war and ethnic cleansing, as was the case in the former Yugoslavia throughout the 1990s. The centralization of state power following the terrorist attacks of 9/11 put the US state back in focus. The failure to get the European Union Constitution ratified by individual member states in 2005 showed that the awareness of national identity within the European region was strong. The spectacular growth in China, led by an autocratic state, has provided grounds to question the importance of the "free market" for economic prosperity. The collapse of the US mortgage market in 2008 and the following financial and economic crises brought the importance of state "back in" yet again.

Not surprisingly, then, the book you are reading comes at a time when attention to the role of the state, generally, and the role of the state in the economy, specifically, is quite high. We dare to predict that it will reach its peak and then decline yet again. Yes, it seems that attention to state-centered analyses and the perceived importance of the role of the state moves in waves. What we want to argue is that this reflects political events and the prevailing *Zeitgeist*, the spirit of the time so to speak, more than something intrinsic in the nature of how important nation-states really are.

Finally, we want to clarify a couple of terms that we will be using when we discuss the role of the state in the economy. The first is the distinction between government and state. In common speech we use "government" more frequently than "state." But, in its strict meaning, government refers to the body which carries out the administrative tasks of the state. If you will, the state is like a firm and the government is like its management team. When we refer to the administrative tasks of the state, we will use the term government. The second clarification we want to make is about the relationship between state and law. Throughout the book we will refer to law and legal regulation as a product of state action and analyze them as state influences on economy. Stating this, we acknowledge three caveats. For one, when they are applied, laws are interpreted, sometimes variously, by legal experts, so a link between state adoption and implementation is not necessarily straightforward. Second, courts can be more or less independent from the rest of the state, especially when judges are elected (such as in the US) as opposed to appointed as civil servants (such as in Europe).

Third, in principle, laws are subject to judicial review and can be overturned. On account of all these reasons, there is an extra layer, so to speak, between the action of state and the impact of law that complicates the immediacy of this relationship. We recognize this. Still, it is a fact that all national legal provisions need to be accepted by national governments to go in effect, and, in this sense, the state works though law to impact social life, including the economy. In the subsequent chapters, we will highlight how states do so in the governance of property relations, money, labor, and firms, and to influence economic development and internationalization.

Conceptualizing Economy–State Relations

Questions about the role of the state in the economy have generated many debates and countless pages of writing. The issue about the appropriate state involvement in economic affairs is extremely politically charged, inspiring controversies between the liberal and conservative poles. It goes to the core of the debate about the virtues of socialism vis-à-vis capitalism. Moreover, the research on the topic is voluminous because there are so many ways in which states can be involved in economies. Not surprisingly, theoretical conceptualizations of these relationships are multiple as well. Handling this controversy and complexity, at the risk of oversimplification, we will outline (only) two ways in which economy–state relations have been conceptualized. This does not allow us to specify nuances of different middle-range theories, but it does help us make core distinctions at the level of basic assumptions about the nature of the economy–state relationship. From one perspective, which we term **economy–state dualism**, these two spheres are conceived as separable entities operating with contrasting logics. The key question here is: To what extent should states intervene in the economic sphere? From the other perspective, which we term **economy–state embeddedness**, these two spheres are mutually constitutive, so that states always play a role in economies, enabling and constraining their operation in different ways. The key question from this perspective is: In what ways are states involved in the economy and with what consequences?

Economy–state dualism

A classical view on state–economy relations is characterized by an assumption that the state and the economy are two separable entities with distinct logics of orientation. The state's preoccupation is the governance of public affairs. The economy, especially the market, is about managing resources for maximization of private interests. The public versus private orientations are in opposition. Hence, we can call this conceptualization economy–state dualism.

If we conceive of state and economy as two distinct spheres, then a state's involvement in the economy, imposing its hand over a private sphere, is seen as an intervention, a market manipulation. Such a state is called an **interventionist state**, and the key question is: How much should it intervene in the economy? To what extent should governments be involved in economic affairs? The focus is on the *quantity* of state control over the economy. The concern is also normative: How much control is desirable? Should it be as minimal as possible, or considerable? Answering this question allows us to align societies along an analytic continuum from those with the lowest to those with the highest level of state interference. Along this continuum, as Fred Block (1994) proposed, we can distinguish five different types of state intervention in the economy: public goods state, macro-economic stabilization state, social rights state, protectionist state, and socialist state.

From a classical economic perspective dating back to the writings of Adam Smith, the father of modern economic science, states should have minimal interference in the economy. Smith's idea of markets as guided by an invisible hand is probably one with which even those with no background in economics are familiar. This idea implies that economic activities will perform best if they are simply left to their own devices. The activities of buyers and sellers on the market will spontaneously adjust so that everyone will be best off. Prices will equilibrate where demand for goods and their supply meet. Most economists prefer this self-regulating market idea, without state interference. To be clear, only the very few most radical of thinkers would want to get rid of state involvement in economic and social affairs altogether. Those who do so subscribe to anarchism, which considers compulsory governments as unnecessary or even harmful, and prefers anarchy or the absence of the state. Rather than promoting an anarchist stance, classical economists, including Adam Smith, subscribe to the view that the intervention of states is justified in the provision of goods, commodities, and services that markets cannot produce by themselves. These are called public goods, and such a state is referred to as a **public goods state.**

Following an article by a Nobel Prize winning economist, Ronald Coase (1974), a lighthouse has often been used as a classic example of a public good. It is not possible to blindfold the crew of some ships and only let others benefit from the signaling beams. That is, a characteristic of a public good is that it is difficult to exclude people from using a service, once provided. Moreover, a lighthouse's beams do not shine less with each additional ship passing by; no one's use detracts from the use of others. However, the provision and maintenance of public goods still requires financing. Why should we expect anyone to contribute money if they can enjoy the benefits without paying for them – that is, catch a free ride? Actually, this is called a free rider problem. Free-riders are those who consume a resource without contributing to its upkeep. State intervention is the primary mechanism by which societies address free-rider problems – in the form of taxing citizens and then using the revenues to finance public works and infrastructure such as railroad or interstate highway systems, airports, public schools, hospitals, and water purification and sewage treatment centers. In addition to taxation, other kinds of state regulation attempt to deal with the free-rider problem for goods that do not need to be provided but require attention because of their vulnerability, such as clean air. To protect the public good of clean air, governments pass environmental degradation regulations.

The second type of intervention by the state encompasses its role in alleviating the impact of the business cycle, characterized by periods of growth and downturn, or boom and bust. This intervention is also called macro-stabilization. The **stabilization state** is charged with controlling economic growth and managing the downturns so that they don't result in serious economic crises. Provision of a stable supply of money is a relatively minimal kind of such intervention. According to the influential economist Milton Friedman, government's role should be primarily to control the money supply in the economy (Friedman and Schwartz 1963). This view espouses monetarism, a perspective which argues that excessive expansion of the money supply inherently leads to inflation and that containing inflation should be the central goal of **monetary policy**. Paul Volcker and Alan Greenspan, former chiefs of the Federal Reserve Bank, are both considered to have promoted policies in line with monetarism.

In its more extensive version, the role of the stabilization state is akin to the type of economic governance promoted by the British economist John Maynard Keynes. Keynesian economics advocates interventionist government policy. Government should promote monetary policy actions by the central bank beyond simply targeting the money supply, as well as fiscal policy actions, for example by using government spending in times of hardship to mitigate the adverse effects of the business cycle (Keynes 1936, 1937). We discuss this further in box 1.1.

Third, the social rights state focuses on the state's role in the provision of protection to citizens. The British sociologist T. H. Marshall (1893–1981) provided the most influential argument along these lines in his essay entitled "Citizenship and Social Class" (1950). In this essay he introduced the concept of social rights, claiming that a citizen is only a full citizen if she or he possesses not only civil and political but also social rights, and that possession of all three rights is linked to social class. Social rights meant protection from the market forces and provision for illness, injury, and old age that should be assured by the state. States' roles thus would be to provide working people with sources of income other than those that they can gain from their participation in the labor market. We discuss further the redistributive role of the state in providing social protection in chapter 4, suggesting how the development of the modern welfare state can be conceptualized

Box 1.1 John Maynard Keynes's boom and bust cycle of influence

The commonplace notion of a free market leads many to believe that the general economic view is to abhor government intervention in the economy. However, not all economists think alike on this topic. A famous individual whose theory seems to fall in and out of favor with time is the British economist John Maynard Keynes (1883–1946).

Growing up, Keynes enjoyed a privileged lifestyle. His father was an economics professor at Cambridge University and his mother was Cambridge's first woman mayor. Not surprisingly, Keynes attended the finest prep school and then proceeded to enroll at Cambridge himself. He was given the honor of representing the British government at the Versailles Peace Conference at the end of World War I, but soon afterwards became quite disenchanted with what he called the economic consequences of the peace (which he later used as the title for a book).

Keynes's experience in negotiating the postwar peace and the Stock Market Crash of 1929 were seminal events that convinced him that capitalism was inherently unstable and that this "boom and bust" cycle would continue to occur if governments did not intervene. His rejection of classical economic policies was made clear in his most famous work, *The General Theory of Employment, Interest and Money* (1936). Though some consider this book difficult to read because of its reliance on technical language and wordy prose, it is widely considered to be of immense theoretical import. In it, Keynes provides the rationale for "big government" and active intervention in the economy whenever necessary. Tariffs, protectionist measures, government spending on social programs, and unbalanced budgets were all policies that Keynes saw as appropriate ways of mitigating the excesses of the market. For Keynes, the capitalist system would not self-regulate in the interests of general prosperity. Employment and consumption would never reach the equilibrium that classical economics promised. During times of economic hardship, Keynes offered a controversial recommendation: spending. He thought that scrimping and saving, by individuals and by the government, only prolonged the problem. If consumers and the government spent, this would increase economic growth and bring an end to economic troubles. This example illustrates one of Keynes's most central contributions to economic theory: that, without government intervention, capitalism would inevitably lead to hardship and deprivation.

It is interesting to consider how Keynes's influence on popular economic thought falls in and out of favor over time, creating a sort of boom and bust cycle of its own. Keynesianism was strong after the Great Depression and all through the 1970s, which was the time of big government, social spending, and active intervention in the economy. This changed after the 1973 oil shocks, and Keynesianism was quite out of favor until the economic downturn following the 2007–8 financial crises, which stimulated its revival.

not only by the state dualism but also by the state embeddedness perspective.

A fourth type of intervention of the state in the economy is to act in a protectionist manner. The most famous instance of a **protectionist state** is mercantilism of the sixteenth to eighteenth centuries, where states put in place policies such as tariffs on trade in order to encourage national economic development. The American statesman and political theorist Alexander Hamilton is known to have argued for government intervention in support of business, including imposing tariffs, building infrastructure, and providing financing to private firms (Chernow 2004). A leading German economist, Georg Friedrich List, was also influenced by Hamilton's thinking, arguing that Germany could catch up with England only through a pursuit of active policies to encourage and protect industry.

The postwar Japanese government has also been cited as

an instance of a highly protectionist state. The key role in the postwar Japanese economy was played by the Japanese Ministry of International Trade and Industry (MITI), which reacted to the Anglo-American pro-competition policies and took comprehensive and deliberate action to protect domestic industries in Japan by limiting imports, providing access to foreign technology, and offering financial help, tax breaks, protection from competition, and other services to chosen industries. Johnson (1982) and others conclude that Japan's strong interventionist state policies after World War II are part of the explanation for the economic miracle that occurred there in terms of economic growth in the 1960s through the 1980s.

Fifth, the **socialist state** may be thought of as an extreme example of the social rights and protectionist states. According to Marxist–Leninist ideology, the goal of society is to dominate both the economy and the state in the final stage of societal development – communism, where people will be free to work out of interest not out of need. Socialism is an intermediary stage on the way to communism where the state's role is necessary to alleviate the injustices of inequality that are involved in the capitalist mode of production, as well as the human alienation that results from subjecting people to inherently dehumanizing market transactions (Gouldner 1980). This is why socialism as experienced in the former Soviet Union and in Eastern Europe is often termed state socialism. To accomplish these goals of fairness and equality, private property needs to be abolished, economy centralized, and social protection, including full employment, assured. We discuss more about the nature of socialist states in chapter 2.

Economy–state embeddedness

The five visions of the state's role in the economy as described above are preoccupied by the question: How much state intervention in the national economy is advisable? In answering this question, studies ultimately rest on normative assumptions. They presuppose to a greater or lesser extent that states are parasitical and wasteful, and/or that markets are inherently dehumanizing and unjust (Block 1994). There is very little empirical research, however, that would substantiate these assumptions. While some state activities can be inefficient, this is not invariably the case. More likely, different kinds of state involvement contribute to different kinds of economic outcomes. This requires a focus that moves beyond the preoccupation with quantity or the extent of state intervention to asking questions such as: How does the state shape the economy? What are the *different kinds* of state involvement in the economy? What combination of conditions produces a state that parasitically feeds on the economy, a so-called **predatory state**? What combination promotes economic growth as a result of **developmental state** actions? What combination helps reduce poverty and ameliorate inequality, such as in a strong **welfare state**? Moreover, analysts working from this perspective assume that social forces shape governments' decision-making about economic affairs. They ask: What is the role of ideas, politics, and institutions for shaping economic policy-making and thus the course of economic development, domestically and globally?

The fact that economic phenomena are strongly dependent on social forces is often termed economic embeddedness. One of the most influential classical writers in economic anthropology, Karl Polanyi, is credited for this notion, writing that "economies are embedded and enmeshed in institutions economic and non-economic" (1957). You may have come across a somewhat different use of the term "embeddedness" to reflect that economic action is influenced by networks of social ties (Granovetter 1985), which is its application at the individual and firm level. We will, however, use the term in the Polanyian sense to refer to the macro-institutional environment in which economies are situated and treat the state as a key macro-institution. For this reason, we also use the term "economy–state embeddedness" for the economic sociology perspective on state and economy relations.

From the economy–state embeddedness perspective, states and economies are not two separate spheres but connected worlds. States are seen as constitutive of economy, meaning that economic activity is viewed as continuously shaped and managed by the state and political institutions: "State action always plays a major role in constituting economies . . . [so] it is not useful to posit states as lying outside of economic activity" (Block 1994: 696). States' role in the economy should not be understood as a mere *constraint through regulation* but also as something that is needed to *facilitate economic processes to enable the workings of markets*.

The notion of **fictitious commodities**, as developed by Karl Polanyi, illustrates these concurrent enabling and constraining properties of states most effectively. Polanyi argued that land, labor, and money are not commodities in the same sense as those things produced by firms to be sold on the market. We understand Polanyi's notion in two ways. On the one hand, it is a fiction that land, labor, and money are inherently produced to be supplied for sale on the market; thus, state action is needed to *constitute* them as commodities on the market. In another sense, it is also illusory that land, labor, and money can be easily multiplied should demand increase; in fact, state action is needed to *constrain* demand in preventing the destruction of these resources. Let us elaborate on both points. Land, labor, and money are not "manufactured" in order to be sold: land is not produced but given, people do not reproduce with the intention of providing more labor power, and money is an agreed-upon medium of exchange. The demand for land, labor, and money has to be regulated so as to protect the exhaustion of these resources to the point of annihilation. Just consider, if all land and natural resources were allowed to be fully privatized and the state did not retain any control over them, we would soon witness overpollution and overextraction. If human labor were to be treated as any other commodity to be sold on the market, then there would be no limit to the kinds and extent of its use by employers, resulting in inhumane exploitation and overexhaustion. In terms of money, if we could continually print it as needed, it would become worthless and no longer function as a legitimate claim on value. Economic actors would have to resort to barter trade instead of market exchange. This makes clear that, if we want economies to be sustainable, state *regulation* is necessary to put limits to the use of land, labor, and money. At the same time, it is undeniable that, for markets to function in the first place, it is necessary to put institutions in place that allow land, labor, and money to be bought and sold at some price – that is, to treat them as commodities. By allowing land to be privately owned, as through the enclosure movement in England in the eighteenth and nineteenth centuries (see chapter 2), and by establishing labor markets as opposed to the socialist policy of guaranteeing full employment, for example, the state *enables* the operation of markets. This is why we say that states are both regulatory and constitutive of market activities, and therefore cannot be placed outside markets. It is the balancing act of having simultaneously to regulate and constitute the use of natural, human, and money resources, as core market objects, that lies at the heart of the state's role in economy. States have to manage fictitious commodities, otherwise market exchange is untenable. Because natural assets, labor, and money are central objects related to all spheres of the economy, either directly or indirectly, it follows from the state embeddedness perspective that states continually manage, directly and indirectly, all spheres of the economy.

But while the involvement of state in economy from the embeddedness perspective is a given, the research focus is on *the kinds* of such involvement: to identify the different types of state–economy relations and their consequences, and to consider which among the multiple ways of state–economy relations induce more or less "productive synergy between states and markets," as stated by two very prominent sociologists working in this tradition, Fred Block and Peter Evans (2005).

The possibilities are more numerous than we can summarize. Instead of offering a characterization of state involvement types, as we did in the section on economy–state dualism, it is more appropriate to offer a characterization of the type of questions about economy–state embeddedness at different levels of analysis: individual, organizational, and system. These are summarized in figure 1.2. The first two sets of questions are about how states shape different economic actions, including production, distribution, exchange, and consumption, at the level of both the individual and the firm. The third set of questions is about how

Introduction

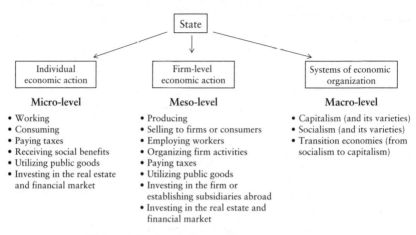

Figure 1.2   The influence of state on economy

states shape the whole system of economic organization, such as different kinds of capitalism or socialism. Another set of questions that motivates economy–state embeddedness research recognizes that the decision-making of states about their involvement in economic affairs is itself influenced by multiple social forces, such as politics, ideas, or institutions. These types of questions are about the role of social forces on state decisions about economy (see figure 1.3), which in turn influence economic outcomes.

In sum, the central message of the economy–state embeddedness perspective is that the state always plays an integral role in facilitating and regulating, directly and indirectly, economic outcomes. The nature of this influence, its kind and type, varies across time and space and for different political inclinations of governments, but economy and state are never conceptualized as divorced from each other. Rather, they are seen as connected worlds. This basic assumption has major consequences for thinking about the operation of markets. Remember that a well-known trope of the economy–state dualism perspective, the self-regulating market, envisions that markets operate principally without government intervention. In fact, it prefers it to be so. From the embeddedness perspective, however, markets cannot function without state provision of structures that define who can make claims over assets

Introduction

Social forces		State decisions about economy		Economic outcomes
• Values • Norms • Activist groups • Institutions • Social networks • Domestic political struggles • Allocation of power in the world-system	⇨	• About nature (property rights laws, environmental protection, etc.) • About money (printing of money, managing money supply, taxation, government spending, banking laws, financial regulations, etc.) • About labor (social protection, employment provision, imprisonment regulations, immigration policy, etc.) • About firms (firm incorporation procedures, employment law, corruption law, bankruptcy law, corporate governance, inter-firm relations, industrial policy, innovation policy, business regulation to protect consumers, etc.) • About economic development and internationalization (privatization policy, industry or sector protection and subsidies, tariffs, international economic cooperation agreements, etc.)	⇨	• Economic growth • Inflation • Interest rates • Currency exchange rates • Balance of trade • Unemployment • National debt • Income or earnings inequality • Poverty levels • Productivity levels • Standard of living • Consumer spending

Figure 1.3 The influence of social forces on state decisions about economy

and what the rules of competition and cooperation are. States also create and implement rules about what can be bought or sold on the market and under what conditions. In practical terms, this elucidates why, for instance, there is no formal market in human organs and why some countries have national universal health coverage but others don't.

Moreover, the focus on embeddedness rather than dualism in economy–state relations makes clear that a variety rather than a single (right) mix of government involvement in the economy can produce economic prosperity. That is, research on comparative development has established that the powerful role of an authoritarian state can bring about economic development, such as in China or Singapore, as can the developmentalist states of South Korea or Taiwan, or a minimalist regulatory state such as in the United Kingdom or the United States. We discuss this further in chapter 6.

Introduction

Finally, the notion of embeddedness, in particular embeddedness of state decision-making about the economy, highlights that development and prosperity need to be measured by multiple indicators, which are often untenable simultaneously, rather than by a single indicator. Different political orientations of elites, such as those of Republicans and Democrats, and different social groups or institutions, such as anti-globalization movements or international financial organizations, promote different economic and social goals. In the end, the focus on any particular desired goal, be it economic growth or economic equality, is a matter of power struggles and the ideational commitments of those groups that prevail.

Overview of the Book

Based on the theoretical review, we identify two central economic objects – property and money – two crucial economic subjects – labor and firms – and two consequential economic processes – development and internationalization/globalization. This produces six issue areas of economy–state interaction that we want to discuss in the book, and we take each of them in turn. The first one is property, because defining who has rights to own assets is a fundamental role that institutionalizes systems of macro-economic organization. Taking property as its point of departure, chapter 2 explains the role of the state in capitalist systems of private property rights and socialist systems of collective property rights. We also discuss postsocialist societies. The second issue we tackle is money. As chapter 3 discusses, states set the money rules by providing the means of payment for economic transactions, determining the availability and cost of money circulating in the economy, and setting taxation and spending policy. The third issue of economy–state intersection is labor. Chapter 4 covers issues related to the state's redistributive role in protecting economic actors through social transfers and labor regulations and policies that indirectly shape who is allowed to participate fully in the formal labor market. The fourth issue is about firms and industries. Chapter

5 reviews how states provide business and industry governance and enforce rules of exchange among economic actors to manage the production, distribution, and consumption of goods and services. The fifth issue we present is about economic development. Chapter 6 discusses the different perspectives on the role of the state in fostering – or not – a country's economic development and prosperity. The sixth issue transcends national borders to discuss international and global economy. Chapter 7 covers the state's role in managing the territorial boundary both in response and with a goal to shaping global economic developments. Chapter 8, in conclusion, summarizes the main arguments of the book.

2

Property: The State's Role in Capitalist and Socialist Economies

What do capitalism and socialism have in common? *Do* they have anything in common? Capitalist economies use markets as the main form of economic organization. Exchange between buyers and sellers who buy and sell assets on the market depends on entitlement to private ownership – the fact that economic actors can rightfully possess assets to sell them to others who become their rightful owners. In stark contrast, the main form of socialist economic organization is not **market exchange**, but **redistribution** by a central authority. This is because the central institution of socialism treats property rights as collective and not private. The abolition of private property rights precludes market exchange and necessitates that economic production and distribution be organized in alternative ways. It should be clear, then, that defining who has rights to own assets determines the fundamental features of economic systems – capitalism in case of private ownership and socialism in case of collective ownership. Systems as diverse as capitalism and socialism, therefore, have one thing in common. The definition of property rights is consequential for how both organize economic production, distribution, and consumption. Who defines property rights? It's the state: not only do states define property rights but they also serve to protect them. This is the most basic role of the state that even the strongest of market fundamentalists recognize.

Taking property as its point of departure, this chapter examines the role of the state in capitalist and socialist economies as well as in those societies that underwent a transformation to market in the 1990s. We specify the characteristics of capitalist, socialist, and postsocialist systems and the differential roles that states play in institutionalizing and maintaining their macro-economic arrangements.

Classical Perspectives on Capitalism

Capitalism generally refers to an economic system in which the means of production are mostly privately owned and operated for profit and in which economic activity, including the production, distribution, consumption, and pricing of goods and services, is determined through the operation of a free market. Several classical theorists, economists and sociologists alike, wrote on the origins and character of the capitalist economic system, and we proceed to discuss briefly their work and how they envisioned the role of the state in the economy.

Smith and Ricardo

One of the key authors who wrote about capitalism is Adam Smith (1723–1790), whose best-known work, *The Wealth of Nations* (1776), a book that took him ten years to write, is considered to have sparked a revolution in economic theory. Although he did not use the word capitalism per se, Smith devised a set of concepts that remain strongly associated with capitalism today, particularly his notion of the **invisible hand** of the market, through which the pursuit of individual interest produces a collective good for society. He criticized monopolies, tariffs, duties, and other state-enforced restrictions of his time and believed that the market is the most fair and efficient arbitrator of resources. Because of this, Smith is viewed today as one of the most important advocates of free-market ideology. But this doesn't mean that he did not imagine any role for the state. As he actually carefully outlined in *The Wealth of Nations*: "Political oeconomy [sic] . . . proposes two distinct objects: first, to provide a plentiful revenue or subsistence

27

for the people, or, more properly to enable them to provide such a revenue or subsistence for themselves; and, secondly, to supply the state or commonwealth with a revenue sufficient for the public services" (Smith [1776] 2000: 455). So, while he rejected the protectionist role of the state, he did believe that the state had a role in providing the following "public services": defending the country against invaders, maintaining justice and protecting property rights, and providing public works such as roads and harbors, as well as some elementary types of education and religious instruction (Swedberg 2003: 162–3).

Smith's view that the market is the most efficient arbitrator was shared by David Ricardo (1772–1823), who, in *Principles of Political Economy and Taxation* (1817), developed the law of comparative advantage, which aimed to explain why it is profitable for two parties to trade, even if one of the partners is more efficient in every type of economic production. The core argument is that each can gain by specializing in the good where they have relative productivity advantage, and trading that good for the other on a free market. Any kind of government regulation messes these principles and renders trade inefficient. In fact, Ricardo spent much time campaigning against the corn laws, English regulations between 1815 and 1846 that prescribed high tariffs on agricultural imports. For Ricardo, these laws contributed to the stagnation of the British economy of that time. Only trade that was free and unregulated would ensure the greatest amount of prosperity for the most people. Ricardo also felt that wages should be unregulated so that each person would specialize in their own development to maximize the return they would receive from employers. Ricardo's ideas clearly fall in line with Smith's in terms of their emphasis on economic freedom.

Marx and Weber

Smith and Ricardo, with their focus on free trade and the invisible hand regulating the demand and supply of goods, are considered the founders of the classical liberal economic doctrine which sees the economy as largely separate from society, operating by its own laws and better left untouched by the state. In contrast, classical sociological writers viewed economy as a social system, influenced by social relations, distribution of power, and the meanings that people attach to economic actions. We will discuss two classical sociological figures here, Marx and Weber, who each emphasized the role of different social forces in the economy and held different views on the role that the state plays in it.

Karl Marx (1818–1883), a German intellectual trained as a philosopher, understood capitalism primarily as a mode of production characterized by specific social relations – that is, the conflict of interest between the owners of the means of production – the bourgeoisie – and the workers that they exploit. This conflict creates an inherent tension in capitalism, which, according to Marx, will lead to its collapse. The fact that laborers have to give up the ownership of their own labor and sell what Marx called their labor power to capitalists is inherently dehumanizing. Moreover, capitalists have no incentive to alleviate this alienation because they can profit from labor exploitation. The more surplus value they can extract from labor – that is, the greater the price they can receive for products in comparison to what they pay laborers to produce them – the larger the profits. For this reason, capitalism is a system prone to overproduction, overaccumulation, and inherent inequality, and therefore needs to be overthrown. In the spirit of these ideas, Marx wrote with his collaborator, Friedrich Engels, *The Communist Manifesto*, where the authors encourage the proletariat from all over the world to unite in a revolution to overturn capitalism and bring about a classless society where private property rights will be abolished and people will not have to sell their labor power on the market. This would be a communist society.

It is mistakenly believed that Marx advocated a strong role for the state in the economy. In fact, the classless society of communism would also be a stateless society. The quote from *The Communist Manifesto* about the state says that it is "but the executive committee for managing the affairs of the bourgeoisie" (Marx and Engels 1978: 475). Hence he imagines that, once private ownership of the means of the production is abolished, it will be possible, and desirable, for the communist society members to organize and control economic activity without a powerful state apparatus.

However, Marx recognized that communism cannot follow capitalism directly. A transitional period of socialism is needed. Marx and Engels never wrote much about how this transition should occur, in fact. This was left to those who followed their ideas in practice, including the Russian revolutionary Vladimir Ilyich Lenin, the leader of the revolution in 1917 and the founder of the Union of the Soviet Socialist Republics. Under Lenin's and later Stalin's socialism, the party-state – that is, the state apparatus controlled by the Communist Party – was to act as a vanguard for the interests of the working class. The party-state commands the economy by abolishing private property, centralizing production, and using redistribution as the primary principle of economic organization. As we will discuss later, this kind of economic system is called state socialism.

The other classical figure is Max Weber (1864–1920), who made a distinct contribution to the understanding of the role of states in capitalism with his work on rationalization and **bureaucracy**. In *Economy and Society* (1922), Weber emphasized the fundamental value of bureaucracy as an institutional foundation for capitalist growth. For Weber, bureaucracy was a set of administrative organizations with specific structural features which included the focus on (a) *rules* that guide transparent operations; (b) *roles* that clearly define the division of administrative labor among persons and offices; (c) the keeping of *records*; and (d) a meritocratic assignment of *rewards* based on consistent patterns of recruitment and the assurance of stable long-term careers. For Weber, bureaucracies are, above all else, rational, and the rules, roles, records, and rewards that comprise bureaucracies lead to an impartial functioning of the state apparatus. No person is above the rules, and the impartial, rational nature of bureaucracies is one of the key dimensions on which Weber focuses. The operation of bureaucratic systems is predictable and calculable, not left to whim and emotion. Bureaucratic organization, for Weber, was one of the most important aspects that enabled the development of the capitalist system. Once some began to work and manage their labor supply bureaucratically, other industries did so as well. But it is not only industrial enterprises that can benefit from bureaucratic organization. Weber also claimed that the state organization that follows bureaucratic structures paves the way for the development and expansion of capitalism.

Following Weber, a subject of empirical study has been to what extent bureaucratic state structures influence economic growth. One such study by Peter Evans and James Rauch (1999) examined thirty-five developing countries and noted regional differences in bureaucratic state organizations and the degree of economic development in the period from 1970 to 1990. In this period, Africa was at the lower end of the scale of Weberian bureaucratic state organization and also at the bottom of the scale of economic development, while the East Asian countries that industrialized quickly after World War II were at the higher ends of both scales. Evans and Rauch demonstrated that at least two elements of Weberian bureaucracy, meritocratic recruitment and the provision of predictable and rewarding career ladders, helped create the conditions for economic growth for the countries in their study. The authors showed that the Weberian bureaucratic state can play a key role in stimulating economic growth around the world, a feature identified with the developmental role of states, discussed further in chapter 6.

Central Institutions of Capitalism

The market is the central institution of capitalism. We can define markets as places where buyers and sellers come together to exchange property stakes in various assets. Buyers and sellers could be different kinds of firms or individuals. You are engaged in market exchange when you buy a used Ford from an acquaintance. But, obviously, the Ford Motor Company is also a market actor by producing cars and buying raw materials from supplier companies in the US and abroad. The Ford Motor Company is also in the role of a seller when it sells cars to dealerships, which, in turn, act as sellers of cars to people. Because there are multiple dealerships that can sell you a car, and multiple car producers to begin with, we say that economic actors exchanging in a market are in **competition** with each other. In consumer markets, multiple firms target a similar group of consumers. In labor markets, multiple individuals compete for a single job position. Markets and competition represent the central logic of capitalism.

It is important to note, however, that market exchange is not the only way to participate in an economy. The economy could be organized by **redistribution** if, to continue with our car example, the Ford Motor Company were to be financially supported by the central authority and in return provide a certain quota of cars back to this authority, which, in turn, would allocate cars, for instance, to individual families, and for a lower price than they could purchase on the market. This redistributive kind of economic action would have the combined function of distributing goods among a population while also reinforcing social order through the communal nature of the exchange. This is, in fact, the major characteristic of socialist economies that we discuss later in this chapter.

Alternatively, if you engaged in exchange with people relatively close to you and would not necessarily expect anything in return for your economic activity that also benefits them – at least not immediately – your relations would be described as reciprocity. These reciprocal symmetrical exchanges would not occur out of a desire for profit but out of a commitment to a communal social order.

Redistribution and reciprocity have been very common ways of economic organization throughout history. It is only since the late nineteenth century in countries such as England and the United States that the great bulk of production – food, clothes, and so on – has been in the form of commodities which are exchanged in the market, and **market exchange** is the primary principle of economic organization, more important than reciprocity and redistribution. For example, in 1790, 80 percent of all clothing in the United States was made in the home (Boorstin 1974). A couple of hundred years later, you probably know hardly anyone who doesn't buy the majority of their clothing in stores.

How did markets become the most prevalent form of economic organization? As we describe in Box 2.1, Karl Polanyi provided an important explanation for the rise of free-market exchange in the early nineteenth century, or, as he said, the great transformation, and pointed to the crucial role of the state in creating markets and capitalism. Polanyi gives a prominent role in the state-led creation of free markets to the enclosure movement in England, which led to privatization of the previously commonly shared land and forced disposed farmers to migrate to fledging industrialized areas, which facilitated the rise of labor markets. Until the eighteenth century, farm land in England was largely communally operated (hence it was often referred to as "commons" and the peasants as "commoners"). General Enclosure Acts ordered land to be "enclosed," or privatized. These controversial orders met with active resistance from the English commoners most affected by the changes, and those who disobeyed were fined or otherwise punished. However, despite this resistance, the enclosure movement had great importance as an early instance of privatization and was a crucial condition that drove the rise of markets (Neeson 1993). After all, holding private property rights, such as those fostered by land privatization, is a key requirement for functioning markets, as sellers need to own assets legally to be able rightfully to sell them to buyers on the market. In case of communal ownership of assets, this is not possible.

What exactly are **private property** rights? According to economists, private property rights have three components. First, they determine who controls a resource and how it may be used. Second, they offer exclusive access to the services of a resource. Finally, they include the right to sell, give, or rent any part of the rights at whatever price the owner desires and a buyer will pay. From a sociological perspective, Weber explains, property can be conceptualized as a specific form of a closed social relationship. More precisely, it represents a relationship that allows the actor to exclude other actors from the opportunity to use some item or some person. This right is also alienable and can be inherited. Property is typically legally protected, which means that, if it is infringed upon, coercion can be used to restore it (Weber [1922]

Property

Box 2.1 Karl Polanyi and the role of the state in construction of markets

Karl Polanyi (1886–1964) was a Hungarian scholar who argued against the "naturalness" of self-regulating market capitalism. In his book *The Great Transformation* (1944) he provides a historical analysis of the revolutionary rise of free, laissez-faire markets in nineteenth-century England. For Polanyi, the "laissez-faire economy was the product of deliberate state action" (1944: 147). He emphasized the role of industrialists, neoclassical economists, and liberal politicians in influencing the British state to set up structures that turned land, labor, and capital into "fictitious commodities" and enforced allocation by the market mechanism in all spheres of the economy.

According to Polanyi, the commercialization of land was greatly facilitated by the enclosure movement, which began in the eighteenth century. Important General Enclosure Acts were passed in 1836, 1840, and 1845 that ordered land to be enclosed, privatized, and no longer operated communally. This led to the dispossession of peasant cultivators, forcing them to migrate to urban areas to sell their labor. This pressure was initially moderated by the measures that the British state enacted to protect the poor and to maintain standards of workmanship and quality of craft. However, the Poor Law Amendment Act of 1834 gave legal sanction to the price-making market for the fictitious commodity of labor. By eliminating the provision of assistance to the able-bodied, the New Poor Law sought to make public assistance so undesirable and degrading that only the most desperate of individuals would submit to its provisions, effectively forcing those who could no longer use common land to farm and ceased to be protected by state's social measures to choose between work, however miserably remunerated, and the stigma of the workhouse. Under its provisions, those receiving welfare were not only confined to a workhouse but also deprived of their political and legal freedoms through strict programs of

34

discipline, celibacy, and forced separation from family members (Somers and Block 2005). The New Poor Law was instituted by the reform parliament of 1832, which subordinated the landed oligarchy to the urban and industrial bourgeoisie. The majority of the population had no voice and no vote. The result was the unleashing of capitalist accumulation on a scale never before experienced in human history.

Nevertheless, in face of the ever expanding role of the unimpeded functioning of markets and laissez-faire economics, society responded with a protective countermovement designed to keep the expansion of the market in check through measures and policies that would prevent market principles from dominating and thus re-embed its structures in society. Polanyi calls this logic the "double movement." Examples of policies and legislation brought about by society's countermovement are things such as minimum wage legislation, child labor laws, and environmental protection for land, all of which protect these resources from being subject completely to market principles. Polanyi feels that, when the capitalist system reaches too far on the scale of excess and the market becomes too distant from society, citizen protest and advocacy can spur change in the other direction, countering the push for free markets and working against the disembedding of markets from society.

1978: 22, 44). Weber's view is close to the economistic definition, except that the element of social relations as integral to the concept of property rights is more strongly emphasized. But both economists and sociologists agree that credibly enforced property rights have been crucial for the development of capitalist economic systems.

In earlier modernity, confiscatory governments could seize the wealth of individuals at will. New institutions of representative government, such as a parliamentary body and an independent judiciary, emerged in the aftermath of the Glorious Revolution of 1688 in an express attempt to redesign fiscal and governmental institutions to inhibit the capricious state actions that dominated in earlier times. The interlocked political structure produced by these changes, with neither parliament nor the sovereign being able to achieve their will unilaterally, limited the use of arbitrary power and firmly entrenched the security of property rights as a key part of this new system. As a consequence of the increased confidence in the state's commitment to the protection of individual wealth, governmental borrowing after the Glorious Revolution escalated considerably, demonstrating the new trust of lenders that the state would honor its agreements rather than violate the terms of the loan for its own gain (North and Weingast 1989). In fact, one of the key issues in the relationship between the role of the state and economy, according to the Nobel laureate economist Douglass North, is precisely the challenge for a state to be strong enough to guarantee the enforcement of property rights but not too strong to expropriate them (North 1990).

In the contemporary economy, one of the main ways in which governments control property rights is through the enforcement of regulatory decisions. Manipulation of property rights in the US telecommunications industry, for instance, helped create a situation of monopoly and one of competition at different points in history. AT&T monopolized the US telephone market in the late nineteenth century largely because its patents were legally upheld by court decisions, which prevented other companies from breaking into the long-distance phone market. In the mid-twentieth century, however, Federal Communications Commission (FCC) regulations allowed for the development and use of new technologies by all carriers, not just AT&T, and offered other companies access to AT&T's vast infrastructure. By allowing all companies access to new technologies and AT&T's infrastructure, the FCC helped create a situation of competition that replaced the era of AT&T monopoly in long-distance phone service (Campbell and Lindberg 1990).

These examples make clear that it is the role of the state to institutionalize and enforce private property rights, but its function in facilitating markets does not stop there. Sociologist Neil Fligstein (1996, 2001) delineates three other institutional preconditions of markets beyond property rights, including governance structures, rules of exchange, and conceptions of control. These define how power is distributed and therefore determine how actors organize to compete or cooperate. According to Fligstein, property rights are the rules that determine who can profit from firms and are necessary to society because they determine the boundaries between the owners and the rest of society. Patents and other types of protection for intellectual property are examples of property rights that regulate who is entitled to the profits of an enterprise (patent holders) and who is not (non-patent holders). Governance structures determine how firms should be organized in addition to prescribing rules for competition and cooperation among firms. Antitrust laws are examples of governance structures that regulate how firms can interact with each other by prohibiting market monopolization and other practices that work against market competition. Rules of exchange determine which actors are eligible to engage in economic transactions and under what conditions this may occur. An example of rules of exchange is the standardization of products by regulatory bodies, such as health and safety agencies. Only those who produce goods in accordance with these regulations are able to engage legally in economic transactions for profit. Finally, conceptions of control are pieces of market-specific knowledge used by economic actors to guide the internal organization of firms or to set forth strategies for competition or cooperation with other firms. Conceptions of control are world views, or understandings of how things work in a particular industry at a particular time, and are adopted by other firms when they are seen as profitable and advantageous. Fligstein identifies various types of conceptions of control, including the "sales and marketing conception of control" that was dominant among US firms in the post-World War II era, and the "finance conception of control" which is dominant currently. Overall, Fligstein's emphasis on the institutional preconditions of exchange highlights the role of states in markets, since it is states that institute governance structures and rules of exchange that guide market transactions, as well as legitimize certain conceptions of control over others.

Property

Varieties of Capitalism

We explained private property rights and markets as defining institutions of capitalism, but, even with these institutions in place, the actual socio-economic organization in capitalist societies is not one of a kind. The literature in the varieties of capitalism perspective focuses on the observation that there are different institutional arrangements of capitalist organization and that there is no single or uniform set of economic institutions that is superior in its efficiency. This is because different national contexts offer different endowments to economic actors and exhibit different kinds of social regulations, laws, and industrial agreements.

Broadly, then, varying systems of capitalism can be classified according to whether they rely on economic logics of market competition or strategic coordination. Consider the comparison between British, French, and German capitalism. Historical analysis shows that, in Britain, strong institutions of formal legal contracting supported competitive market relationships. In Germany, by contrast, cooperation and collaboration was needed to rebuild the country after World War II and the state played an active role in providing support for strategic collaboration between firms toward this goal. The French state was guided by yet a different organizing logic. In an effort to modernize itself, it took an active hand in the economy by directly regulating and coordinating wages, technological development, and corporate governance (Hall 2007).

Paying attention to the type of coordination among firms in a national context, two political economists, Peter Hall and David Soskice (2001), proposed to distinguish two main types, or varieties, of capitalism: liberal market economies (LMEs) and coordinated market economies (CMEs). An example of an LME is the United States, where markets are the primary way of coordinating economic action. In a CME, such as Germany, firms depend more on non-market modes of coordination, relational contracting, network monitoring, and a greater reliance on collaboration than on competition. Although the LME and CME distinction speaks to the macro-organization of an economy, Hall and Soskice based it on the action of firms and what firms need to do in different systems to exploit their core competencies in the areas of industrial relations, vocational training and education, corporate governance, relations with employees, and interfirm relations. Where is the role of states in all this?

Generally, it seems that the role of the state is more pronounced in countries that rely on strategic coordination. In these cases, the state may regulate the economy directly or set up institutions and agencies that help solve the problems of coordination, such as regularized collective bargaining or agencies for worker training. However, in countries based more on market mechanisms, the state also has an important role, though it is not so directly visible. In LMEs, the state is charged primarily with protecting the preeminence of markets as a key coordination mechanism between economic actors. LME states do so principally through the kind of legislation that favors market coordination and constrains the opportunities for economic actors to engage in strategic coordination. Ultimately, it is the state that enforces the key principle of economic organization, be it strategic coordination for CMEs or market mechanism for LMEs. For example, a state could provide framework legislation and supporting incentives for wages either to be regulated through collective bargaining by sectoral representatives (in CMEs) or to remain controlled by companies themselves (in LMEs).

The discussion categorizing capitalist economies into LMEs and CMEs is relatively recent. However, the distinctions between different capitalist economic systems were noted already in the 1970s. One of the classic works is Ronald Dore's (1973) comparison of the British and the Japanese factories. In Japan, Dore noted, the state takes an active role in regulating and facilitating the training of workers – a skilled workforce is seen as a benefit to the entire economy, and as such is a high priority for Japanese state action. The British state does something quite different. It sees skills as belonging to each individual worker as a representation of his or her personal advantages on the labor market, so an active role in general training is not a priority of the state. What is important, according to Dore, is that the different organizing economic logics present in Japan and the UK lead to far different economic actions and policies.

The notion of different national logics of economic organization, or different national economic cultures, is actually more popular among economic sociologists, while the LME/CME distinction is used mostly by political economists. Because they tend to understand institutions more broadly than strategic or market coordination, sociologists prefer the notion of logics. Generally, national economic logics refer to historically institutionalized patterns of authority, which make some kinds of economic actors (such as big firms or small family firms) and some kinds of interactions between economic actors (such as alliances with foreign firms or domestic firm networks) more or less appropriate and desirable. This leads to a great variety in national economic organization. Thus, networked small business firms might form the core pattern of economic organization in Taiwan, while *chaebol* based on a patrimonial principle dominate in South Korea, and foreign multinationals linked to international technology and marketing channels exist in Spain (Biggart and Guillén 1999). Not surprisingly, the role of the state in any of these economic cultures varies. In Korea, for instance, the state actively promotes the rise and expansion of huge and stable empires by subsidizing new firms under the auspices of existing *chaebol*. In Japan, the state actively promotes exports and plans industry expansion, while in Taiwan and Hong Kong the state leaves firms largely to their own devices (Whitley 1992).

Socialist Economies

Capitalism can be contrasted with socialism, which is a system characterized by (a) the collective ownership of the means of production; (b) redistribution, rather than market exchange, as the main principle of economic organization; and (c) a goal toward economic equality for all individuals. We will refer in this section to those socialist systems that were established in the Soviet Union, Central and Eastern Europe, and China, in addition to other countries where the communist parties rose to power after World War II (see map 2.1). As we discussed, Marx envisioned a classless and stateless communism. However, on the road to communism, socialism

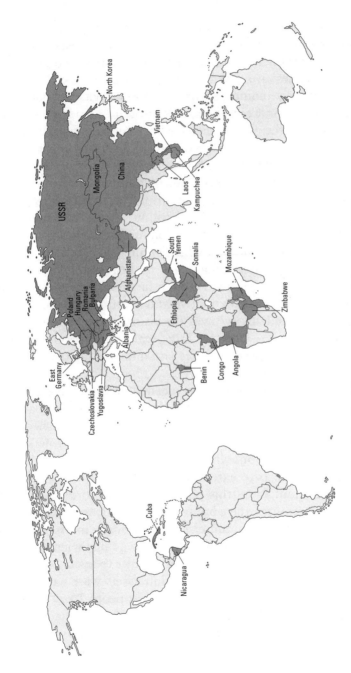

Map 2.1 Socialist countries across the globe, 1987

would be the intermediate stage in which states would play an important role, acting on behalf of workers and having control over the means of production, or "command" of the economy. Hence, socialist countries are often called state-socialist or command economies. Because communism was imposed with the help of the Soviet Red Army on Central and Eastern European countries after World War II – the Soviets helped liberate these countries from fascism – the state-socialist systems there are often referred to as Soviet socialism. Chinese socialism initially imitated the Soviet style of planning but soon developed in its own directions.

Marx envisioned that socialism would be the transitory stage before communism, which would follow as the last stage after advanced capitalism. However, the communist parties took power in underdeveloped economies which wanted to catch up with the West and so committed themselves to heavy industrialization. This would be accomplished through large-scale factory production with an emphasis on extractive and manufacturing industries. "One Nation, One Factory" was the vision of the socialist system (Róna-Tas 1997). To facilitate large-scale production, the party developed elaborate bureaucracies and imposed factory discipline on the entire population.

Three major institutions were needed to fulfill the goals of state socialism: collective property, centralized planning, and full employment. First, private property had to be abolished. You will remember that, according to Marx, private ownership of the means of production, which forces workers to sell their labor and pushes capitalists to extract ever more profit, is the culprit of labor exploitation. From this point of view a more humane and equal society requires the abolition of the institution of private property. Moreover, Communist Party leaders in state-socialist countries thought that private property was inefficient and thus an impediment to their goal of industrial expansion and large-scale production. Hence, all production assets were nationalized, becoming the property of "the whole of the people" or "the whole of society" (Kornai 1992: 71).

Second, and following from the lack of private property rights, the economy was organized as a redistributive system based on central planning. This would also help eliminate the inefficiencies associated with markets. Thus, instead of relying on market competition, party-appointed economic planners fixed output targets and prices and consequently made decisions about production, consumption, investment, and employment. Party-appointed administrators controlled the execution of the plan.

Third, the whole adult population was needed to achieve large-scale industrialization. The policy of universal employment was a solution on several grounds: it would help concentrate production, eliminate the inefficiencies and injustices of labor markets, and fulfill the promise of prosperity to the people by guaranteeing jobs. Full employment was also in line with the overarching motivation of the socialist economies, which was to maximize not profit but production (Szelényi, Beckett, and King 1994).

From the perspective of capitalism, the design of the socialist economy may seem irrational. However, such an assumption misunderstands socialism's purposes. Planning and control were put in place precisely to achieve rationality and to undo the inefficiencies associated with market fluctuations. Nevertheless, there were clear differences between the rationality of the socialist redistributive system and that of market capitalism (Szelényi, Beckett, and King 1994). The most explicit difference was the proclaimed goal of economic activity. While market competition and profit-making are extolled in capitalism, redistribution and equality were valued in socialism. Because of these different goals, firms operated under different conditions. As economist János Kornai characterized it, the key difference was in the budget constraints. Private firms strive to maximize profits. They operate under "hard budget constraints," meaning that, if they lose money, they go out of business. State-owned firms operate under "soft budget constraints"; if costs are higher than revenues, firms can continue to operate, since the state will bail them out. The state does so to ensure that the whole system functions. Any enterprise in a socialist economy is highly dependent on others for industrial production, and redistribution eliminates competition. Large state-owned firms, the most important socialist property form, are generally monopolies, and the system cannot tolerate the failure of any particular entity if it wants to advance the general interest (Kornai 1980). This principle is an instantiation of the grander cultural logic of the socialist system where collective interest supersedes self-interest. The case for socialism is thus made on both economically rational and moral grounds.

Centralized planning of the economy implies that uncertainties in economic production will be eliminated, since all activities are carefully planned and controlled. In fact, in the initial decades after World War I, socialist economies were catching up well with the West in terms of economic growth and industrialization. The Soviet economy, for instance, became industrialized at a rate that surpassed that of Germany and Japan at comparable moments in history (Róna-Tas 1997). However, this economic progress was hard to sustain. In the long run, large-scale production proved to be too inflexible, and plans too rigid, for the economy to meet the expectations of both the planners and the people. While the central committees designed five-year plans, the targets set sometimes changed, and supplies and raw materials needed for production would often not arrive on time or in the right amounts. To manage uncertainty, they padded budgets and hoarded materials. All this resulted in chronic shortages (Kornai 1980).

The Transformation of Soviet State Socialism

By the end of the the 1980s, communist rulers in most Central and Eastern European countries had introduced some economic reform, which included experimentation with economic decentralization and liberalization. While there were economic reasons for changes, we need to emphasize that calls for reforms had political and moral foundations. People were dissatisfied because their experience of socialism was moving further and further away from the proclaimed Marxist goals of freedom, equality, and social justice. The legitimacy of the system was becoming weaker and weaker.

In addition, external conditions after 1970 were not favorable to socialism. The explosion of oil prices after the OPEC crisis and developments in Western economies, which were moving away from heavy industry to information technology and services, were key economic factors that undermined the Soviet-style command economy. Faced with pressures to restructure their industries in addition to internal tensions, the Soviet state-socialist countries started borrowing heavily from the West and soon were drowning in foreign debt. The economic and political crises, aggravated by a constellation of domestic and international forces, induced grass-roots mobilization and mass protests. A significant large-scale mass mobilization began in Poland, where the Solidarity workers' movement mobilized an estimated 10 million members, about one-third of the Polish adult population (Jenkins and Benderlioglu 2005). They were supported by the Catholic Church and Pope John Paul II, a native of Poland, and emboldened by the unwillingness of the reform Soviet leader Mikhail Gorbachev to intervene militarily in Poland. (The Soviet army held a strong hand over the Central and Eastern European region throughout the postwar period.) In February 1989, the Polish government announced formal roundtable talks with Solidarity, with the Catholic Church mediating. The Polish Communist Party agreed to semi-free elections, facilitating what turned out to be a negotiated transition from communism. After six weeks of negotiations, a historic accord was reached in April 1989. Opposition political associations were sanctioned, legal rights were conferred on the Catholic Church, the party's media monopoly was lifted, and a new constitution, based on both socialist and pluralist principles, was drafted. In the subsequent elections, held in June 1989, the communists were defeated and Solidarity took over the government. In what some call a cascading effect, similar changes occurred throughout Eastern Europe, symbolically marked by the fall of the Berlin Wall in November 1989.

In retrospect, the collapse of Soviet socialism may have seemed inevitable, and this is the popular view. However, social scientists by and large did not see this major transformation coming (Przeworski 1991). Therefore, for many the question of socialism's collapse – whether inevitable because of the internal contradictions of the system or caused by historical contingencies beyond the system's control – is still not settled. The answer depends largely on one's understanding of what Soviet socialism was. If this system is considered an inefficient detour on the universal road to capitalism, then its fall was inevitable. But if, like the capitalist market, it was a particular institutional order that needed to be created, then the major reason for the crisis of Soviet state socialism was the weakening of the legitimacy of its core institutions – caused by contingent historical events – not inherent inefficiencies of a command economy (Szelényi and Szelényi 1994).

The revolutionary acts of 1989, and the subsequent collapse of communist regimes throughout the region, were followed by different ideas about how to transform socialist economies and the role that postsocialist states should play in this transformation, which could be characterized as the shock therapy and gradualist approaches. Neoliberal economists from the West who offered advice to these countries largely argued for the necessity of rapid changes, "a shock therapy," "a big bang" approach, with a goal to create markets quickly by eliminating state command of the economy and the supposed irrationalities of redistribution. They emphasized that the most efficient way of economic organization is a self-regulated market. Societies that ousted communists were advised to develop a private property rights regime swiftly through mass privatization. According to economic theory, once prices and currency controls are released, state subsidies withdrawn, and trade liberalized, this will give rise to a depoliticized economic system coordinated through market prices and competition, with a clear incentive structure that will induce efficient corporate governance and the rapid restructuring of firms (Boycko, Shleifer, and Vishny 1996).

Advocates of gradualism criticized shock-therapy recommendations for assuming *tabula rasa* conditions, an institutional vacuum after the fall of socialism, and they questioned the ability to design market institutions via a blueprint at a systemic level. They argued that the process of change is about gradual market institution-building, which requires the role of the state, depends on experimentation and evolutionary learning, and incorporates the existing social and economic networks and forms of practice (Stark and Bruszt 1998). As sociologist David Stark (1992) famously put it, capitalism should be built not on but *with* the ruins of socialism.

The shock therapy view of postsocialist transformation rested largely on a conviction that "markets [will] spring up as soon as central planning bureaucrats vacate the field," as a prominent economic advisor to the region, Jeffrey Sachs (1993: xii), put it. In contrast, economic sociologists studying economic changes in Central and Eastern Europe and the former Soviet Union agree that the state continues to play a very important role in postsocialism even if it does not have direct power over economic production and distribution. Postsocialist states played a key role in creating private property rights, regulating enterprise restructuring, creating consumer markets, and liberalizing economies to foreign investment. Much as Polanyi described for the nineteenth century in England, postsocialist states were charged with establishing the institutional framework that has enabled markets to function since the fall of communism. Most basically, private property rights needed to be institutionalized in the process of privatization which was led by states. But the role of the postsocialist states did not end there. As King and Sznajder (2006) reported in the case of Poland, for instance, the state was crucial in the transformation of the economy because it selected which firms would be extended credit and, therefore, had a higher likelihood of survival; it implemented an extensive industrial policy to guide the reallocation of resources; and it acted as an active owner of the thousands of state-owned enterprises, restructuring them before privatizing them in competitive auctions.

One key aspect of the postsocialist transition was also market liberalization – that is, allowing foreign economic actors to participate in the postsocialist economies as investors. In this regard, also, postsocialist states turned out to be quite important. Not only did they institute the regulatory framework that encouraged foreign investors to look out for opportunities, but they also helped create professional agencies that were charged with attracting such investment and which facilitated prominent foreign privatization deals that increased the legitimacy of foreign investment as an appropriate and desirable behavior for domestic business actors to emulate (Bandelj 2008).

As we can judge from economic performance after the first two decades of the collapse of communism in Central and Eastern Europe and the former Soviet Union, postsocialist states have led the transformation from plan to market more or less successfully. While the Central and Eastern European countries have done quite well and earned their membership in the EU, the collapse of the socialist state in Russia resulted in the involution of society, bringing anarchy to production and bargaining in external relations (Burawoy 1996). This has been attributed to the weak institutional capacity of the Russian state to carry out reforms, thus allowing some businessmen to amass wealth in so-called tycoon privatizations at the expense of the general welfare of others and intense increases in social inequality.

Indeed, a crucial aspect of postsocialist transformations linked to the role of the states is about social redistribution. Remember that the official ideology of socialism portrayed it as a system that ensures social justice and equality. The party-state would secure full employment and take care of the population's basic needs by providing universal education, healthcare, subsidized housing, and cultural goods (Kornai 1992). While socialist systems did not in fact erase inequalities, scholars overwhelmingly agree that income inequality was substantially lower during socialism than that in other systems at comparable levels of industrial development (Heyns 2005). Indeed, the state's role in guaranteeing pensions, free education, and healthcare has been one that people living in postsocialist countries had most difficulty forgoing in the transition to a market economy. Consequently, many Eastern European countries maintained relatively extensive social protection after the collapse of communism (Haggard and Kaufman 2008). Not all countries remain equally generous, however. The nature of the postsocialist state's role in maintaining social equality, and how much social protection they continue to offer to their citizens, depends on domestic politics and historical legacies and varies across different countries. Table 2.1 shows trends in income inequality across a variety of capitalist, socialist, and postsocialist countries. Note that countries where communist rule collapsed register higher levels of income inequality across the board between 1990 and 2000. Although there are many reasons for this, the retrenchment of the redistributive role of the state is one of them (Bandelj and Mahutga 2010). Differences in the types of welfare protection that states provide also partially account for variation in inequality among capitalist economies. We will return to this in chapter 4.

Chinese Socialism and Beyond

Chinese socialism evolved quite differently from Soviet socialism. The Chinese Communist Party took power in 1949, after the Chinese Civil War, with Mao Zedong as its leader. Like that of the Soviet regime, Mao's goal was to transform the largely backward Chinese economy into a modern agricultural and industrialized nation using central planning. After successfully imitating the Soviet style of planning for five years, Mao forged ahead with a program known as "the Great Leap Forward" to achieve simultaneous agrarian and industrial progress, including establishing people's communes in the Chinese countryside, together with backyard steel furnaces to foster steel production. This all led to a major economic disaster, with widespread famine that left tens of millions dead (Yang 2008). Mao's successor Deng Xiaoping initiated economic reforms in 1978 which aimed at liberalization and the decentralization of the Chinese economy, but strongly supervised by the communist state. Over a period of several decades, these reforms spearheaded continuous rapid economic growth which propelled China to the ranks of the top three world economies in terms of nominal GDP value.

How has China been able to accomplish such economic transformation? Conventional wisdom holds that clearly defined and enforced private property rights are essential to economic growth. From this perspective, the success of the Chinese economy presents a puzzle because the majority of productive assets are still state-owned. However, reforms have enabled rapid growth of private ownership and reliance on markets.

Chinese economic reforms were quite different from the process that occurred in Eastern Europe, which sought to move toward

Table 2.1 Trends in income inequality in capitalist, socialist, and postsocialist states (Gini indices)

	Capitalist						Socialist and postsocialist				
	1960	1970	1980	1990	2000		1960	1970	1980	1990	2000
Argentina	—	38.7	41.3	44.4	50.4	Armenia	—	—	—	—	48.6
Australia	27.8	28.0	24.0	37.7	35.5	Azerbaijan	—	—	—	—	40.4
Chile	—	50.1	51.9	54.0	57.4	Belarus	—	—	—	—	28.9
Costa Rica	—	—	—	45.8	47.9	Bulgaria	24.5	20.0	23.4	22.1	30.8
Denmark	—	—	41.3	34.2	37.1	China	—	29.9	24.4	28.7	32.4
Finland	—	—	—	26.9	30.2	Czechoslovakia	—	21.2	20.6	—	—
France	—	40.1	—	28.0	28.2	Czech Republic	—	—	—	—	25.4
Greece	41.1	45.3	—	—	32.3	Estonia	—	—	—	—	36.8
Indonesia	—	32.6	33.3	32.3	—	Hungary	—	22.9	20.7	29.2	25.0
Italy	—	39.0	37.5	—	34.6	Kyrgyz Republic	—	—	—	—	42.3
Japan	—	41.4	27.7	35.0	—	Latvia	—	—	—	—	34.3
Jordan	—	—	40.3	—	—	Lithuania	—	—	—	24.8	34.7
Mexico	—	49.1	—	—	54.0	Moldova	—	—	—	—	41.5
Nigeria	—	60.8	44.5	—	—	Poland	27.2	23.1	23.1	26.3	34.2
Norway	—	31.0	—	31.2	30.9	Romania	—	—	—	22.9	35.4

Philippines	—	—	—	—	47.5
Singapore	—	—	—	44.8	48.1
South Africa	54.0	51.0	49.0	63.0	56.5
Sri Lanka	—	33.8	36.1	—	40.4
Sweden	54.3	44.0	24.0	26.1	28.2
Turkey	—	—	—	—	39.8
UK	35.4	29.7	25.2	33.5	33.1
US	42.3	39.1	39.7	40.4	41.7
Mean	42.5	41.0	37.1	38.5	40.7
Russian Federation	—	—	—	—	43.7
Slovak Republic	—	—	—	—	24.3
Slovenia	—	—	—	—	25.9
Ukraine	—	—	—	—	41.3
USSR	—	—	26.8	28.1	—
Yugoslavia	—	25.0	21	31.6	—
Mean	25.9	23.7	22.9	26.7	34.8

Source: United Nations University World Institute for Development Economics Research, World Income Inequality Database.

a market economy rather quickly. Instead, Chinese economic reforms "grew out of the plan," to quote Barry Naughton's famous phrase. Even if Chinese planners did not really intend to develop a market system, they began to reform the economy in several important ways. The reforms began in agriculture and in the creation, in 1980, of four special economic zones to promote foreign investment on terms attractive to the outside world. The "Agricultural Responsibility System," which took three years (1979–82) to be pushed through nationwide, entailed dismantling the communes and contracting a small parcel of land to every household. Farmers could sell their produce on the open market after they had fulfilled the sales quota for which they had contracted with the collective, which still owned the land, at least nominally (Solinger 1993).

Beginning in the mid-1990s, important further reforms were enacted, such as requiring the equal treatment of state-owned and private firms, a unified exchange rate, uniform tax rates, and the restructuring of state-owned enterprises (Naughton 1999). The country was also opened up more and more over time to foreign investment. While there had been practically no foreign companies in China before the 1980s, by the new millennium it had become the most popular FDI destination in the world (Wang 2001: 11).

As a consequence, the degree of state ownership in the Chinese economy has begun to decrease. By mid-1995, 90,000 small state-owned enterprises had been transferred to the non-state sector by merger, sale, or lease. This represents full privatization rather than partial privatization understood as the diversification of ownership. The "Five Year Plan" for 2006–10 is explicit in its desire for a "people-centered" development strategy that balances economic growth with distributive, environmental, and social concerns. Despite greater moves toward privatization, the existence of growth plans exemplifies the great control and direction that the state still has over its economy, and thus many resist labeling the Chinese economy as a market economy. Gallagher (2005) points to the fact that the state still monopolizes key industries, such as banking, telecommunications, and energy, as important reasons why China is not a full-fledged market economy, even though in recent years it has introduced key policies promoting elements of private ownership and market capitalism.

Conclusion

The central tenet of chapter 2 is that the state's definition of property rights is fundamental to a country's macro-economic organization, be it capitalism or socialism. Private property rights in capitalism enable markets to function because buyers and sellers can exchange property stakes in assets. Adam Smith was one of the first economists to espouse the benefits of markets and argued that they should be led by the "invisible hand" rather than by government. Classical sociological writers did not focus on the efficiency of markets as price-setting mechanisms but on the economy as a social system, influenced by social relations, power distribution, and the meanings that people attach to economic actions. For Marx, economic relations determine all other aspects of society, including the state, so it is not surprising that in his view the state served the bourgeoisie, the capital. His vision of communism was a classless and stateless society. Max Weber made a distinct contribution to the understanding of the role of states in capitalism with his writing on rationalization and bureaucracy. Building on his work, contemporary sociologists find that the bureaucratic character of a state, in particular meritocratic recruitment and the provision of predictable and rewarding career ladders, is positively related to economic growth. Bureaucratic structures are essential to carry out developmentally oriented policies, but the power relations between different branches of the state bureaucracy must be organized in a way that also supports coherent state action.

The central institutions of capitalism are a free market and private property rights. Sociologists and economists agree that protection of private property rights is the duty of a state. For political and institutional economists, the key issue in the relationship between the role of the state and the economy is precisely the challenge for a state to be strong enough to guarantee the cnforcement of property rights but not too strong to expropriate them. Sociologists' understandings of the role of states in the capitalist economy go beyond this issue. This is because they view states as crucial not only in the provision and protection of property rights but also, as Neil Fligstein asserted, in determining rules of exchange, governance structures, and conceptions of control.

Even if markets and private property define the system in actually existing capitalist countries, there is significant variety in how capitalism is organized. The varieties of capitalism school in political economy traces differences to the various prevailing principles of economic coordination, distinguishing between societies that emphasize market competition or strategic coordination. Sociologists prefer to view capitalism's varieties in broader terms and point to the role of national logics of economic organization that are sustained by institutionalized patterns of authority relations within countries, which makes some kinds of actors and economic relationships more legitimate than others.

We contrasted the capitalist system of economic organization with socialism, which appears as antithetical to capitalism because it calls for the abolition of private property and relies on redistribution rather than market exchange. Just before the collapse of communist regimes in most socialist countries in 1989, one-third of the world's population lived under socialism. Socialist principles are still important in several countries today, most notably China. In common parlance we often think of capitalism as a rational and socialism as an irrational economic system. However, such an assumption misunderstands the latter's purposes. In fact, socialist planning and control were put in place precisely to achieve rationality and to undo the inefficiencies associated with market fluctuations.

Socialist economies showed some real economic progress but, on the whole, large-scale production proved to be too inflexible, and plans too rigid, for the economy to meet the expectations of the planners and the people. The economy suffered from severe shortages, and limits on individual freedom were becoming more and more oppressive. By the end of the 1980s, communist rulers in most Central and Eastern European countries had introduced some economic reform, which included experimentation with economic decentralization and liberalization. Socialist economies were reformed following the defeat of communist parties in the first free elections after World War II. Two different approaches were advocated: shock therapy and gradualism. The former was claimed to have produced more harm than good, and the latter is often declared as the reason for the success of the Chinese economy, which is among the top three in the world today, and the fastest growing, retaining socialist principles and with communist rule still in place.

In sum, the state plays a fundamental role in organizing macro-economic systems, be they capitalist or socialist, because it defines and upholds who has rights over property. By defining property rights as either private or collective, the state promotes – or not – the functioning of markets. Beyond the definition of property rights, the role of states in different kinds of capitalist and socialist systems is qualitatively different. In socialism, the state controls the great bulk of the economic resources and decides how they will be used. In capitalism, the state's primary function is to set the rules and norms. Both the rise of markets in nineteenth-century England and the role of the postsocialist states in guiding the transformation from plan to market after communism exemplify how crucial state action is in the creation of capitalism.

3

Money: The State's Role in Monetary Policy, Government Spending, and Taxation

Polanyi claimed that modern money is a fictitious commodity. In one sense, this refers to the fact that money is essentially a bookkeeping entry validated by a social agreement and enforced by law. In another sense, money is not a genuine commodity because it is not "manufactured" to be exchanged in the marketplace. Even though, today, any national currency can actually be bought and sold at a particular price on international exchange markets, money's primary function is not to be traded but to serve as medium of trade. Moreover, equilibration of supply and demand forces alone cannot produce more money. That is, the US government does not start printing more US dollars if suddenly more foreigners wish to hold larger amounts. The production of money is not subject to such supply–demand market rationality. Instead, national governments retain ultimate control over when and how to manipulate a country's supply of money and, thus, influence its value.

Before the mid-1800s, the state guaranteed that coins contained the appropriate amount of precious metal so that their value could be reliably ensured to those engaging in economic exchanges. One of the main reasons why this is no longer done is that currencies made out of valuable material are easy to manipulate for personal gain. Small portions of gold and silver coins can be shaved off, for instance, while economic exchanges based on their full value continue to be carried out. Central governments thus began to look for new materials out of which currency could be produced. The first paper money was little more than an IOU that represented a certain amount of precious metal, usually gold. But, over time, states have introduced "fiat money," where the paper money we exchange is not intrinsically valuable, nor does it necessarily correspond to a certain value of precious metals. Instead, the value comes from the social agreement that notes and coins are worth something, just like cigarettes in prison, subway tokens, baseball cards, or poker chips, which have an agreed upon rather than a natural value (Zelizer 1999).

In the 1800s, states generally began to expand in size and to become more centralized in their operations. At this time, the control of currency became an increasingly important function of the state. By monopolizing the money supply, states were able to raise revenue and fund public expenditure as well as to regulate economic transactions within and across their borders. This link between currency and statehood is one that has guided the development of national currencies throughout history (Helleiner 2002). It is also quite evident in the visual representations of the monies used in different countries. Consider US currency, for instance. Dollar bills and coins are decorated with portraits of presidents and other public figures, and some carry with them the slogan "E pluribus unum," which means "from many, one," emphasizing national unity.

This chapter examines what role states play in monetary and fiscal policy and the financialization of contemporary economy. When does the state decide to issue more currency? How are decisions made about taxation and spending? What happens when manipulation of money itself becomes the major source of productive activity? These are the questions addressed here.

Money, Money, Money

Why do we need money? In non-market economies long ago, people obtained various items through reciprocal exchange. For instance, if you were a farmer and needed clothes, you could offer your grain to a tailor, who would give you a pair of pants in return. Ultimately, however, such barter exchanges became untenable because they limit the range of goods that one can acquire, make saving rather difficult (as many goods have an expiration date) and pose issues of commensurability and divisibility. (What is the commensurate amount of grain for one pair of pants? But if I have only half of that grain amount, I can't really get half the pair of pants, as pants are not a good that is easily divisible.) For many reasons, therefore, it made sense to start using some medium of exchange in economic transactions. The earliest forms included cowrie shells, cacao beans, jewelry, and spices, which all functioned as money during some period of history. These goods were valuable in and of themselves, and as such they carried with them a sense of compensation for the individuals who received them as payment for an exchange. Not surprisingly, precious metals, such as gold and silver, were also particularly important as early forms of money (Cohen 1998).

In the mid-1800s, the right to monopolize the money supply was seized by rulers, and only in this period did truly territorial currencies arise. Many have emphasized that currencies came into being alongside the development of the modern state and the corresponding nationalistic sentiments (Cohen 1998). We can find more current evidence of the link between sovereign statehood and currency in the almost immediate proliferation of national currencies among newly independent ex-colonial states as well as the postsocialist states of Central and Eastern Europe, which established unique currencies as part of their assertion of independence.

In the case of the US, the dollar has been the national currency since 1861. Interestingly, it was introduced at a time of national disunity expressed through the Civil War. This draws our attention to the political symbolism of money. Introducing a common currency at a time of war and division helped emphasize that the US should remain a united territory. Importantly, the Confederacy also recognized the unifying function of currency, and Confederate dollars circulated in the US South during this time. It took about fifty more years after 1861 before the money supply was standardized and regulated by a central bank (Cohen 1998; Bensel 1990; Markham 2002).

Money

Up until the 1970s, each dollar represented a certain amount of gold reserves kept by the state. In this regard, the US was no exception. The fact that each state government produced currency that was tied to its own reserves of precious metals is called the "Gold Standard." However, the turmoil and hardship of the Great Depression and World War II increased the degree to which monetary stability became an international concern, and in 1944 representatives of major nations gathered together in Bretton Woods, New Hampshire, for the United Nations Monetary and Financial Conference. What emerged from this meeting was the Bretton Woods Agreement that created rules and institutions for the international monetary system. Notably, one part of this agreement was the formulation of a new exchange rate system replacing the individual gold standards with a system of fixed exchange rates, where all international currencies were pegged to the US dollar, which was itself pegged to reserves of gold. Additionally, the International Monetary Fund (IMF) was established as an international lending agency to support the central banks of individual states. This system existed until the 1970s, when fixed exchange rates were replaced by floating exchange rates, where the value of currency was determined by international markets. Under floating exchange rates, money is tied only loosely to gold (Carruthers and Babb 2000; Helleiner 1996).

Finally, who prints the money? In the US, money is "manufactured" by two government agencies, the Bureau of Engraving and printing (BEP) and the US Mint, which are both a part of the US Treasury. The BEP prints paper currency and the Mint creates coins. The printing of money is an immense undertaking, employing 2,300 people. In the fiscal year 2008, the BEP printed over 28 million pieces of paper currency with a face value of over $629 million. $1 bills make up almost 45 percent of the production of paper notes, and over 95 percent of paper currency produced each year replaces old currency that is taken out of circulation. Currency does in fact have a lifespan, and it is constantly pulled from circulation and replaced with new bills. $1 bills, for instance, have an average lifespan of twenty-one months (Bureau of Engraving and Printing 2009). After money is printed, it is then transported to the Federal Reserve for processing and distribution. The Fed actually buys money from the US Treasury at the manufacturing cost, currently about 4 cents per bill for paper currency. The twelve Federal Reserve banks then distribute the money to other financial institutions.

Monetary Policy

Monetary policy is the process by which the monetary authority of a country controls how much money circulates in the economy (the so-called supply of money) and the cost of money (expressed in the interest rate). The government's goal is to encourage economic growth and stability, and to do so it relies on different kinds of monetary policy actions, such as changing the interest rate or printing more money. These actions generally respond to the business cycles – that is, economy-wide fluctuations that contribute to periods of expansion in the economy (boom), followed by periods of relative stagnation or decline (bust), before economic production, investment, and consumption grow yet again.

The workings of monetary policy are complex and sometimes confusing, but crucial to the lives of those throughout the country. The average person encounters monetary policy when he or she applies for a loan, buys a car, or receives a mortgage to purchase a house. The terms for such agreements are set by the Federal Reserve Board, which is a central monetary authority in the United States.

In order to influence economic stability and employment during periods of economic boom and bust, monetary policy can be either expansionary/loose or contractionary/tight. As these words indicate, the expansionary policy increases the total supply of money available in the economy and a contractionary policy decreases it. Increasing the money supply is traditionally used to combat unemployment in a recession, because increased amounts of money circulating will be associated with lower interest rates, encouraging people to invest and consume rather than keep their money in the high-interest-earning bank accounts. In contrast, contractionary policy leads to higher interest rates, which help to combat rising prices, or inflation, that may accompany periods of economic growth.

Which official body regulates the supply of money? Institutions called central banks perform this function, as they have the ultimate authority over their nation's money, its convertibility, and the overall health of the national banking system. In the US, the Federal Reserve System is the nation's central bank, also called the banks' bank or the government's bank. The European Central Bank (ECB), based in Frankfurt, Germany, plays this role for the countries using the euro. The Bank of Japan, the People's Bank of China, and the Bank of England are central banks for their respective countries. Central banking institutions were established primarily to regulate the money supply and the behavior of banks and other lending agencies to prevent instability, such as during the Great Depression when the banks could not pay all those who wanted to withdraw their money (Markham 2002). (See box 3.1 on the role and history of the Federal Reserve System, or the Fed.)

What are some of the specific ways in which the Fed can control the supply of money? As is reported on its website, the Fed uses three major monetary tools. The first is via open market operations. This refers to the buying and selling of US Treasury securities, which are the bonds issued by the US Department of the Treasury, also referred to as T-bonds or T-notes. When the Federal Reserve Bank of New York purchases T-notes, for instance, it supplies the market with dollars, and thus increases the nation's money supply. The second mechanism is discount window lending, which refers to the normal behavior of banks – i.e. lending to customers – except that here the Fed's customers are banks themselves. The rates at which it lends at the discount window, its lending facility, are set by the twelve Reserve banks, which are part of the Fed and approved by the Fed's Board of Governors. The third mechanism is manipulation of reserve requirements. US banks and other depository institutions are required to keep funds in *reserve* at the Federal *Reserve* against deposits made by their customers (including you, if you have a savings account). If the Fed raises these requirements, banks need to keep more funds in reserve,

Box 3.1 What's the Fed got to do with you?

Have you ever turned on a news program and heard a statement such as, "Today, after much speculation, the Fed lowered the interest rate . . ." If so, and you were somewhat confused by this declaration, you are certainly not alone. The Federal Reserve System, commonly known as the Fed, is a crucially important but often misunderstood institution in the United States.

So what has the Fed got to do with how much money costs if you borrow it – that is, the interest rate? If you tried to get a loan to finance a car, a house, or your education, you were quoted an interest rate. This rate was based on what is known as the "prime rate," which is set by the banks. However, this "prime rate" is strongly influenced by the rate set by the Federal Open Market Committee (FOMC), a decision-making body of the Federal Reserve, known as the "federal funds rate." This is the rate that banks charge each other for overnight loans out of the *reserves* they are required to keep in the Federal *Reserve* Bank. Banks would need such loans, for instance, when they do not have enough reserves of their own to cover the withdrawals of their customers. (Yes, the money you put in the bank doesn't just sit in that account, always available for you to withdraw. The bank circulates that money to offer loans and participate in financial markets.)

The federal funds rate and the prime rate generally move in tandem in that they rise and fall together: the prime rate is generally about 3 percent higher than the federal funds rate and is published in the *Wall Street Journal*. It is up to the banks to change their posted rates after the announcement about the federal funds rate change from the FOMC. Once 75 percent of banks introduce new rates, the *Wall Street Journal* reports a new prime rate. Practically, this means that when twenty-three out of thirty of the United States' largest banks change their prime rate, the *Wall Street Journal* prints a prime rate change.

This is why consumer loans were not suddenly free when the FOMC decided to lower the federal funds rate to near zero in

December 2008 to address the economic recession. This was a historic move by the Fed, and many thought that this drastic and extraordinary cut went far beyond what experts speculated it would do. This act, however, is one that should remind us why the Federal Reserve System was established in the first place: it was in 1913, in response to the widespread financial instability, panic, and bankruptcies of private banks that had occurred in the nineteenth and early twentieth centuries. The Fed is intended to increase the safety of the financial and monetary system, and in today's globally connected world its influence actually extends far beyond US borders.

and consequently less money is available for circulation in the economy.

By buying or selling Treasury securities, lending to banks, or changing reserve requirements for banks, the Federal Reserve System influences the federal funds rate, which is the interest rate charged by one depository institution on an overnight sale of balances at the Federal Reserve to another depository institution. What matters for any one individual living in the US, as we also explained in box 3.1, is that changes in the federal funds rate will influence the rate that lending institutions charge when business or individuals borrow money from them, called the prime rate. This is why we may mistakenly believe that the Fed actually sets the interest rates. It doesn't. It sets the federal funds rate, and this influences prime interest rates. Figure 3.1 shows how these interest rate trends move in tandem. Overall, the changes in interest rates will influence the amount of money and credit in the economy and ultimately a range of economic outcomes, such as employment and the prices of goods and services. Why is that? According to a general economic theory, if the interest rate is higher, more people will be interested in saving their money rather than spending it, which will lower the level of investment and consumption in the economy, and therefore the prices of goods and services. If the interest rate is lower, people will be encouraged to spend and invest, which will open up jobs and raise employment in the

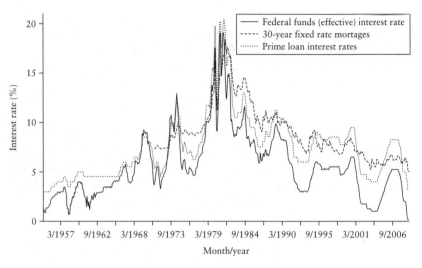

Source: www.federalreserve.gov/releases/h15/data/Monthly/H15_FF_O.txt.
www.freddiemac.com/pmms/pmms30.htm.
http://research.stlouisfed.org/fred2/data/PRIME.txt.

Figure 3.1   Interest rate fluctuations in the US, 1955–2008

economy. If interest rates change from high to low, or vice versa, this can help reduce the impact of fluctuations stemming from the cycles of growth and contraction of the economy, or the business cycle.

The actions that the Fed undertakes will also have an influence on the international market by impacting exchange rates and the balance of trade. For instance, if the Fed decides to lower deposit reserve requirements for banks, banks will have a greater amount of money to invest. This causes the price of investments such as US bonds to rise because there is higher demand for them. The increases in bond prices will have an effect on the exchange market because they will prompt investors to sell American bonds and buy bonds in other international markets. So an investor will sell his American bond to buy, say, a Japanese one, and in so doing will exchange American dollars for Japanese yen. Foreign exchange markets will therefore see an increased supply of American dollars and a decreased supply of Japanese yen. These shifts in the supply of the one currency and demand for the other will lead to a devaluation of the US dollar relative to the Japanese yen. This has an influence on the balance of trade (the ratio between exports and imports) because the lower exchange rate makes American-produced goods cheaper in Japan and Japanese-produced goods more expensive in America. Exports from the US will therefore grow and imports from Japan will decline, causing the balance of trade to increase.

So far, we have assumed that countries have official authorities which act to shape the money supply to influence alternations between periods of boom and bust in the economy. (This is not an unwarranted assumption because almost every country has one.) However, it is important to mention that some influential economists do not believe that central banks really serve their intended function because they doubt that the banks can get it quite right. Milton Friedman, for instance, believed that the central bank would always get it wrong, leading to wider swings than if the economy had simply been left to organize on its own, without government intervention. This is why he advocated a non-interventionist approach to the economy (Friedman 1962). And there are cases where central banks "don't get it quite right" which can have significant detrimental effects on an economy and the society that depends on it. The consequences of a failed monetary policy include hyperinflation, stagflation, recession, high unemployment, shortages of imported goods, an inability to export goods, and even total monetary collapse and the adoption of a much less efficient barter economy. This happened in Russia in 1998, for instance, when the Russian government had defaulted on its domestic currency debt, an event that is also known as the "rouble crisis."

In 2004, Ben Bernanke, who two years later took over as chairman of the Federal Reserve Bank, suggested that, since the late 1990s, modern central banks have become skilled at the manipulation of the money supply, leading to a smoother business cycle, with smaller and less frequent recessions than in earlier decades, a phenomenon he called "the Great Moderation" (Bernanke 2004). However, the financial crisis that took place less than two years into Bernanke's term lends a bitter taste to his speech. The heated discussions debating the role of the Fed in causing the crisis, as well as the actions in which the Fed engaged to address it, indicate that what central monetary authorities do – whether they attempt to jig interest rates up or down or have a wider set of economic functions – is not as clear cut as economic laws of money supply and demand lead us to believe. Mitchel Abolafia (2004, 2005) offers a very rare sociological study of decision-making at the Fed, analyzing publicly available transcripts of meetings of the FOMC, and shows that "policymaking at the Fed is not only an exercise in discovering [what economic decision should be made] but also in shaping what is known in financial markets" (2005: 227). The stage of meeting, existing customs, and prior decisions all matter in what the FOMC decides, and the stock market traders and the banks respond to even the slightest of its moves as a sign of what is going on in the economy, which influences the amount of trading and borrowing and lending. But the definition of market conditions is anything but certain. According to Abolafia, chief economists at the Fed engage in interpretive politics – that is, a struggle over the framing of ideas, attempting to have their definition of what is going on in the market prevail. This is consistent with a basic tenet of economic sociology that markets are socially constructed institutions and not some objective mechanism that adjudicates demand and supply curves. An integral part of the social construction of markets is ongoing interpretation and sense-making of market actors. Abolafia's remarkable research shows that, in order to function, markets require interpretation and sense-making not only of buyers and sellers who partake in exchange, but also, and crucially, of those who are appointed to govern markets, such as the decision-makers at central banks.

Fiscal Policy

In addition to providing the medium of exchange used in economic transactions and controlling the availability and cost of this money, states engage in **fiscal policy**, which refers to government borrowing, spending, and taxation. An advocate of active fiscal policy was John Maynard Keynes, who suggested that the government should spend during a recession in order to stimulate investment that will resuscitate the economy, rather than leaving it to the market to work it out by itself in the long run – because, as he famously put it, "in the long run, we are all dead" (Keynes 1924).

Government spending

There are two key aspects to a fiscal policy, government spending and taxation. Let's first consider government spending, which is something that varies significantly across countries (map 3.1). Even the harshest critics of the role of the state in the economy, such as Adam Smith, agree that the state has a role to play in providing public goods, national defense, and education. These are the very basic things that are included in government spending. Governments also spend on healthcare, research and development, social protection, and the military. But they vary widely on the resources they allocate to each of these purposes. Consider figure 3.2.

How are government expenditures funded? The most obvious source is taxes, which we discuss in the next section. But the government can also obtain money by consuming fiscal reserves kept from times of economic growth, when it may have removed funds from the economy to stave off inflation. The government can also sell assets that are in state hands, such as land or state-owned corporations – which happened on a large scale during the process of privatization in Eastern Europe, for instance – and can borrow from the population by issuing bonds such as T-bills. We may all own government-issued bonds, which are considered a safe investment, albeit yielding a lower rate than stocks. Curiously, most of the US Treasury bonds are actually owned by the Chinese government.

How are decisions about spending made? As it becomes patently obvious to anyone who follows government budget debates, political parties and interest groups have different priorities and push for different kinds of spending. The blatant truth is that the

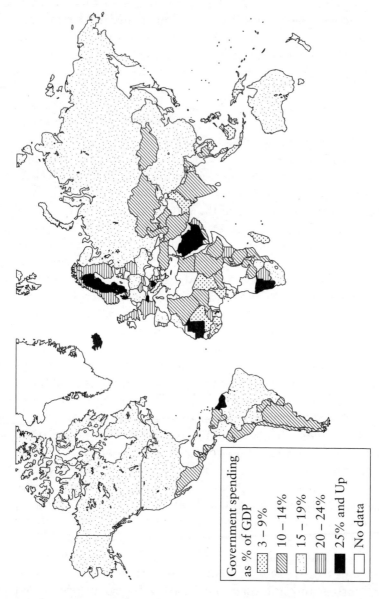

Source: World Development Indicators, 2005.

Map 3.1 Government expenditure across the world

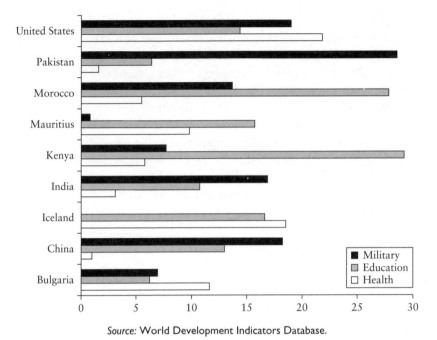

Source: World Development Indicators Database.

Notes: Iceland spends 0% of government expenditure on the military.
Education data for India are for 2003 and China for 1999.

Figure 3.2 Government expenditure on the military, education, and health, 2004 (%)

government's resources are limited, so decisions to spend more on defense, for instance, mean that less is spent on other social issues, such as education or healthcare. After fierce debates in senates, parliaments, or assemblies, a government budget is written into a legal document that is often passed by the legislature and approved by the chief executive or president.

One of the issues debated among politicians and scholars is that of balanced budgets, a situation where there is neither a deficit (too much spending) nor a surplus (too much extraction through taxation). Should governments always aim for balanced budgets? There are dissenting views on this, with the mainstream economic position that balanced budgets every year are actually not desirable. In American politics, the issue seems especially central, so much so that all US states other than Vermont have a Balanced Budget Amendment of some form. As far as the US federal government is concerned, however, budget deficits seem to be more of a rule than an exception. The US has generally run a deficit since the late 1960s, with estimates at an unparalleled $1.2 trillion for the 2009 budget year, marking one of the highest deficits in recent history. Wars in Iraq and Afghanistan, the recession, the stimulus, and the rising costs of social security and Medicare because of the aging US population have all contributed to this colossal figure. The proposed solution likely lies in both reductions in future government spending *and* increases in taxation (Leonhardt 2010).

Taxation

If the only things certain are death and taxes, one of the most obvious ways in which the state matters for individuals economically is by extracting taxes. States may levy taxes on goods and products that we purchase in stores, on the income we earn, on the capital gains we may receive, on the property we hold, on the inheritance to which we may be entitled, on imported goods from another country, and on things that may pollute the environment, among others.

Issues of taxation are central to the relationship between a state and its citizens. As part of their membership in the state, individuals have rights to property and some other liberties, but they receive these things in exchange for serving the state, either physically in times of war, through services in kind, and through contributions to the state's revenue base via taxation. The taxation process, then, can be envisioned as a relationship, a social contract, between the heads of state and the citizens of the state.

How much do different countries pay in taxes? Many Americans think their taxes are high, but analyses show that total tax revenue as a share in GDP has been generally lower in the US than in all other affluent countries except Japan. Sweden, for instance, collects more than half its GDP in taxes (Dreier 2007). This doesn't mean that income taxes are generally low in the US and so much

Table 3.1   Taxation rates across countries (%)

Country	2000			2007		
	Personal taxes	Corporate taxes	VAT taxes	Personal taxes	Corporate taxes	VAT taxes
Australia	26.10	34.00	10.00	23.40	30.00	10.00
France	28.80	37.76	20.60	27.80	34.43	19.60
Germany	44.50	42.20	16.00	42.80	26.38	19.00
Hungary	35.70	18.00	25.00	38.70	20.00	20.00
Ireland	20.30	24.00	21.00	13.90	12.50	21.00
Japan	17.00	30.00	5.00	20.10	30.00	5.00
Korea	9.00	28.00	10.00	11.90	25.00	10.00
Mexico	2.40	35.00	15.00	5.20	28.00	15.00
Sweden	33.70	28.00	25.00	27.60	28.00	25.00
UK	25.50	30.00	17.50	27.00	30.00	17.50
US	24.90	35.00	n/a	24.50	35.00	n/a

Source: OCED Online Statistics

Notes: Personal taxes figures refer to average personal income tax rates for a single person with no children. Corporate tax figures are basic (non-targeted) central, sub-central and combined (statutory) corporate income tax rates. Where a progressive (as opposed to flat) rate structure applies, the top marginal rate is shown. VAT taxes are "value-added taxes" or "goods and services taxes" that are assessed on the value-added to goods and services. Figures reported here refer to the standard rates. Some countries also have reduced rates for different regions and/or different goods and services categories. There is no VAT tax in the US.

higher in Sweden. There are many different kinds of taxes that the state can impose, and those figures reflect the overall picture. Table 3.1 shows some tax rates for various purposes and for different countries. These figures provide averages for ease of comparison. We should note, however, that actual tax schemes are rarely flat (i.e. with one rate for all income categories), but either progressive or regressive. The difference captures the extent to which the rate increases or decreases, respectively, as the taxable base amount increases. Progressive personal income taxes, for instance, place a greater burden on the rich than on the poor, while regressive taxes accomplish the opposite.

So, what determines the taxation policies that a government

adopts? Economists frame the answer to this question primarily as a matter of minimizing cost and maximizing benefits. That is, taxation should strike a balance between minimizing the loss of economic welfare and maximizing the efficiency of wealth redistribution in a country. Sociologists are not convinced that tax policies are best understood as a cost–benefit calculation. Rather, they focus on how taxation is a socially constructed phenomenon, a social contract between society and state, and shaped by political, cultural, and institutional factors.

Historically, much of the initial impetus for tax policy comes from geopolitical conflicts, such as wars (Tilly 1985). This suggests that there are important political bases to this economic behavior. Even during times of peace, researchers point to political conflicts and struggles for power as a way of explaining differences in taxation policies across nations. Morgan and Prasad (2009) argue that decisions about tax structure in the United States and France were shaped by resistance to the concentration of economic power in the former and the centralization of state power in the latter, producing something that seems quite counterintuitive: more progressive income taxation (which implies a greater control of capital) in the US, a country otherwise believed to be one of the starkest defenders of the free market, and an ineffective income tax and regressive sales taxes (which implies lesser control of the state) in France, a country believed to be strongly statist. The adopted taxation responds to nineteenth-century political movements that tried to counter the rapid concentration of economic power in the US and the centralization of state power in France, leading to support for an income tax with redistributive purposes in the former but not in the latter.

Politics enters into decisions about taxation today as well. Consider that taxes may be lower in industries with large firms that can exercise political clout over legislators, and that the presence of a strong labor movement tends to indicate tax breaks for the working class. However, the relationship between class power and fiscal power is not always straightforward on account of the bargaining and lobbying that takes place during the legislative process: though the labor movement would prefer that corporations have higher taxes than the working class, labor organizations sometimes concede tax breaks for the wealthy to help promote economic growth and expand employment to benefit workers. Another illustration of the influence of politics over taxation would seem to be the promises made by political candidates either to lower or raise taxes. While the tax issue is on almost everyone's campaign platform, research shows that tax policy does not in fact change radically in response to electoral cycles, as might be expected, but rather changes only incrementally so that political constituents are not upset by radical tax shifts (Campbell 1993).

Particular aspects of taxation also reveal cultural understandings of what society considers valuable. Think about tax deductions and incentives that are offered for charitable giving. While altruistic acts such as charity donations would seem to be at the discretion of any single individual, the taxation framework can influence the extent of giving to a significant degree. The fact that you are able to deduct your charitable donations on your income tax return indicates that the state, through its taxation policy, encourages you to do so. Research also finds that corporations in states with higher corporate tax rates give more to charity. This is partly because statutory law allows corporations to deduct up to 10 percent of their taxable earnings, but it is also partly for normative reasons; higher state tax corporate rates signal that it is important to create and maintain the health of a local community, and greater engagement in corporate philanthropy is in line with this goal (Guthrie et al. 2007). Tax credits are another example of how a state conveys what is considered valuable. The aims for which a government provides tax credits can help steer research and development into chosen directions. For instance, the government can respond to calls for ecologically friendly technologies by providing tax credits to businesses that conduct research and development in this area, effectively steering the course of technological development (Backhaus 2002). Tax provisions also intersect with intimate spheres such as family. Providing tax credit for children is one way of institutionalizing hierarchy among the different kinds of families, placing those who are childless in a disadvantage under the law. Related, several features of US tax law could be understood as favoring traditional, single-earner families over dual-income, married couples with children (McCaffery 2009). Moreover, recent research has pointed to how tax policy is influenced by the institutional forces that diffuse across international borders. One such example is the flat tax rate scheme. Flat taxes mean that household income and sometimes corporate profits are being taxed at one marginal rate, in contrast with progressive taxes that vary by different categories of income level. Because a flat tax rate is applicable also to the corporate profits of foreign investor firms, it can be considered as consistent with the neoliberal goals of lowering the costs of cross-country investment. The flat tax scheme gained unprecedented popularity in postsocialist Eastern European countries. Out of the twenty-three countries that currently have a flat tax rate, nineteen are former socialist countries. International diffusion processes encouraged by the emulation of peer states has a lot to do with why so many neighboring countries have adopted this procedure, coupled with the right-wing political orientation of the governments in power (Baturo and Gray 2009). Kiser and Sacks (2009) present another example of the role of international diffusion processes but for a very different region: sub-Saharan Africa. The authors show that many countries in this part of the world have widely, and largely uncritically, adopted "modern" tax administration, which is ill-suited when resources are scarce and means of communication and transportation so poor as to make monitoring and sanctioning tax collectors all but impossible. Practically, this means that many states in sub-Saharan Africa are unable to raise revenues to provide the most basic conditions for peace and prosperity. Kiser and Sacks argue that, under certain conditions, contemporary developing countries may actually benefit from tax-farming arrangements similar to those implemented in early modern Europe, whereby the burden of tax collection is assigned to private individuals or groups rather than to the state bureaucracy. (These private parties must invest their own money initially to pay off the tax debt, against the hope of subsequently collecting, or "farming," a larger sum.)

The social consequences of tax policy

Once tax policy is formed, it has important social ramifications. Historically, political rebellion and resistance have been the chief consequences. Not only might citizens take action against their state for excessive taxation, but undertaxation might weaken state capacity, creating a fiscal crisis ripe for revolutionary activity (Skocpol 1979; Goldstone 1991). Taxation also serves as a key input in the process of state formation and maintenance over time (Tilly 1978; Ardant 1975). The particular kind of taxation helps specify the type of state structure that develops (Mann 1988). For instance, the bureaucratic apparatus in countries that tax international trade is not as extensive as that in other states, because the collection of taxes is less onerous and there are fewer collective goods to be distributed through government agencies (Ardant 1975; Poggi 1978). Taxes also influence the structure of economic activity: depending on how tax burdens are distributed among organizational forms, a particular type of firm (i.e. small or large) might come to dominate the economy on account of the tax benefits it receives from the state (Lindberg and Campbell 1991; Lazerson 1988). Finally, levels of income tax can influence who does or does not participate in the labor force. If married couples are taxed on their communal earnings, they might be placed in a higher tax bracket, which could discourage the participation of both spouses in the labor force (Steinberg and Cook 1988; Leader 1983). On the whole, this research makes clear that taxes are not simply a product of economic calculation in which rational state actors engage to maximize wealth and minimize costs, but instead are the result of complex processes that mediate the formulation of tax policies and produce a variety of consequences for social life.

One of the key consequences of taxation is economic inequality, in terms of both the amount of wealth that a person can accumulate during their lifetime and the size of the inheritance a person's heirs can collect. In the US, specifically, wealth is extremely concentrated in the hands of relatively few (Keister and Moller 2000), and policy instruments such as tax breaks for the rich seem to work further to encourage the accumulation of wealth among those who are already wealthy. Inheritance is one of the main ways through which a person's wealth can be augmented without any particular effort, skills, or labor market activity required. For this reason, inheritance tax, as laid out by the state, plays a crucial role in determining the transfer of wealth across genera-tions. However, whether a country should have an inheritance tax and, if so, how high it should be is not an obvious thing. Jens Beckert (2008) compared the development of inheritance laws in Germany, France, and the United States to find that, despite the commonalities that these modern, Western capitalist countries share, distinct differences came to exist because of the differences in political culture and institutionalized understandings about the nature of property, the state, and the family. The US has the fewest restrictions on the autonomy of the testator to determine the inheritance of wealth, based in part on the low priority given to the redistribution of wealth and the general distaste concerning the intervention of the state in private economic affairs. In Germany, however, social and familial relations are prized above economic freedom, so the government limits individual choice of how to dispose of wealth after death in an effort to protect the family unit. Different again, France is a country where the government per-ceives an obligation to uphold the general welfare of its population but strives to remain neutral in regard to private property. Rising out of the principles of equality and liberty that guided the French Revolution, inheritance policy was used by the state as a way of organizing society along these principles.

The State's Enforcement of Debtor–Creditor Relations

Much of the discussion in the monetary policy section of this chapter focused on the influence that state actions have on the cost at which money can be borrowed. We assumed that individuals and firms readily borrow money and take out loans, including the "short-term" borrowing that our credit cards afford us, even if we pay the balance at the end of the month. However, the fact that economic subjects (debtors) borrow money from other economic subjects who lend it (creditors) is not at all straightforward. The debtor–creditor relationship is marked by uncertainty and requires an element of trust in order for some to lend money to others with a reasonable assurance that the debt will be repaid. A predictable legal system is one means through which the state helps to enforce debtor–creditor relations by creating enforceable contracts regulated by commercial law. Mortgages and other loan contracts are specific examples of formalized expressions of debtor–creditor relations which are enforced through state regulations to ensure that each party will fulfill its obligations to the other.

There also are other state actions and regulations that impact debtor–creditor relations more generally. These include bankruptcy and insolvency laws that determine what course of action creditors can take when a debtor becomes bankrupt. Bankruptcy law provides a framework within which creditors receive payment from their insolvent debtors and is a general regulation that impacts the relationship between debtors and creditors. Creditors, for instance, might be more reluctant to lend money in legal environments that offer extensive protection to debtors out of the fear that they might not be able to collect payments in all cases. The legal framework of predictable, enforceable contracts as well as regulations specific to debtors and creditors are instances of how states regulate this lending and repayment of money and credit (Carruthers 2005).

While lending and borrowing have always been an integral part of economic life, the recent decades have witnessed a profound change in the scope of this activity at the global level. We want to spend the concluding part of this chapter discussing how the manipulation of money and credit – that is, investments in financial instruments and lending and borrowing – became a more and more prominent way of making profit in the contemporary economy, a phenomenon called **financialization**.

The Prominence of Finance

We can define financialization as the increasing dominance of financial services over productive activities in the economy (Krippner 2010). Financial services and transactions are those that involve the extension of capital with the assumption of returning a profit on the exchange, through interest rates, dividends, or other means. Production, on the other hand, refers to the activities that are required to produce or trade commodities. Of course, while production does still occur, when we speak of financialization we are referring to the relative weight of financial services when compared with productive investments. In the US, financialization is a drastic departure from times past, when production and, specifically, manufacturing were the backbones of economic growth (see figure 3.3). Consider the Ford Motor Company, which is a prime example of a company that used to obtain its profit through the manufacturing and sale of automobiles. A recent study has shown that Ford's profits today come primarily from the provision of loans to purchase cars – a financial service – rather than from the production of the cars themselves (Froud et al. 2006).

How can we explain the dramatic rise of financial services as a central economic activity in the United States? Scholars have identified several factors that matter. The most important for our discussion concerning the role of state in economy is Krippner's (2010) argument that financialization was propelled by actions taken by the US state. Three sets of government policies and regulations worked together to produce the conditions under which it would emerge: deregulation, the encouragement of foreign capital inflows to the US, and the introduction of higher interest rates and other elements of "tight" monetary policy. These worked together to create something of a "hurdle" for productive investments, especially in industries that were no longer protected by government regulations. Under a high interest rate system, these productive investments are much less profitable than financial transactions, on which the profit margin increases as interest rates are raised. Additionally, because of the high interest rate regime, foreign capital became increasingly attracted to the US, and the US

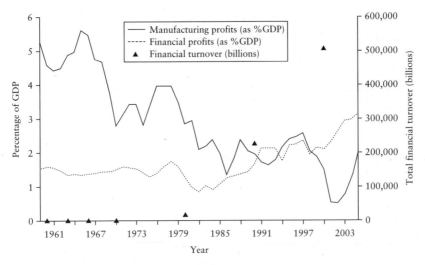

Source: *Economic Report of the President: 2007 Report Spreadsheet Tables.*

Figure 3.3 Financialization of the US economy

enacted policies to encourage further foreign investment. The policies of deregulation, encouragement of foreign capital inflows, and tight monetary policy worked together to produce a disincentive for productive investments while encouraging financial services, both within the US and from global investors.

We have now explained how financial services rose to prominence in the US economy, but we have not yet determined why this shift occurred. In short, we have shown that the state brought about economic financialization but we have not yet discussed why it acted in this way. Basically, the policies supporting the financialization of the economy rose out of a crisis faced by the US in the 1960s and 1970s. As Greta Krippner (2010) argues, achieving financialization was not the goal of state policy during this time, but rather was a byproduct of the way that the state chose to react to the crises it faced. In the 1960s and the 1970s, the erosion of the US economy and the pressures from increased global competition were placing the state in a tough position as it tried to figure out ways to meet its commitments to society, in the form of welfare state policies that had expanded during the post-World War II era, on a much less extensive revenue base than ever before. This caused it to seek new ways of facilitating economic growth while providing for its citizens. Thus, the state was challenged fiscally but also on other grounds, as economic hardship caused citizens to question its legitimacy to fulfill its mandate as the guardian of social welfare.

It was at this historical moment that the state began to enact policies that supported the rise of financial services in the economy. Policies stipulating deregulation, foreign capital inflows, and higher interest rates generally increased the amount of money and credit available in the US and provided a new way for the state to finance its budget deficits. Its very legitimacy and its ability to promote economic growth were coming into question and, instead of bringing society into its decision-making process, it turned to the market to resolve its problems. Initially, this strategy seemed to work, as the economic troubles of the 1970s gave way to a time where capital flowed freely. Economic problems were seen less as the product of state actions than as a result of the workings of impartial and impersonal market forces (Krippner 2010).

However, recent economic troubles, exemplified in the financial crisis that began in December 2007, suggest that financialization did not provide a long-term cure for the state's troubles, but rather served to aggravate them.

Monica Prasad (2009) writes that one of the reasons for the financial crisis is the fact that the financial market deregulation that spurred financialization allowed an explosion of experimentation and innovation in new ways to make money and a predominant use of financial instruments that derive their value from other financial instruments, *aka* derivatives. For instance, banks would start selling home mortgages owed to them to derivatives market investors. Securitization meant that these bank "assets" were not sold "whole" but combined into a pool, where parts are of different reliability, which is then split into shares – securities. The shares are sold to investors, who can make profit if debtors pay the mortgages on schedule but do not if they default on their loans. One consequence of this is that, if more risky mortgages can be sold to someone else, then the original investor (a bank in our case) suffers few penalties if the debt is not honored. This can create a perverse incentive to offer more and more risky loans. This is a bad idea because, eventually, there will be dire consequences when more and more people default on such loans, as happened with the home mortgage market collapse. (How ironic, in fact, to call these financial instruments *secure*-ities.)

Another aspect of financialization related to the 2008 crisis was the ever increasing rate of leveraging. Leveraging means that an economic subject borrows money, not simply for a house or car, but with the goal of investing in the stock market – for instance, with the expectation that the rate of return will be greater that the cost of interest for the initial loan. You can see how this aims to have the potential positive effect of borrowing magnified, but the potential negative effect is also enhanced should things go wrong, and the stock investment fails to perform as well as initially thought.

In the home mortgage market, this leveraging was shown in the fact that home-owners were taking out loans against the value of their house to invest in a second home or the stock market, for instance. As long as property values were rising, this was sustainable, as was giving mortgages to borrowers with poor credit ratings or those who didn't even provide proof of their income. However, when the prices of property began to decline, more people started to default on their loans, leading to foreclosures and, therefore, further declines in property values. Now remember that many securities were built on these very home mortgages that people could no longer continue to pay back. So all the investors, from all over the world, who had put money into these securities based on mortgage debt lost their money. This includes individual investors as well as institutional ones, such as big banks and insurance companies, some of which went bankrupt; others were prevented from bankruptcy only because of bail-outs from the government. This all led to a general cycle of reduced spending and disinvestment, and hence unemployment, and marked the most severe economic downturn in recent history.

Conclusion

"Money makes the world go round, the world go round . . ." is not simply a tune from *Cabaret*. Many of us would agree. Still, we rarely think to what extent money matters depend on the role of the state. The state not only gives legitimacy to the notes we use as the medium of exchange, it also controls, through monetary policy, the availability of money in the economy and influences, through the actions of central banks, the cost of this money when we want to borrow it. Monetary policy actions are the primary way states respond to and manage the tendency of market economies to alternate between periods or boom and bust, or the business cycle.

The state also collects money from its citizens, and fiscal sociology considers taxation as the central function of states. Conceptualizing tax policy as a social contract, fiscal sociologists emphasize that changes in taxation are not merely a reflection of social change but that they have the potential to transform significantly the relationship between state and society (Schumpeter [1918] 1991; Martin, Mehotra, and Prasad 2009). Such an analysis of tax policy goes far beyond economic considerations of cost and benefit to uncover fundamentally social and political bases of taxation. A great deal of attention is also paid to the social consequences of taxation, such as its influence on state building, labor force participation, and the distribution of wealth in society and across generations, as well as charity and philanthropy, for instance. Generally, what or whom states tax, and how much, is a consequence of a political struggle between various social groups and reflects what society considers valuable. This is true also for decisions about government spending.

Importantly, recent decades have seen a rise in money and credit as chief money-making instruments. That is, more and more activities these days that contribute to a share of GDP come from the financial sector rather than from the production of goods. This phenomenon, the financialization of the economy, has been responsible for significant economic growth after the 1980s because it has contributed to increasingly high levels of

Money

investment. However, it was also responsible for the economic bust starting in late 2007, when loans audaciously taken out could not be repaid and the hyper-risky derivative investments built on them were lost. All this happened in a particular institutional context where trading in derivatives – "financial weapons of mass destruction," as Warren Buffet presciently announced in 2003 – went unregulated by the state. Ultimately, and returning to the first point we made in this chapter, this economic crisis makes the argument about money as a fictitious commodity all the more salient. Disastrous consequences ensue when market actors and regulators forget that money is not a true commodity, manufactured to respond to demand and supply, but a fictitious one that requires continual management by the state.

Money

investment. However, it was also responsible for the economic bust starting in late 2007, when loans audaciously taken out could not be repaid and the hyper-risky derivative investments built on them were lost. All this happened in a particular institutional context where trading in derivatives – "financial weapons of mass destruction," as Warren Buffet presciently announced in 2003 – went unregulated by the state. Ultimately, and returning to the first point we made in this chapter, this economic crisis makes the argument about money as a fictitious commodity all the more salient. Disastrous consequences ensue when market actors and regulators forget that money is not a true commodity, manufactured to respond to demand and supply, but a fictitious one that requires continual management by the state.

4

Labor: The State's Role in Redistribution and Employment

You lose a job and don't find one for a while. Should you just "suck it up" (it's your own fault, after all) or should you receive some help from the government in the form of unemployment benefits, because there may be other reasons, beyond laziness or merit, that make it difficult for individuals to find and hold a job? People tend to have strong opinions about this issue and they have had them for centuries. For instance, Thomas Paine (1791), a famous British intellectual, wrote extensively on this subject two hundred years ago, noting that provision by the state for the welfare of its citizens was the mark of a civilized government. In his account, Paine emphasizes that the government had more than enough funds to provide instruction for the youth, to support the elderly, and to improve the condition of the impoverished, and that not providing these services was a detriment to the entire nation. In contrast – and moving to much more recent history – Charles Murray (1984), a conservative American academic and researcher, also wrote on this topic, emphasizing the inefficiencies of state intervention in private life and calling for a reintroduction of the ethic that would hold individuals accountable for ensuring their own economic welfare, rather than expecting it from the state.

Considering the words of Thomas Paine and Charles Murray provides clear evidence for each side of the debate over the state's role in the labor market. Recall that human labor is yet another example of the fictitious commodities we discussed earlier. Along with land and money, human labor would be annihilated if it were allowed to be fully commodified like other goods produced for market sale. Instead, some state regulation is necessary to put limits to the use of labor. The key question, then, is not whether states "should" regulate human labor, but rather about the various ways in which this is done. What actions does the state take to prevent the exhaustion of human resources, such as social protection, welfare provision, and labor market regulation? How do these actions vary among states and with what consequences? How does the state influence who participates in the labor market? What do the penal system, immigration policies, and informal economy participation have to do with this? These are the questions that this chapter addresses.

Resisting Labor Commodification

In an agrarian system, citizens typically provided many of their own goods and services by growing or making them as a family. Trade and bartering with local craftsmen and merchants supplemented the household. With the rise of a market society, as we described in chapter 2, people left farming and started to work in factories for subsistence. Hence, under conditions of capitalism, labor becomes a commodity that can be sold (by laborers) and is purchased (by factory-owners) at a certain price. Capitalists purchase a person's labor and put it to work making a variety of goods for sale. Because workers have "sold" their labor to the capitalists, this means that the products of the laboring process (i.e. the goods) belong to the capitalists, who get to sell these items and keep all of the surplus profit for themselves. The nature of capitalism entails labor commodification because workers are constantly forced to sell the only thing they possess – themselves and their labor – while the profits and surplus of production accrue only to the capitalists. However, as Karl Polanyi aptly put it, labor is not like any other commodity. It is a fictitious commodity. The reason behind human reproduction is not to supply more labor power to the market. Moreover, protection must be in place to prevent the complete exhaustion of labor at the mercy of profit-oriented capital.

Indeed, different strategies exist that limit the extent of labor commodification. The first strategy of possible resistance is the organization of **labor unions**. Scholars emphasize that labor movements grow and strengthen themselves where they are institutionally protected from the market forces that encourage competition among workers, specifically through working-class political parties cooperating with the state; centralized industrial relations, which reduce employer hostility toward unionization; and union-managed unemployment insurance, which integrates peripheral members of the labor market into the mainstream. Labor unions exist between class and the market, and their presence and success at any particular time depends on the relative weight of market forces and class-based politics (Western 1997). In 2003, union density expressed as a percentage of union members per total labor force was only 12 percent in the US. In Finland and Denmark these figures were 74 and 70 percent, respectively (Visser 2006).

Second, labor can resist commodification in situations of **corporatist bargaining** that contribute to its protection against pure market forces of competition. Corporatist bargaining can be defined as institutionalized tripartite bargaining between so-called social partners: the state, labor, and capital. The inclusion of representatives from labor movements as legitimate actors gives more power to labor in determining how productivity gains they have helped to create in the economy should be distributed (Hicks 1999; Swank 2002; Wilensky 2002).

Third, commodification of labor is lessened also through the process scholars have termed **decommodification**, meaning the protection of workers, through the **welfare state**, from the pure forces of market. In other words, labor is decommodified when state benefits allow individuals to maintain their standard of living when they are unable or otherwise separated from the labor market through old age, disability, or illness (Esping-Andersen 1990; Huber and Stephens 2001). In essence, labor is decommodified when workers are shielded from the labor market through social protection and thus not wholly dependent on the market for survival. The provision of social protection is part of the welfare function of states. We devote the next section to the discussion of the welfare state, recognizing that states do not provide social benefits solely to labor. Rather, as T. H. Marshall has famously argued, being a citizen of a country, whether part of the labor force or not, entitles one to claim not only civil and political rights, but also social rights. Civil rights include rights of individual freedom, such as rights to property, free speech, and the like. Political rights include rights of political participation, either directly in political matters or as a voter or elector of political officials. Social rights include rights to economic welfare and security, and the institutions most closely connected with social rights are the educational system and the administration of social services.

Welfare States: The Provision of Social Rights

For the most part, the need for the state to provide some modicum of social rights is not controversial in capitalist democracies. What does remain highly contested however, is the *extent* to which the state should be responsible for the welfare of its citizens. Public opinion data show significant variation across nations. For instance, as we show in table 4.1, Svallfors (1997) found that higher percentages of citizens in the Scandinavian and other social democratic countries (discussed in more detail below) indicate support for redistributive economic policies by agreeing with such statements as "The government should provide everyone with a guaranteed basic income." Are these differences in opinion consequential? Indeed, in their study of OECD countries, Brooks and Manza (2006) found this to be the case. Their results show that countries whose citizens express a high level of support for welfare state expenditure in public opinion data tend to have higher percentages of GDP allocated to social spending.

Before we discuss the characteristics, determinants, and consequences of welfare states, let us address where the term "welfare state" comes from. Most accounts indicate that it was popularized

Table 4.1 Opinions on redistribution

	It is the responsibility of the government to reduce the differences between people with high incomes and those with low incomes	The government should provide a job for everyone who wants one	The government should provide everyone with a guaranteed basic income
Sweden	54	74	46
Norway	60	78	78
Germany	66	66	58
Austria	70	72	51
Australia	43	39	51
New Zealand	53	49	61
Canada	48	40	49
US	38	47	34

Source: Svallfors (1997).

Note: Figures represent the percentage of the population in each country that agrees with each of the three statements.

in Britain during World War II, though related terms had been used in Germany and a few other countries in the late 1800s. World War II was a time of crisis, devastation, rampant militarization, and the conquest of Europe waged by power-seeking Nazi Germany. Britain, as a national priority, focused much energy on remaining untouched by the expansion of the war-making German state. It was in this context that the term "welfare state" was first used in 1941 by Archbishop William Temple as a means of drawing a contrast between "warfare" states, like Germany during this time, and "welfare" states like Great Britain. Warfare states were concerned principally with conquest and power, and used warfare as a means to gain influence and territory throughout the world. Welfare states, on the other hand, resisted such impulses, and the archbishop and other leaders used this image as a way of sustaining the national spirit during the war, emphasizing the differences between the British state and the German

one. Increasingly, the term "welfare state" began to be associated
with the social benefits the British state hoped to be able to offer
its citizens after the war was over (Briggs 1961), and the association with social benefit provisions is central to how the notion of
welfare state is understood throughout Europe. As we explain
in box 4.1, this is in contrast to the US, where "welfare" is most
often associated with the assistance from the government for the
unemployed, which, in a country that strongly favors individualist
explanations of one's economic circumstance, has mostly negative
connotations.

Most scholars apply Esping-Andersen's (1990) classification of
welfare states into three kinds of regime: social democratic, conservative, and liberal. In social democratic welfare regimes, such as
in Sweden, citizens are legally entitled to extensive social services
from the state, including wage replacement benefits, elderly care,
generous family policies, and sometimes job protection policies,
all of which tend to be funded from the state's general revenues. In
contrast, social protection in conservative welfare regimes, such as
in Germany, are less extensive and tend to be financed from wage-
based contributions. Common forms of protection are passive
family policies structured around the role of men as "breadwin-
ners," healthcare, education, and vocational training. In these
countries, rights to social protection are awarded based on class
and status. Finally, liberal welfare regimes, such as in the United
States, provide means-tested social benefits for certain groups,
which are also funded out of a state's general revenues. Aside
from healthcare and education, other social services are minimal.
Family policies, job protection, and vocational training are underdeveloped. The differences between the social democratic model
and the conservative model lie mainly in the structure of the
conservative welfare regime as something that is based around
workers and traditional forms of the family. Conservative regimes
are financed through wage contributions, tying the welfare regime
to the system of wage labor, and family policies assume that the
primary worker is the male breadwinner. In line with their underlying ideology, social democratic welfare regimes finance more
universal benefits from general state revenues and offer extensive

Box 4.1 What is a welfare state?

In the US, many of the popular images of welfare programs and recipients are negative. We have all read articles or seen news reports that characterize welfare recipients as lazy individuals who are looking to receive handouts from the government. In such accounts, the welfare state is alleged to be a drain on the state's economy that only perpetuates unemployment and supports laziness.

However, welfare policies encompass much more than the provision of income to those who cannot sustain employment. Unemployment insurance, social security, public healthcare, maternity/paternity benefits, public education, disability benefits, childcare, and job opportunities in the public sector are only a few examples of contemporary welfare benefits. Here, we can see that some welfare state policies, such as maternity/paternity leave benefits and public education, are used by people of all social backgrounds, while other policies provide a safety net to individuals who are unable to work as a result of illness or old age.

A comparison of the US and other industrialized countries is illustrative. Though the US is the second richest state in this group of countries, it also has the highest levels of inequality and poverty among them. The vast wealth of the country is not reaching those at the lowest end of the income spectrum. Consider these trends in light of the fact that the US generally offers more limited social benefits that are available on a means-tested basis to those who can prove need. This stands in contrast to the Scandinavian countries, which tend to have more generous and universal welfare policies. Some feel that expanded welfare state benefits can come only at the expense of economic productivity and prosperity, but research shows that industrialized countries with more generous welfare states, such as Norway and the Netherlands, also have higher rates of productivity and lower rates of unemployment than the US.

It would be incorrect to assume that welfare states have no

shortcomings. American welfare policies, in particular, have been criticized for their confusing nature (Stuber and Kronebusch 2004). The welfare state is often said to be fragmented, and a host of programs, each with their own set of complicated procedures, exist to offer support to the poor and low-income individuals, including food stamps, Temporary Assistance for Needy Families, and Medicaid, to name only a few. Studies show that many of those who are registered for these programs have limited knowledge of how they work, and many who are eligible for them do not understand how to register to receive benefits.

Though welfare policies vary considerably across countries and suffer from shortcomings in their implementation, all of these endeavors are unified by states' recognition that they must, to some degree, shield individuals from pure market forces and assume some responsibility for their economic well-being.

social services and family policies. The liberal welfare regime does not see social services as protected rights but rather as things that are available to those who can prove extreme need. If we are to arrange these three welfare regimes in terms of the level and generosity of benefits they provide, social democratic systems offer the most benefits and liberal welfare regimes offer the least, with conservative regimes falling in between the two (Esping-Andersen 1990). Figure 4.1 shows social spending in different countries.

What determines welfare state expenditure

There is a wealth of research on the determinants of welfare state expenditure, from various theoretical perspectives, emphasizing the role of demographic forces and industrialization; state capacity, state structure, and policy legacies; and power distribution in civil society and government, in particular the incumbency of left parties or Christian democratic parties as crucial for welfare state development. Culture and gender have also been discussed as determining factors.

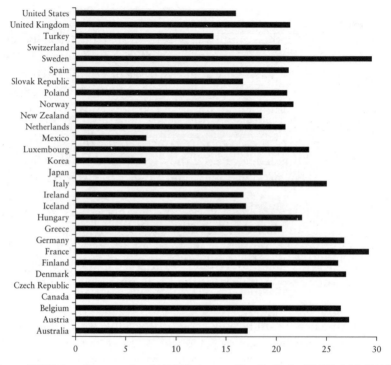

Source: OECD, http://stats.oecd.org/WBOS/Index.aspx?DataSetCode=SOCX_AGG (2009).

Note: These figures include combined expenditures for:
- old age – pensions, early retirement pensions, home-help and residential services for the elderly;
- survivors – pensions and funeral payments;
- incapacity-related benefits – care services, disability benefits, benefits accruing from occupational injury and accident legislation, employee sickness payments;
- health – spending on in- and out-patient care, medical goods, prevention;
- family – child allowances and credits, childcare support, income support during leave, sole parent payments;
- active labor market policies – employment services, training youth measures subsidized employment, employment measures for the disabled;
- unemployment – unemployment compensation, severance pay, early retirement for labor market reasons;
- housing – housing allowances and rent subsidies;
- other social policy areas – non-categorized cash benefits to low-income households, other social services – i.e. support programs such as food subsidies, which are prevalent in some non-OECD countries.

Figure 4.1   Social expenditure as a percentage of GDP, 2005

Industrialization and its resulting demographic shifts, such as population ageing, have been credited as the main impetus behind welfare state development. In such accounts, industrialization and economic growth place states on a path that requires the development of welfare policies to manage the new needs thus generated. The expansion of the state and its social provisions was more or less automatic in response to the needs generated by expanding capitalism. This perspective is sometimes referred to as the "logic of industrialism" because it posits that the welfare state emerges in response to industrialism and the social changes it engenders (Wilensky 1975).

Policy legacies, state structures, and state capacities are another set of variables that have been shown to influence welfare state expenditure. For example, the legacy of the New Deal in American politics, in terms of its successes and shortcomings, has powerfully influenced the evolution of the welfare state in the United States and has sparked decades of debate about what the appropriate amount and coverage of social spending should be. In this sense, "what came before" in terms of social policy influences "what is to come" (Skocpol 1988). Legislative majorities of those supportive of welfare and social protection have also importantly determined the resulting welfare state expenditure in the US throughout its history (Amenta 1998). An effective state bureaucracy is also thought to be positively associated with the development of welfare state provision, as it provides the means to administer social programs to the population (Orloff 1993).

The third explanation for welfare state development includes factors such as the political orientation of the government and the power distribution among social actors (Korpi 1983). Researchers have found that the political party of the government leads to dramatically different welfare state provision. The most extensive welfare states tend to exist in countries ruled by or with powerful Christian democratic parties or other leftist parties and in situations where socialist or wage-earner political parties exist, are strong, and work closely with the state. Huber and Stephens (2001) show that extensive welfare states develop in countries governed by both social democratic parties and Christian democratic parties on account of the support they receive from the working and lower classes. However, specific provision in these states varies, such that social democratic regimes, for instance, create welfare states that offer many social services and emphasize maximum labor force participation, while Christian democratic parties focus more on the basic aim of alleviating poverty through social insurance and income transfers. With this in mind, we can see how the distribution of power resources matters for the extent and scope of a welfare state.

Recently, sociologists have also emphasized the role of culture, including the values and norms held by individuals – both citizens and government officials – as a powerful influence on the kind of welfare entitlements that a state does or does not offer. Brian Steensland's book *The Failed Welfare Revolution* (2007), on the rise and fall of guaranteed income policies as a strategy to reform the American welfare system in the 1960s and 1970s, argues that attempts at instituting a minimum level of economic protection to Americans through guaranteed income provision failed not simply because of powerful opponents and political structures. Instead, cultural norms about poverty in America and notions about who, among the poor, "deserved" assistance was a key part of the explanation for its failure. Prevailing notions about "the availability of jobs for anyone who wants to work," the emphasis placed on individual responsibility for one's life and one's family, and the meritocratic ideals that promised advancement and economic mobility to "anyone who works hard enough" are examples of the cultural understandings of poverty that cast some as "deserving," unfortunate, or down on their luck, while others were viewed as "undeserving," lazy, and unwilling to work. Proposing radical reforms to the American welfare state challenged these cultural notions and understandings by placing all of the country's poverty-stricken individuals in the same category, questioning the political, economic, and cultural status quo of the time.

Gender is yet another force that has been implicated as an influence on the development of welfare state expenditure. Researchers have found that traditional understandings of gender are an overarching influence on the types of welfare provision offered by a state. For instance, in Germany, assumptions that women would raise the children and men would work prevented the development of paternity leave policies, limited public childcare, and generous unemployment benefits. In Sweden, however, the assumption that women would work meant that government spending and policy focused on providing employees with flexible hours, extensive childcare, and generous parental leave. Longitudinal cross-national research also shows that women's representation in both the national legislature and the labor market increases overall social spending (Bolzendahl 2009).

Much of the literature that we have reviewed so far has concentrated on the development and expansion of welfare states in Western European countries. However, social policies of this sort exist in countries all around the world, and a vibrant body of scholarship is beginning to emerge that details the ways in which the welfare states in, for example, Latin America, Eastern Europe, or East Asia are similar to or different from those that exist in Western Europe. The Latin American economy after World War II, for instance, was organized around the import-substitution industrialization strategy, which was a development model in which state support and subsidies were offered to domestic firms to produce goods rather than having to import them. There was room in this system for firms to accommodate the social welfare of their workers and to provide entitlements for the urban working class. This led to a dualistic system of welfare and social insurance in Latin America, one that provided benefits to urban workers while excluding agricultural and other rural workers. This is only one example of how the organization of the economy can produce a particular kind of welfare regime. Political institutions, too, influence the development of non-Western welfare states. As Haggard and Kaufman (2008) find, both democratic and dictatorial regimes have different impacts on the formation of social policy. Democracy, with its electoral competition and interest group organization, has long been thought to be associated with developing and expanding welfare entitlement. However, the existence of welfare provision depends not on regime type alone, but also on the underlying coalitional alignments and economic interests present in a state. Authoritarian regimes, in East Asia, for instance, expanded welfare benefits as a way of limiting insurgencies, and the communist regimes of the socialist states in Eastern Europe were firmly committed to redistribution as part of their socialist economic organization.

The consequences of welfare provision

It is commonly argued that welfare state policies constitute a burden on the state and its resources. Indeed, critics have often alleged that social policies drag down the state, limiting its potential for growth and success. Empirical evidence, however, does not provide clear support for such propositions. Some researchers have found that welfare state policies "cost" a state's economy by reducing the size of its GDP, sometimes by up to 25 percent (Browning 2008). However, other studies have yielded contrasting results and indicated that welfare state policies do not have to mean negative economic consequences. For instance, some countries have focused on increasing productivity and the skills of workers while protecting the social rights of their citizens (Streeck 1992). Here, increasing productivity and skill development are seen as a mutually beneficial strategy for both citizens and the state. By focusing on industries that need highly skilled workers, industrial growth can occur while individuals still retain their protection. This is an alternative to short-term strategies used by firms to maximize profit, including relocating production to low-wage countries. In contrast, another strategy pursued to increase economic growth in the presence of an expansive welfare state is to focus production in high-value economic sectors (Pontusson 1992). Countries that pursue this strategy, such as Sweden, try to produce items of higher value to increase their economic growth while allowing for the maintenance of various kinds of social protection offered to their citizens. Cooperation at the firm level also plays a role in contributing to economic growth (Hicks and Kenworthy 1998). Neocorporatism is both conducive to economic growth and equalizes income distribution. In all these cases, the welfare state does not necessarily lead to either economic prosperity or decline.

In terms of the social consequences of the welfare state, the findings are more straightforward. Brady (2005) found that social security transfers, healthcare expenditure, and social wages significantly reduced poverty among populations in eighteen Western nations between 1967 and 1997. These findings demonstrated that welfare entitlements are particularly important to those outside of the labor force – for example, groups such as children and the elderly, who specifically benefit from transfers from the government in the form of social security and healthcare. Importantly, studies have also found no evidence that the existence of welfare state policies causes recipients, as some critics have claimed, to grow dependent on aid from the state, increasing the magnitude and scope of poverty. Scruggs and Allan (2006) obtained similar findings with regard to unemployment, pensions, and sickness policies, all of which decrease poverty. Generally, we can say that welfare state policies do reduce inequality among populations. We present data in figure 4.2 reflecting the positive impact that welfare state policies, such as income transfers, have on reducing child poverty rates.

Challenges to the welfare state

Others have questioned the welfare state, namely its ability to sustain its entitlements as the age structure of populations change (Coleman 2006). Population ageing is sweeping the globe, resulting from the combination of falling birth rates and longer lifespans. If fewer babies are being born, and people are generally living longer, a situation arises in which a state's population is made up of many more elderly than younger people. This can be a problem for existing welfare states in that larger numbers of older people require an increase in the material resources that underlie welfare entitlements, such as pensions and healthcare. This can become even more of an issue since a falling birth rate means that the size of the working population will be smaller and will thus limit the state's ability to expand its fiscal resources to support social policies, such as through taxation.

Yet another challenge for welfare states can be found in the

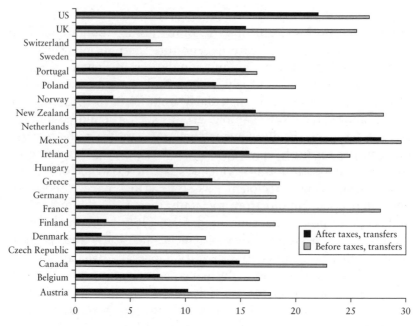

Source: UNICEF, www.unicef.gr/reports/rc06/UNICEF%20CHILD%20POVERTY%20
IN%20RICH%20COUNTRIES%202005.pdf (2005).

Figure 4.2 Child poverty rates, 2000 (%)

structure of administrative agencies and other bodies that are necessary to administer the variety of social programs. Such administrative bodies have costs of their own in that they require funds to exist and function on a day-to-day basis (Offe 1982; Browning 2008). Thus, one of the costs of the welfare state system is the increased burden in governmental support required to maintain it. A key challenge in this regard is for welfare states to operate as effectively as possible so as not to waste resources while attending to the day-to-day basis of the administration of policies.

Globalization has also brought challenges to welfare states. First, increased mobility across borders poses the issue of whether states should extend benefits to immigrants or undocumented persons. To address this issue, Yasemin Soysal (1994) posited the concept of "postnational citizenship," which would base citizenship and the rights it entails on the recognition of each individual's universal personhood and humanity rather than their specific national affiliation. Of course, such a proposition challenges the dominant conception of welfare as protection offered to citizens by the state, but postnational citizenship and the corresponding openness of social benefits is one way of reducing inequality and poverty while meeting the challenges posed by increased cross-border mobility and migration. Second, globalization has also been seen as a threat to the welfare state. Some heated debate in the literature has been generated with arguments that globalization leads to a crisis and retrenchment of the welfare state because it expands the role of capital and requires neoliberal restructuring to foster flexibility and competitiveness. Still, others argue that globalization actually contributes to the expansion of the welfare state in order to compensate domestic labor that may be harmed by economic openness. Empirical research has substantiated portions of each of these arguments for different aspects of the welfare state. This means that any bold statements about the influence of globalization on the welfare state, in either the positive or the negative sense, are largely unsubstantiated (Brady, Beckfield, and Seeleib-Kaiser 2005).

The role of employers

Labor's role in the "double movement" (Polanyi 1944) has contributed significantly in the development of welfare state policies to shield against market commodification, often acting as its impetus. However, it is important to consider the role of business interests and employer organizations – and not just labor – in the development of welfare states generally and in the selection of particular types of welfare provision specifically (Block and Evans 2005). Mares (2001) finds that firms and employer organizations guided the development of the German welfare state. In particular, large business interests in the iron and steel industries whose workers suffered many workplace accidents supported compulsory disability insurance, while firms in risky industries proposed unemployment insurance and large manufacturing interests were key in the development of old age policies. Similarly, business interests played a role in the development of welfare state policies in the US during the New Deal (Swenson 1997). Though the pressure for social reforms during the 1920s and 1930s came from other social groups and mass movements, key successful business executives signaled their support for social and labor policy reforms, paving the way for protective legislation to emerge.

As well as the business interests of employers potentially contributing to the development of social policies provided by states, employers can play a very direct role in welfare benefits provision. In spite of conventional wisdom that depicts the US as something of a welfare state laggard when compared with Western European states, some scholars have shown that the total *level* of social spending in the country is not as dissimilar from that of other countries as the *source* of this spending (Hacker 2002). In other countries, social policies are administered by the government, but in the US these tasks are assumed largely by private actors, most notably employers. For instance, many who are employed receive healthcare coverage as a benefit of employment, as well as, often, pensions and other retirement benefits. Though many of these benefits come from private actors, it would be inaccurate to say that the American state is uninvolved in the development and administration of these programs. In fact, the US government institutes a variety of subsidies, regulations, and tax incentives to encourage employers to provide such benefits to their employees. We can say, then, that welfare benefits in the US are provided by private actors, most commonly employers, though the state is actively involved in overseeing the development of the system.

What consequences does the private administration of welfare benefits have on the distribution and equity of such benefits? Hacker (2002) acknowledges that there are great distributional consequences from the American system of private welfare, even though it is mainly the source, not the size, of the welfare state that differs dramatically from that of other regimes. According to Hacker, private approaches to welfare benefits are less likely to create a more equitable income distribution than state-sponsored approaches. All private provision tends to be tied closely to employment and to total compensation, which offers a clear benefit to those who have stable, long-term, and highly paid employment. Thus, we conclude that, even though the total size of the US welfare system is not dramatically smaller than those found in Western Europe, the source of provision is distinct, which has ramifications for the redistributive effect of the policies.

One could argue that the tradition of private provision goes back to the spirit of "Fordism," a philosophy developed in the US during the 1910s which argues that widespread prosperity and high corporate profits can be achieved by high wages that allow the workers to purchase the output they produce. "Fordism" was coined to describe Henry Ford's successes in the automobile industry, and also refers to the method where workers work behind a production assembly line, repetitively performing specialized tasks. Ford sold 10 million inexpensive Model T automobiles and made a vast fortune, but his employees also became the highest paid factory workers in the world. They could form unions and assert their rights (Tolliday and Zeitlin 1987). However, the shift from Fordism to the flexible production paradigm (also known as post-Fordism), induced by the use of new information technologies, the rise of services, and the globalization of financial markets, has contributed to the fragmentation and dualism of the workforce, fracturing the state–society alliances against market forces, not only in the US but worldwide. These developments are thought to have changed the relationship between capital and labor in favor of (global) capital, which is one of the reasons behind the fears, discussed above, that globalization has undermined welfare states.

Labor Market Regulations

Even if the focus of our discussion on the welfare state was labor decommodification, it should be clear that welfare state provision broadly mediates the relationship between economy and society, and is thus related to labor not only directly but also indirectly. In this section, we want to return to our chapter's central theme to look at specific provisions enacted by states to regulate the labor market, such as a minimum wage, statutory vacations, child-rearing leave, and flex-time policies. These are by no means the only labor market regulations, but they showcase the variety of ways in which the state can influence labor conditions.

Minimum wage legislation is one of the most important ways in which the state regulates the labor market to benefit workers. The minimum wage came into existence in the US out of the sweatshop working environments that were part of the experience of industrialization. It functions primarily by setting the lowest level of pay that an employee can receive for his or her work and in this way prevents the exploitation of workers at the hands of employers. Though some contend that such laws decrease economic efficiency and levels of employment by requiring a certain level of wages, they are a common aspect of social policy in many states around the globe.

The state also regulates the labor market through compulsory vacation policies (Dreier 2007). The fact that the state would require an annual, guaranteed, and paid period of vacation time for each worker may sound strange to Americans. But the US is the *only* industrialized country that does not have regulations on the books that offer this benefit to workers. In fact, it stands out in this regard because it offers no compulsory vacations and also because other states that can be considered its peers offer an average of four weeks of paid vacation leave – which is quite an increase over no leave at all. When we take into account the paid holidays offered by other comparable states, the number of weeks of paid leave offered increases to 5.3. It is clear that mandated vacation time in the US is far less generous than that in other peer countries. In most cases, if paid vacation time is offered to workers it is at the discretion of the employing company. This is part of the reason that US employees work four weeks more than the average of those in other countries.

Provision for parents to take time from work to care for children is another way in which the state regulates the labor market, especially where women are concerned. These policies recognize women's particular familial responsibilities and provide them with the means to maintain employment while building a family. Imagine what a woman's work experience would look like without the benefit of maternity policies. If an employed woman wants to have a child and could not utilize such policies, it is likely that she would lose her job as a result. This could make it difficult for this woman both to support herself and to find a job after childbirth.

The maternity leave regulations present in the US are very different to those that exist in other states. As we have already noted, the US mandates only twelve weeks of unpaid maternity leave, which is the lowest level of maternity support offered by any industrialized state. Other countries offer longer periods of maternity leave where workers receive either a full or partial salary for most of the time. For instance, Scandinavian countries tend to offer over twelve months of nearly fully paid leave, while the United Kingdom offers an entire year's worth of leave during which workers receive a portion of their normal salaries (Mishel, Bernstein, and Shierholz 2008).

However, it is not only women whose familial responsibilities may conflict with their position in the labor market. Men, too, may need time away from their jobs to care for children or other family members. Some states have introduced "flex-time" policies into their labor markets as ways for individuals simultaneously to meet their responsibilities to their jobs and to their families (Ezra and Deckman 1996). In short, flex-time requires employees to work the total number of hours required in a day, but allows them to work at least some portion of those hours as is convenient for them. A working parent might be able to arrange some of their hours around family commitments by, for example, spending the first half of the day in the office before leaving to pick their children up from school, and then returning to work later in the evening. Another alternative might be to work four days a week for ten hours each day and take one day off. Flex-time systems are becoming increasingly popular around the world, although in the US it is primarily white-collar workers who benefit from such policies.

Labor Market Participation

We argued that states play an important role in regulating labor markets and in providing protection to limit the commodification of labor. But who is allowed to participate in the labor market is also a matter that states influence. Here we discuss how labor market participation is indirectly related to the penal system, the immigration policies, and the extent of the informal economy in a country.

Imprisonment and the economy

Is there a relationship between the labor market and the penal system? Though these two things might appear not to have very much in common, research shows that unemployment and incarceration are related, especially for black men in the United States (Western, Kleykamp, and Rosenfeld 2006). Incarceration in recent years has risen in relationship to increasing levels of unemployment and decreasing levels of wages. The expansion of the American penal system can be thought to constitute an active intervention by the state into the labor market. In this way, some scholars implicate the penal system as being an institution that works to hide the true level of unemployment in American society by funneling some of the urban unemployed away from public view and official statistics. In fact, the low unemployment figures for the US workforce in the 1980s and 1990s are largely a result of the expanded penal system and an increase in the number of incarcerated individuals (Western and Beckett 1999).

Of course, there are economic and social consequences arising from the large number of prisoners in the US. Over 650,000 people are sentenced annually to one year or more and the American prison population has now reached over 2 million individuals. Clearly, there must be an economic cost associated with supporting a prison population of this size. It is estimated that the US spends over $60 billion per year to fund the system and it costs, on average, over $22,000 to pay for one prisoner for one year (Slevin 2006). In terms of social costs, empirical research demonstrates that, among black American men, incarceration is positively linked to divorce and negatively linked to marriage (Lopoo and Western 2005). This suggests that the consequences of increased incarceration among this population affect other individuals aside from the person who is imprisoned, impacting the nature of families and the very fabric of social structure. Additionally, incarceration has been shown to reduce an individual's subsequent job prospects. The "mark" of a criminal record follows a person throughout their life and work experiences and, insofar as the rate of imprisonment among black men has risen dramatically when compared with that of white men, this may be an important mechanism of economic stratification (Pager 2003). As such, incarceration has significant consequences for affected individuals, for families, and for entire economies.

Immigrant labor

One of the important issues that is shaped by the state and has an impact on the labor market is international migration. We must consider this issue as it relates to both legal immigration and undocumented immigration. In the case of legal immigration, the state defines, encourages, or curtails movement of people across borders. However, closed migration policies encourage illegal migration and illegal employment (and often exploitation) of immigrants. Immigrant populations often form ethnic communities and engage in ethnic economies (Portes and Rumbaut 2006).

Legal immigration has been shown to be a powerful support to the US economy on the whole (Bean and Stevens 2003). Though there is no shortage of popular accounts depicting immigrants as stealing jobs away from the native-born population, research has shown that this is not the case (Chomsky 2007). Instead, the immigrant labor force constitutes a critical factor in US economic success by expanding the working-age population, increasing the labor force and providing skilled and innovative workers (see table 4.2). On account of the ageing of the working population and the retirement of the large number of workers from the "baby boom" era, a hole is being created in the US workforce, one that becomes

Labor

Table 4.2 Growth in the size of the native- and foreign-born population in the US

Nativity and age	Labor force 1980 (millions)	Growth 1980 to 2000 (millions)	Labor force 2000 (millions)	Growth 2000 to 2020 (millions)	Labor force 2020 (millions)
Native-born, aged 25–54	60.1	26.7	86.8	0.0	86.8
Native-born, aged 55+	13.8	2.7	16.5	13.3	29.8
Foreign-born	5.9	9.3	15.2	6.0	21.3
Total	79.8	38.7	118.5	19.4	137.9

Source: Bean and Stevens (2003).

more of a concern as the economy continues to generate new jobs. Between 2000 and 2020, there will be no increase in native-born workers aged twenty-five to fifty-four, yet job increases are projected to continue (Meissner et al. 2006). Satisfying the demand for an expanding and skilled workforce is one of the key dimensions of immigration's impact on the economy. Here, we can see that the policies a state chooses to enact can encourage immigration from certain regions of the world, highlighting the active role that it can have in shaping the future workforce.

Ethnic neighborhoods, such as Little Italy, Little Saigon, and Chinatown, exist in many large cities and are examples of ethnic enclaves to which immigrants are drawn. In neighborhoods such as these, many find employment through networks of immigrants and immigrant-owned businesses (Light 2005). Some researchers have discussed immigrant entrepreneurship as a survival strategy and a way around the barriers that stand in the way of traditional employment, including language acquisition or discrimination. However, many immigrant entrepreneurs also give other immigrants employment opportunities and provide them with other resources to ease their transition to life in the US, and thus can have far-reaching impacts on the patterns of immigrant employment.

Labor

However, it is not uncommon for illegal immigrants to fall prey to exploitative labor conditions. Since they are not supposed to be in the US, employers have a certain kind of leverage over them. Because they lack documentation, such workers are often reluctant to complain about exploitation out of the fear of being removed from the country (Bean and Stevens 2003). You might have seen news footage of veritable sweatshops in large cities, such as Los Angeles or New York, that are populated largely by illegal immigrant labor. Clearly, because of their non-citizen status, immigrant workers are not entitled to any social protection in the event they cannot find work for subsistence.

Employment in the informal economy

Even if they are quite vulnerable to exploitation and deemed undeserving of the social protection reserved for lawful citizens, undocumented immigrants contribute to a country's **informal economy**, part of the economy that takes place outside of the purview of the state (Portes and Haller 2005). "Off the books" employment in factories, as discussed above, but also street vendors, housecleaners, and day laborers participate in the informal economy. As table 4.3 shows, the extent of informal economies varies across countries.

The formal and informal economies intersect through the workings of the labor market, both for corporations and for individuals. Some have shown that those who cannot find or keep a job receive unemployment benefits while working in the informal sector as a means of subsidizing the support they receive from the state and raising their standard of living (MacDonald 1994). In other cases, companies have been shown to fire employees legally and then continue to retain their services unofficially, in an "under the table" kind of manner that frees the company from having to extend the benefits of a traditional employment relationship, such as healthcare and vacation pay (Mingione 1990). Others have pointed to the role played by informal laborers and networks of subcontracting in the formal garment and computer industries (Waldinger 1985; Bonacich and Appelbaum 2000; Benton 1989).

Table 4.3 Estimates of the informal economy (%)

Country	Year	Employment category			
		Workers in micro-enterprise	Own account workers	Domestic services	Total %
Argentina	1998	16	20	5	41
Brazil	1997	10	26	9	44
Costa Rica	1998	11	15	5	31
Mexico	1998	15	21	4	40
Panama	1998	6	18	7	31
Uruguay	1998	11	20	7	38
Venezuela	1994	9	27	4	40
United States	2000	4	4	0.5	8.5

Sources: ECLAC (2000), US Bureau of the Census (1980, 2000a, 2000b).

Though the finished garments and computers are sold through formal economic enterprises, many of the component parts are assembled or created through informal economic activity. This partly explains the continued existence of informal labor, even though one might think that states would actively want to discourage informal economic activities.

Conclusion

Despite oft-raised questions about whether or not states *should* protect labor from ruthless market forces, the particular characteristic of labor as a fictitious commodity makes it clear that states *must* offer some basic decommodification protection. However, how extensive such labor protection – and welfare provision, more generally – is may vary significantly across countries and amounts to different economic and social consequences.

Industrialization, state capacity and policy legacies, and the distribution of power in societies are three of the most common explanations for the expansion of welfare systems, but other factors, such as culture and gender dynamics, also matter. We have little evidence to show that the more generous welfare systems are more costly and thus negatively affect economic growth. Nor can we claim that bigger welfare states increase economic prosperity. Nevertheless, most of the scholarship does show that, generally, there is less social inequality and deprivation among a population in the more generous welfare systems – the social democratic as opposed to liberal ones. This is consistent with the fact that arguments in favor of welfare provision are made on moral rather than economic grounds.

In the second part of the chapter, we discussed some specific labor market regulations, such as the minimum wage and maternity leave provision. These pretty clearly regulate the terms and conditions of the employment relationship. What is less obvious are the kinds of regulations, such as those of the penal system and immigrant policies, that indirectly shape the labor process by influencing who is, or rather who is not, allowed to participate in the labor market. Those left out are often ex-convicts and undocumented immigrant workers, who may be hired "off the books" and therefore become part of the informal economy. While they may have at least some opportunities to engage in licit economic activity, working outside of the state bounds makes informal labor vulnerable to harsh exploitation. It is precisely the merciless conditions that informal employees often have to endure that should make us realize how significant state decommodification provision is for laborers, even in the most modest of welfare states.

5

Firms: The State's Role in Business and Industry Governance

On January 21, 2010, the Supreme Court of the United States, in *Citizens United* v. *Federal Election Commission*, overruled numerous precedents and declared §203 of the 2002 Bipartisan Campaign Reform Act (BCRA, also commonly referred to as McCain–Feingold) to be unconstitutional. The intent of McCain–Feingold was to limit corporate influence on electoral process and increase political efficacy at the individual level; §203 prohibited corporations and unions from directly funding communication that expressly advocated the election or defeat of a candidate. The majority in the 5–4 decision found that §203 abridged the First Amendment right to free speech, stating that political speech is "indispensable to decision-making in a democracy, and this is no less true because the speech comes from a corporation." Justice John Paul Stevens issued a ninety-page dissenting opinion, stating that he found the majority's reasoning "profoundly misguided" in relation to the protection of corporate rights regarding the First Amendment. He declared the decision to be "a rejection of the common sense of the American people," and that it went against the government's historical position of limiting corporate participation in the state. Indeed, as the *New York Times* reported, the court decision "vastly increased the power of big business and unions to influence government decisions . . . by freeing them to spend their millions directly to sway elections for president and Congress" (Liptak 2010).

This fundamental change in US law makes clear that corporations

can have significant control over the state by influencing the outcomes of electoral campaigns through financing. Without ignoring
this issue, nonetheless, the thrust of this chapter is the other way
around – on how state action shapes business. For instance, can
state action account, historically, for the rise of corporations?
What do states have to do with the kind of organizational structures and practices exhibited by firms? How do legal provisions
reinforce, or not, competition between firms? How do industrial
policy decisions and levels of R&D spending stimulate, or not, a
firm's productivity? To what extent does state regulate business
to assure consumer and environmental protection? In answering
these questions we recall themes from chapter 2, in particular the
notions of rules of exchange and governance structures as institutional preconditions for markets to operate. We also preempt
discussions from chapter 6 on state efforts to foster economic
growth.

The Firm and the Law

Why do we have firms? Can't we accomplish all economic activity
by exchanges on the market? Economists suggest that firms arise
because they lower **transaction costs**. Some things are simply less
costly if they are subsumed within an organization rather than
contracted in the marketplace. In particular, for transactions
that are high on asset specificity, uncertainty, and frequency of
exchange, we can expect that hierarchical organizations – firms
– will be used to accomplish economic activity in lieu of markets
(Williamson 1990). In contrast, sociologists see firms as more than
hierarchies that lower transaction costs and focus on their social
character and origins. From a sociological perspective, firms are
social groups – a *company* of individuals – except that they (a)
are designed to achieve certain goals, (b) have established rules,
regulations, and standards of conduct, and (c) are legal entities.
What is meant by a firm being a legal entity? It means that it is
recognized by the law and can act with legal sanctions. The law
provides for different kinds of organizational entities. "In the

United States, these entities include, among others, the business corporation, the cooperative corporation, the nonprofit corporation, the municipal corporation, the limited liability company, the general partnership, the limited partnership, the private trust, the charitable trust, and marriage" (Hansmann and Kraakman 2000: 390). All of these are based on contracts. The law also defines employment relations and specifies a set of obligations, sanctions, and procedures that are quite different from those that govern transactions between buyers and sellers on the market. Practically this means, for instance, that an independent contractor is not compelled to comply with the demands of a firm's executive in the same way as the employees working for that executive, if they want to preserve their jobs (Masten 1988).

The connection between law and firms is not only important because it shapes what firms are allowed to do. Sociologists argue that the large firms that we call **corporations** are, in fact, a creation of the legislature, and not merely a result of market efficiency. According to Roy (1997), three aspects of law contributed to the rise of corporations. The first was the ability of firms to own other firms through intercorporate stock ownership arrangements, the second was the increasing autonomy of directors with respect to shareholders, and the third was the institution of limited liability, excluding shareholders from being liable for the debts of the corporation beyond the amount they invested in the shares (see also box 5.1).

Law is not only consequential for the rise of corporations, it also exerts a significant influence on the functioning of firms through different kinds of regulations. One good piece of evidence that companies really care about state provision is the fact that they try hard to influence governmental decision-making on matters related to their operation. Business lobbying is a staple on the political scene. Lobbyists speaking on behalf of business in areas such as the environment, taxes, energy, trade, and health and safety regulations do their job because they and corporate leaders know that the decisions politicians make and the laws and regulations they pass will have crucial consequences for the functioning of firms (Vogel 1996).

Small Firms, Big Firms

We discussed in chapter 2 that there are differences across capitalist countries in how they organize their economy. Relevant for our focus on firms is the fact that, because of different state actions, big corporations enjoy greater privileges in some countries and smaller firms receive more state protection in others. For example, Orru (1991) reports on the role of small firms as key economic actors in the Italian and Taiwanese economies. He argues that, despite apparent cultural, political, and social differences, these two economies are actually quite similar. In both countries economic success is the result not of large, vertically integrated corporations, but of small or medium-sized firms that engage in flexible production to adjust more quickly to a changing demand for goods. A handful of historical institutional and structural factors are at the basis of economic systems that privilege small firms, including familialism, entrepreneurship and independence, personal ties and business networks, and patterns of household savings. However, as Orru purports, these factors can only partly explain the structural outcomes of the Italian and Taiwanese economies dominated by small firms. State action was important, not only in supporting small firms but also, interestingly, in inhibiting the growth of large ones. Incentives and state ideologies favoring small firms helped these economic actors to proliferate, while a lack of centralized planning, a rigid financial system, and a general distrust of large firms made it more difficult for large corporations to emerge as viable economic actors.

A prominent organizational sociologist, Charles Perrow (2002), explains the difference between privileging small over big firms with the strength of the state: in a weak state, captured more by private interests, private organizations will come to exist and grow to serve their own interests while at the same time coming to influence the structure of the state to serve the needs of organizations better. A strong state, however, would possess sufficient autonomy from economic interests to rein in the power of organizations and to limit organizational influence on the structure of the state and policy-making. For Perrow, the rise of big firms in the US was the result of a combination of a weak state and the influence of

Firms

Box 5.1 The rise of corporations

Corporations are a nearly ubiquitous aspect of contemporary life in industrialized countries and around the world. It is nearly impossible to think of a day's worth of activity that would not require you to encounter some kind of corporation. In recent years, corporations have become larger and more powerful than ever before. In fact, the yearly sales of some corporations are greater than the economies of some states, as measured by GDP. In 2002, for example, Wal-Mart stores constituted the nineteenth largest economy in the world, above those of some well-established industrialized countries, such as Sweden and Austria. Clearly, corporations are an important force in today's economy and society. But this was not always true of the world, at least to this extent. The rise of the corporation has been a relatively modern occurrence. This raises an important question: What accounts for the rise of corporations as opposed to other forms of economic organization that existed in the past?

Several explanations have been offered in response to this question. A common argument among economists is that corporations rose to prominence because they were the most efficient mode of organization for economic activity. Here, corporations emerged because of the organizational improvements that they offered to the economy. Such accounts note that, in the past, economic activity in the US tended to be dominated by smaller enterprises and concentrated on local markets. But beginning in the mid-1800s, expansions in technology, transportation, and other innovations produced the conditions for a true national market to grow – and the corporation emerged as the mode of economic organization that was best suited to deal with this new landscape of economic life (Chandler 1977).

Sociologists, on the other hand, have disputed the notion that corporations emerged because they offered an upgrade in economic efficiency. Rather than seeing their rise as a natural, inevitable, and ultimately beneficial economic process, some scholars have emphasized the role that state action and legislation has played in encouraging the development of the modern corporation. One of the most important of these, for instance, was the formulation of antitrust regulation. Large corporations came to exist as small firms merged together to harness the opportunities of price setting as a conglomerate under antitrust laws. But antitrust legislation also had a further impact by bringing about a sea change in the nature of business culture and norms so that more of a financial view was taken of the business world, where managers sought to diversify companies to increase profitability. For sociologists, there was nothing more natural or efficient about corporations as compared with other forms of economic organization. Instead, the market conditions set by states were important forces underlying the rise of corporations to their current position of economic prominence (Roy 1997; Fligstein 1990).

organizational interests on its structure, thus allowing large economic organizations to come to dominate the economy.

Perrow is not the only one to take on the rise of large corporations in the US. Actually, economists and sociologists vary significantly in the kinds of explanations that they provide and the emphasis they put on the role of state in this process. Box 5.1 summarizes this debate.

The Organization of Firms

What influences a firm's structures and its functioning? Sociologists have proposed different explanations, focusing for instance on the role of resource dependence, or environmental pressures. Those working in the **neo-institutionalist** tradition of organizational analysis, following a seminal article by Paul DiMaggio and Walter Powell (1983), have focused on the fact that, over time, organizations have become more and more alike in their structures and functioning, exhibiting organizational isomorphism. DiMaggio and Powell identified three mechanisms that account for this trend: normative, mimetic, and coercive isomorphism. The central actor behind coercive isomorphism that mandates (coerces) the adoption of similar, isomorphic, structures is the state. For instance, as Baron, Dobbin, and Jennings (1986) found, government intervention in manpower activities in the US between 1939 and 1946 spurred the development and expansion of bureaucratic labor control. Throughout the war, the government was more actively involved in the labor process than it had ever been before. Official agencies, such as the War Production Board (WPB) and the War Manpower Board (WMB), were created to intervene in labor markets, labor unions, and work processes. These agencies often sought to standardize employment conditions in key industries and advocated bureaucratic models for doing so. Direct contact with these bureaucratic methods caused many other organizations to choose similar procedures for managing their own labor force. In this case, the intervention of state agencies produced and contributed to the spread of a new organizational outcome – bureaucratic labor control.

Isomorphic outcomes are also evident in how states regulate hiring practices, not only within individual countries, but also internationally (see table 5.1). In this respect, organizational scholars and economic sociologists have conducted extensive research on the impact of the American Civil Rights Act and the Equal Employment Opportunity (EEO) legislation – one of the most significant pieces of legislation that regulates American organizations – on the employment practices of US firms. In response, corporations created new workplace departments that we now consider commonplace, including those dealing with personnel, antidiscrimination, safety, and benefits. Over time, the existence of these departments became widespread among organizations and evolved into a larger human resources paradigm (Dobbin and Sutton 1998). Although managers and other officials first developed new organizational forms in response to state pressures and regulations, they later formulated "efficiency rationales" that justified the continued existence and institutionalization of these changes. Hence, while human resource organizational features started out as a response to state action, they spread quickly across organizations because they became viewed as efficient practices.

Firms

Table 5.1 Anti-discriminatory hiring regulations across countries

Country	Anti-discriminatory labor regulations
Australia	Australian law requires non-discriminatory hiring practices through the following legislation: Racial Discrimination Act (1975), Sex Discrimination Act (1984), Disability Discrimination Act (1992), Human Rights and Equal Opportunity Commission Act (1986). These laws prohibit direct discriminatory hiring practices and also indirect practices that create conditions that favor one group in the hiring process over others, even if this is not the explicit aim. Institutions to deal with complaints regarding workplace discrimination are publicly available.
US	Job discrimination is prevented through the following legislation: Title VII of the Civil Rights Act (1964), the Equal Pay Act (1963), the Age Discrimination in Employment Act (1967), Title I and Title V of the Americans with Disabilities Act (1990), Sections 501 and 505 of the Rehabilitation Act (1973), the Civil Rights Act (1991). All of these laws are enforced through the Equal Employment Opportunity Commission (EEOC). This legislation requires employers not to discriminate against employees based on race, color, national origin, religion, sex, age, and disability and provides compensation for individuals who have been willfully discriminated against by their employers.
Singapore	Though Singapore protects workers in many ways, by offering workers compensation and maternity leave, for example, it has not passed legislation that regulates discriminatory hiring practices on the part of firms. The Singaporean constitution states that all people are equal before the law and the state's labor department, the Ministry of Manpower, has produced "Good Business Practices and Guidelines" that emphasize non-discriminatory recruitment practices for workers, but no specific laws have been passed regulating hiring practices.
Egypt	Egypt's Labour Code states that all workplace policies apply to men and women equally except for the class of legislation that deals specifically with female employment. Female employment provisions set out specific maternity policies, such as those giving women workers two rest periods a day to feed their children. Additionally, these laws prohibit women from working nights and in certain kinds of occupations that

Table 5.1 (continued)

Country	Anti-discriminatory labor regulations
	can be physically or morally harmful. The Egyptian case provides few anti-discriminatory or equal opportunity laws for male and female workers.
Sweden	Sweden provides extensive anti-discriminatory legislation that applies to hiring and general workplace behavior through the Equal Opportunities Act (1991) and other laws. In addition to prohibiting discriminatory hiring policies, Sweden requires businesses actively to recruit and train both male and female workers to ensure an even sex balance in the workplace. When the sex balance is uneven, Swedish employers must actively try to recruit applications from the under-represented group.

Sources: Australia: www.workplace.gov.au/workplace/Organisation/Employer/ EmployerResponsibilities/Avoidingdiscriminationinemployment.htm; US www. eeoc.gov/facts/qanda.html; Singapore: www.mom.gov.sg/publish/momportal/en/communities/workplace_standards/good_employment_practices.html; Singapore, Egypt, and Sweden: data come from the International Labour Organization's Equality at Work Database.

This action is termed the strength of a weak state: "the US state is administratively weak but normatively strong" (ibid.: 441) – which fits well with the pattern that is typical in the US, where **market fundamentalism** is relatively strong and government intervention in business is not considered appropriate.

It is important to note that firm-related legal provisions often have unintended consequences. For instance, the passing of the civil rights law that prohibited sex discrimination encouraged firms to start offering maternity leave programs. Kelly and Dobbin (1999) note that it is curious that maternity leave benefits began to spread through organizations in the 1970s and 1980s, even though the Family Medical Leave Act (FMLA) was not passed at the federal level until 1993. As the courts passed such legislation throughout the 1970s, organizations began to offer maternity leave benefits as a way of complying with the sex discrimination provisions. This means that almost 50 percent of large employers provided family leave benefits years *before* the federal government

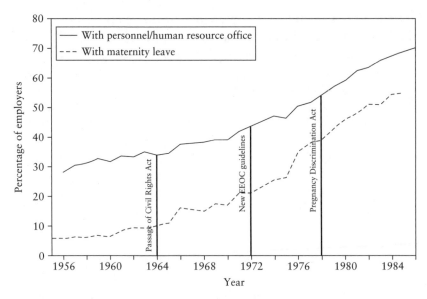

Source: Based on data from Dobbin and Sutton (1998) and Kelly and Dobbin (1999).

Figure 5.1   Consequences of the Civil Rights Act (1964) on structures and practices in American corporations

explicitly called for childcare provision through the FMLA legislation. We portray these trends, together with the rise in HR offices (as discussed in the previous paragraph), in figure 5.1. While the creation of maternity leave programs is a positive unintended consequence, it is important to keep in mind that a firm's adoption of any piece of legislation does not mean that these rules are necessarily going to be respected in practice. Law is often quite ambiguous, open to multiple interpretations, and what counts as compliance is ill-specified (Edelman 1992). Hence, firms' practices may often be decoupled from official provisions.

Corporate Governance

The set of procedures, policies, and laws affecting the way a corporation is directed, administered, or controlled is called **corporate**

governance. This includes governance of the relationships among the many stakeholders. The principal stakeholders of a firm are the shareholders – those who hold stocks (shares) in this firm – the management, and the board of directors. Others are employees, customers, creditors (such as banks), suppliers, regulators, and the community at large. There are differences across countries in which entities have more say in controlling a company. In the Anglo-Saxon world, shareholders have more power than employees, for instance, and the reverse is true in continental Europe. In Japan, managers have a lot of control over how the companies are run, more than in countries where supervisory boards or boards of directors control the work of managers (Luo 2007).

What determines the corporate governance regimes across countries? As Ruth Aguilera and Gregory Jackson (2003) propose, national corporate governance will depend on property rights established through corporate law, bankruptcy law, and contractual articles of incorporation. These will define mechanisms through which shareholders can exert control (such as voting rights and provisions for information exchange) and how control is balanced with managerial discretion. For example, in contrast to the Japanese or German corporate governance regimes, the United States exemplifies a liberal market approach facilitating market-oriented mechanisms of control. Liberal property rights provide strong minority shareholder protection owing to relatively high disclosure requirements and norms of one share, one vote. Overall, different regulation of property rights shapes the degree of capital's control in the firm, favoring different interests within corporate governance (boards, shareholders, or management).

There has been renewed interest in the corporate governance practices of modern corporations since 2001, particularly after the high-profile collapse of a number of large US firms, such as the Enron Corporation. Enron's fall was a result of revelations that much of its profits and revenue stemmed from deals with entities that it controlled. This meant that many of its debts and losses could go unreported in its financial statements. Enron's executives lied about the performance of the company, misleading shareholders, and its accountants colluded by creating faulty financial statements. The dire consequence of this corporate misconduct was an enormous drop in the price of Enron's shares, which cost stockholders about $60 billion. Employees with long-term tenure lost more than $2 billion in pension funds, and 5,600 people lost their jobs (Booth Thomas 2006).

Based on what went wrong in cases such as Enron's, in 2002 the US federal government passed the Sarbanes–Oxley Act (SOX), intended to restore public confidence in corporate governance and securities markets. According to President Bush, who signed it into law, the Act represented "the most far-reaching reforms of American business practices since the time of Franklin D. Roosevelt" (Bumiller 2002: 8B). SOX amplified regulations on publicly traded companies as well as accounting firms. On the one hand, the law requires public companies to report more information to the public. Companies are also required to maintain greater independence from their auditors, and their executives are criminally responsible if the company's accounting is flawed. On the other hand, the law provides for increased regulation of accounting practices through the creation of the Public Company Accounting Oversight Board, charged with overseeing and disciplining, if need be, accounting firms in their roles as auditors of public companies (Holt 2008). Overall, this law represents one of the strongest regulations pertaining to American corporations, unprecedented in a country which privileges the freedom of capital above the intervention of state.

Inter-Firm Relations

Should states try to prohibit firms from forging alliances with other firms that may result in collusion? Answering in the affirmative reinforces the assumption that markets operate best when **competition** between different actors engaged on the market is high. However, not all countries have similarly strict competitions laws. They also regulate differently the formation of business groups and may or may not outlaw interlocking directorates, for instance. We discuss each of these in turn.

Firms

The Roman Empire introduced a form of competition regulation by imposing heavy fines on anyone who deliberately interfered
with grain supply ships (Wilberforce, Campbell, and Elles 1966).
In their modern form, competition laws became widespread in
the twentieth century. Today, the two most influential systems of
competition regulation are the European Community competition laws and the US **antitrust** law. Sociologists believe that the
antitrust law had major repercussions for the organization of the
American economy. As mentioned in box 5.1, the initial enforcement of antitrust in 1897 had unanticipated consequences and
facilitated the emergence of large corporations (Roy 1997). More
recently, the postwar enforcement of the antitrust law with the
Celler–Kefauver amendments came to play a central role in privileging finance managers within firms and the "financial conception
of the firm" (Fligstein 1990). As we discussed in chapter 2, "conceptions of control" are the ways in which managers evaluate their
situations and decide the appropriate courses of action. They are
frameworks for interpretation and action in the business world.
In the history of American business culture, a progression of four
"conceptions of control" – the direct control of competitors,
manufacturing control, sales and marketing control, and finance
control – have guided managerial action. The passage of antitrust
amendments was a crucial factor leading to the emergence of the
financial conception of control, where financial managers sought
to diversify their companies to increase their profitability. The
antitrust regulation had a larger impact than simply outlawing
cartels and monopolies: it caused a profound shift in business
culture and the conceptions of control that guide economic action.

Organizational scholars also suggest that antitrust enforcement
stimulated corporate mergers. Using the case of railroads, Dobbin
and Dowd (2000) argue that, after the dominant business model
of the time – the cartel – was banned, several alternative ways of
organizing industrial corporations rose to prominence. While the
cartel model dominated, the railroad industry was governed by a
principle of cooperation and mutual benefit: railroad companies
allied themselves into cartels that regulated prices at levels that
allowed all to prosper. Once antitrust legislation outlawed this

form of organization, some railroads began to operate according to the "predator model," where the ultimate goal was to cause competitors to go out of business and acquire their routes. At the same time, the "finance model" emerged and gave rise to mergers between railroads, preventing competitive price-cutting wars that ultimately hurt all involved. It was only after the banking industry threatened to sanction predators that the finance model was widely accepted and mergers became customary.

States also regulate the extent of links formed between firms into so-called business groups. Examples include *chaebol* in Korea, *grupos economicos* in Latin America, and *keiretsu* in Japan (Gerlach 1992; Granovetter 2005). Some business groups are formed independent of state sponsorship and perhaps even in opposition to political elites (Camp 1989). In other cases, groups are assembled by the state and formed from state-owned enterprises, such as in China or Russia (Keister 2000; Johnson 2000). In the US, antitrust legislation effectively prevents the emergence of business groups. Interestingly, Kim (1997) notes that, the more effective the states are in creating successful business groups, the greater the risk that such groups will want to become independent and ultimately resist state control.

Another way in which states regulate inter-firm relations is through provisions that allow or prohibit **interlocking directorates** – that is, the linkages among corporations created by individuals who sit on two or more boards of directors, which allows for information sharing and the diffusion of corporate practices. Interlocking directorates have a long history in the United States. Domhoff (2006) notes that corporate interlocks existed among textile mills in the 1790s, and other scholars have demonstrated that many American industries were tightly interlocked through the early part of the twentieth century. In the early 1900s, scholars and public officials became concerned about the threats that interlocks posed to free-market competition. In response, the US House of Representatives sponsored the Pujo Commission's investigation of the nature and extent of corporate interlocks in several key industries (banking, insurance, railroads, and large industrial firms), which found the clear presence of interlocking directorates, curtailing competition and impeding the functioning of the free market (Windolf 2002: 1–4; Pennings 1980: 1–3). In response to these findings, the regulation of interlocking directorates began with Section 8 of the Clayton Act (1914). Among its provisions, it prohibited any individual from sitting on the board of directors for two competing organizations (McConnell and Brue 2004: 355; Pennings 1980: 2). Some argue that these regulations are not enforced strictly enough to prevent the concentration of power in American corporations, and subsequent government inquiries and scholarly studies have demonstrated the continued presence of interlocking directorates.

Industrial Policy

State provisions to regulate organizational structures and governance rest on different normative principles about economic governance. These vary significantly across time and space. However, what remains constant is an understanding on the part of governments that states have a role to play, whatever that role may be, in supporting the central function of firms as productive units contributing to economic growth. One major way in which states can do so is through industrial policy.

What determines industrial policy? Economists assume that it results from economic efficiency concerns. Political sociologists suggest that different interest groups, such as lobbying groups, have a substantial influence, so that the resultant policy reflects the interest of the group with the greatest political power. As we noted at the beginning of this chapter, lobbying on behalf of big corporations and by professional organizations that link firms in particular industries is widespread (Akard 1992).

In addition to these economic and political explanations of the determinants of industrial policy, sociologists highlight the role of culture. Culture here is understood as the way in which decision-makers understand particular problems and the kind of solutions that they consider plausible and appropriate. This is most evident when one compares industrial policy across countries, as Frank

Dobbin did in his book *Forging Industrial Policy* (1994). Dobbin studied nineteenth-century railway policy in the US, the UK, and France, noting that all these countries were comparable in terms of technological development, and in all of them different interest groups were vying for power. However, the industrial policies that they adopted with regard to railroad development were quite distinct. In the US, political institutions reinforced the value of community sovereignty, which resulted in weak national policy-making capacities. British institutions reinforced the value of individual sovereignty, protecting sovereign firms and individual entrepreneurs. The French placed a premium on state sovereignty and had technocrats in Paris devise a highly centralized national railway system. Overall, the railway policies were different because each country followed fundamentally distinct logics and conceptions of rationality persisting in their political cultures.

Similarly, Bai Gao (1997) examined how Japanese institutions helped shape industrial policy and development between 1931 and 1965. He argues that the Japanese state was guided by an economic logic that prioritized strong productive capabilities along with controls for market forces and a de-emphasis on the importance of corporate profit. Rapid industrialization required the maintenance of social order, and it was necessary for the Japanese state to take decisive action to serve both corporations and workers. The development of the *keiretsu*, a cooperative grouping of businesses that served to diminish competition among firms, is a prime example of how the state encouraged a particular kind of economic organization.

We want to make a point that industrial policy takes different forms around the world as a result of not only economic but also political and cultural forces. Decision-makers act upon different ideas about the appropriate role for the state in industrial policy. Hence, states can adopt a developmentalist stance toward industrial policy, directly subsidizing nascent industries or particular sectors where the aim is to achieve competitive advantage. In contrast, decision-makers in regulatory liberal states, such as the US, may see the state's role mostly as setting up the legal and regulatory framework for the development of industry, but not direct subsidizing because that goes against the principles of liberal market competition. We take up the issue of states' role in industrial policy again when we discuss the late industrialization perspective on development and developmental states in chapter 6.

Research and Technology

With the goal of economic growth in mind, states try to regulate, more or less, how productive firms are in contributing to a country's economic output. This is where governmental spending on research development, R&D, comes in. In the initial months of his presidency, Barack Obama promised major investment, claiming that his goal would be to set more than 3 percent of the nation's GDP in research and development for scientific innovation (Revkin 2009). In fact, there are only a few advanced countries that spend more than 3 percent of their GDP on R&D, including Sweden, Israel, and Finland (see figure 5.2).

For Block, in the postindustrial societies where knowledge economy is considered to be the area most generative of economic advances, "governments have played an increasingly important role in underwriting and encouraging the advance of new technologies in the business economy" (2008: 170). They have done so by supporting policies that encourage innovation and facilitate the transformation of innovations into commercial products. However, states have approached this task quite differently, and there is a stark contrast between the policies pursued in the United States and those in Europe. European countries individually and within the European Union are explicit about their developmental goals, while in the US "the developmental state is hidden" (ibid.). It is neither part of political debates nor discussed much in the media. In Block's view this is because market fundamentalist ideas, dictating that markets should operate without governmental involvement, have prevailed in the US since the 1970s. In such a milieu, it is not surprising that developmental policies regarding innovation and research and development remain unacknowledged.

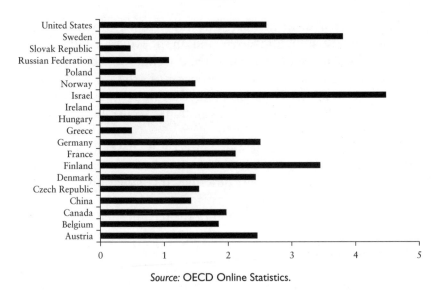

Firms

Source: OECD Online Statistics.

Figure 5.2   State spending on research and development, 2006 (% of GDP)

Their efforts may be more or less recognized, but advanced industrial states, generally, do act to shape innovation policy in multiple ways. One way, for instance, is through state sponsorship of university research or military activities that yield significant innovations (Dorsi, Orsenigo, and Labini 2005). Indeed, Atkinson and Blanpied (2008) discuss research universities as the cornerstone of US technological innovation. Though they did not initially receive federal funding, US research universities have grown substantially since the 1950s with the financial help of the state. Agencies such as the National Science Foundation or the National Institutes of Health give billions of dollars to academics who engage in scientific pursuits. Many university researchers at state institutions are also receiving private industry funding to work on innovative projects. Moreover, military funding of science is widespread across different countries (Geiger 1992). An intricate example of a combination of military funding of science and academic scientific research, all under the auspices of the state, is the Los Alamos National Laboratory (LANL), which is the US Department of Energy National Laboratory, operated by the University of California and three private corporations. LANL is one of the largest science and technology institutions in the world and is one of the two locations in the US where work on nuclear weapons is undertaken. Research conducted in this laboratory includes fields such as national security, outer space, and supercomputing.

Some states have sought more directly to develop indigenous high technology industries, for example in software and telecommunications. O Riain (2004) describes this situation in Ireland, where the state provided employment-based grant aid to firms specifically through the expansion of the technical labor force and by providing investors with incentives. Israel, on the other hand, offered institutional support to firms that develop technology and has pioneered successful strategies to entice capital investment and loss-sharing among innovative firms. Both Israel and Ireland provided direct support and incentives to firms, effectively transforming their local high technology industries into nodes of global production networks.

Particular attention has also been paid to the role that technological innovation plays in the economic advancement of non-Western countries and how the state encourages or discourages this. Govindan (2005) focuses on how the development of the semiconductor industry in Singapore paved the way for its economic advancement. In contrast to some of the cases we have discussed so far, Govindan actually cautions against too much state involvement in technological development. According to Govindan, the developmental state does play a role in encouraging technological development, but it has to be open enough to know that it cannot necessarily determine the next course of technological development, and instead needs to allow it to emerge from the expanding process of innovative development. Specifically, he is concerned about the control that the state has over both academia and innovation policy that might make it more difficult for the emerging biotechnology industry in Singapore. The lesson of Singapore is that there is no one "right" innovation strategy for governments to follow, but instead, flexibility is key.

Firms

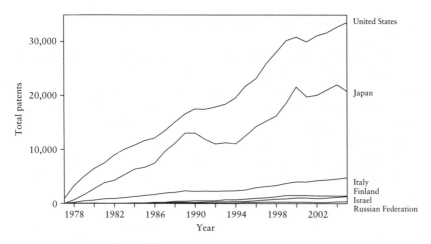

Source: OECD, http://stats.oecd.org/Index.aspx.

Figure 5.3 Number of registered patents across countries, 2009

Indeed, the challenge for the state in influencing innovation is reflected in the fact that overall greater government spending on research and development does not immediately translate into more registered patents, for instance (see figure 5.3 and compare it with figure 5.2) This is also because the relationship between technology and productivity is not very well understood. Technology is related to productivity (Mokyr 1990) but exactly how is still somewhat of an open question. It may be because technological advance is not the only reason for growth in productivity. It has to be coupled with the social organization of work (Roy 1952). As famous Hawthorne experiments show, adjustments to the technology of work (such as the organizations of tasks and equipment used) were less important than paying attention to workers' welfare, a finding that propelled a new theoretical perspective in organizational studies called the human relations perspective (Roethlisberger and Dickson 1939). It is primarily because of the complexities of work organization, owing to its human and technological elements, that initiatives by the state to foster research and development do not have uniform consequences.

Business Regulation to Protect Consumers

So far, we have presented evidence of the state's direct role in regulating firms and industry, mostly to uphold free-market principles or to support developmental aims. But an important way in which states regulate firms is to protect consumers. Through such provisions as those concerning product liability, unfair business practices, privacy rights, fraud, and misrepresentation, the state acts as arbitrator in consumer–business interactions. Why would this be an important role for the state? Consider that businesses are unrestricted in their pursuit of maximum profits. What happens if, in this pursuit, a business finds it most efficient to make their products using components or production processes that pose risks to those who will consume or encounter them? This is where states come in. They enact regulations that protect consumers from the potentially unsafe consequences of business activity. Consider the case of US regulations to limit the amount of lead that can be present in paint and other consumer goods. In spite of the importance of lead to the expansion of the American economy in the first half of the twentieth century and its cost-effective properties for corporations, these products were consistently linked to lead poisoning, which can be especially dangerous to children. Consequently, the US enacted protective regulations in the 1970s and 1980s that required companies to ensure that lead-based products did not pose health risks to consumers, especially where two popularly consumed products (paint and gasoline) were concerned. Comparable regulations with regard to toxic components have been placed on both silica-using and plastics industries (Markowitz and Rosner 1999).

Similar restrictions have been applied to food and drug corporations to ensure that their products do not pose undue risks to consumers and so that individuals can make informed decisions about which products to consume. For instance, have you ever examined the ingredients label on a food or beverage item at a grocery store? The US Department of Agriculture (USDA) and Food and Drug Administration (FDA) have required that the ingredients of food, beverages, and drugs must be specified and available to potential consumers. This has been thought to be a matter of consumer protection. Corporations must now disclose the ingredients in their products (Blanchfield 2000). The protective benefits of this regulation extend far beyond making consumers aware of potentially harmful ingredients in products, allowing those with specific health-related concerns or allergies to minimize the impact any product might have on their condition. Here, we can see that the operations of corporations are curtailed and transparency is increased. We can see similar disclosure laws in the used-car market. In this case, the state specifies the kinds of vehicles that may legally be provided for sale – those whose history and mechanical condition has been completely revealed to their potential buyers (McNeil et al. 1979). These regulations infringe upon the principles of free-market exchange, where a seller should be able to place any good for sale at whatever price a buyer will offer. Instead, the state intervenes on behalf of consumers to protect them against the purchase of damaged goods. By receiving a report of the vehicle's condition at the time of sale, the buying power of the consumer is enhanced.

You might be wondering where regulations for the protection of consumers come from. In other words, why and how do states decide to regulate businesses for more or less benefit of consumers? After all, not all countries have similar regulations imposed on the behavior of firms in order to protect consumers, which requires an explicit and institutionalized recognition of *consumer rights*, not only the civil, political, and social rights of citizens, as T. H. Marshall outlined. Though the genesis of any single piece of regulation is undoubtedly complex, one important force behind the emergence of consumer protection laws has been nonprofit consumer watchdog organizations. These are powerful social organizations that help sustain social order by inspecting the performance of corporations and other actors, lobbying government officials, and educating consumers about their rights. Essentially, these are "watchdog" organizations, analogous to those that exist to protect the environment, animal rights, and other social issues, but their particular mandate is to protect consumers. Research has shown these organizations to be crucial to the development of regulations that favor consumers, both directly and indirectly. In the first case, they can lobby the government directly to address particular causes. But these organizations also raise the awareness of consumers and in some cases create cultural shifts that support the emergence of particular social policies, such as those supporting the removal of unhealthy substances from food, or recycling, both of which are now seen as "acceptable" and therefore "expected" policies in today's times – although this certainly has not been the case historically, nor is it (yet) in all countries (Rao 1998).

Up to this point, we have focused on cases where the state has chosen to enact policies to protect consumers, largely as a result of consumer rights movements. However, there are also cases in which consumers and other forces in society have unsuccessfully tried to influence the government to enact policies to protect their rights in one arena or another. A curious example is the development and subsequent repeal of anti-chain store legislation. Chain stores are ubiquitous today and, from one perspective, are the kind of economic agents that have an equalizing impact on consumerism by making the same goods available to individuals living in different parts of the state. However, chain stores can also be conceived as a powerful challenge to traditional community life, which was based on small retailers who were intimately linked to the locales they served. Still, it is easy to see that business interests would be opposed to legislation that creates limits on economic expansion and profit-making. Indeed, the power of retail has grown drastically in the recent decades, and in 2008 *Fortune Global 500* ranked Wal-Mart, the world's largest global retail chain, as the number one public corporation by revenue. But this rise of chain-retail should not be taken for granted. After World War I, an anti-chain store movement emerged in the US that was staged by small retailers who were hurt by the competition and by interested community members and local activists who saw the growing presence of these organizations as a threat to consumers and their communities. While individual states began to respond to this pressure by enacting anti-chain store legislation, pro-chain store forces in society appealed to the US Supreme Court, and eventually this legislation was repealed. Those who opposed chain stores thought that their existence and spread throughout the country was a threat not only to local business and communities but also to consumers, who would lose out on the experience of patronizing a small, locally invested business. As more local shops go out of business, the consumer's choice about where to shop is essentially made for them. Thus, some feel that the consequences of this state regulation form a substantial issue that works against consumers and community life, though this is by no means settled. The point here is that the state does not always protect all kinds of consumer rights for all kinds of people, and that this is largely a political process, rather than linked to some notion that certain consumer rights are inherently more important than others (Ingram and Rao 2004; Zelizer 2005).

Finally, we want to note that business regulation to protect consumer welfare has also become a more salient issue in developing countries. This is aided by the role of international organizations and is in line with the expected worldwide diffusion of human rights norms by the world polity theory (Meyer et al. 1997). For instance, through the Codex Alimentarius Commission and the subsequent development of the food safety standards into the World Trade Organization, developing countries are increasingly adopting food safety standards similar to those of developed countries. Though the standards of both of these bodies are efforts at regulating food safety internationally, they are in fact agreed to and implemented at the domestic level by the state. In the case of food additives, the standards did diffuse into some less developed countries through the influence of international organizations and powerful countries – the US and Western Europe – that occupy central positions within them (Post 2005). This is the case of how normative pressures at the world-society level operate to shape the adoption of consumption-related policies across the globe.

Business Regulation to Protect the Environment

In this last section of the chapter, we want to discuss the rules that states impose on firms to limit environmental degradation. We want to reiterate one of our central points about the role of the state in managing fictitious commodities, of which nature is one. Firms cannot simply use natural resources as though they can be continually produced for sale on the market. In fact, as with other fictitious commodities, the state is charged with protecting these resources from full exploitation by market forces. Environmental regulation, therefore, benefits all of those who live in a territory and could potentially be affected by environmental hardships, such as pollution.

Thus, some modicum of environmental state regulation is necessary. However, what the appropriate degree of such regulation should be is far from settled. We distinguish three perspectives here: the economic, the managed security, and the ecological. In the economic perspective, the environment is seen as a resource that should be unrestricted and available to any economic enterprise that might bring profit, and the degree to which the state will intervene in the economy to protect the environment is minimal to non-existent. The managed security perspective, on the other hand, recognizes that economic activity comes at the cost of environmental damage, and the state will enact a moderate level of protective regulation so that economic production and profits are not disrupted. Protecting the environment from damage is the highest concern under the ecological perspective, which rejects outright any economic dominance over the environment. Whether decision-makers fall in line with one or the other of these three outlooks will produce different kinds of state environmental regulation in different contexts.

Let us consider the example of recycling solid waste. In Europe, state regulations have mainly required manufacturers to accept responsibility for the waste created by using or consuming their products. In America, on the other hand, the responsibility for recycling was passed on to local governments. There is a clear difference here in the kind of regulation enacted by the state. While European countries dealt with recycling issues by holding businesses responsible, the US state steered clear of infringing on economic profits by assuming a larger role itself. Though both the US and European states have essentially supported the right of consumers to live in a healthy environment by recognizing that waste constitutes an environmental problem, there is a difference in what agents are chosen to resolve this problem. What is clear is that the role of the state and the kinds of legislation enacted vary considerably from case to case, but most states will intervene in some way to protect consumers from the ultimate destruction of the environment (Schnaiberg 2005).

Conclusion

Capitalist markets depend on firms as central agents of production and employment. States' efforts to provide the broad institutional conditions for markets to function, which we covered in chapter 2, translate into specific provisions, namely rules of exchange and governance structures that support the participation of firms as key economic actors in the market. In fact, most sociologists agree that legal regulation enforced by states, rather than economic cost efficiency of large productive entities, was the main cause of the rise of big corporations over the course of the nineteenth and twentieth centuries.

There are many specific state provisions that enable and constrain, simultaneously, the functioning of firms. From an economic perspective, economic efficiency considerations should be central to determining organizational structures and practices. We highlighted, however, that the kind of organizational structures and practices that firms adopt – whether they have a human resources department or engage in antidiscriminatory hiring or offer maternity leave policies – often have to do with the influence of the state providing a key impetus through coercive isomorphic pressures. It is the passage of laws such as the Civil Rights Act of 1964 that impact corporate practices. Both indirect and direct effects are important. What we should keep in mind, however, is that adopting structures mandated by law does not always result in firms' compliance in practice.

The functioning of firms also depends on how they are administered and controlled, and how relations between them are regulated. When discussing corporate and inter-firm governance, we noted the implications of the sanctity of market competition, mostly in liberal states such as the US, for such issues as monopolistic tendencies, the formation of business groups, and interlocking directorates. The practice across nations shows that market fundamentalism is weaker in most other countries than it is in the US. Notably, however, recent corporate financial scandals, such as the Enron or WorldCom debacles, have been followed by the passage of laws that assure stricter state regulation of business.

Implications of different kinds of economy–state relations for organizational structures and governance aside, the central function of firms in any economy is to contribute to growth. States try to influence the productive capacities of firms by direct and indirect provision in research and development. But greater government spending on R&D does not translate directly into new innovations. Scholars make clear that, given the changing nature of technology, states need to remain flexible in providing enough support to firms but not too much regulation.

Finally, the process of production of goods and services links firms directly to consumers and the environment. According to economic theory, and to Marxists, firms – or their owners, to be exact – are most interested in pursuing maximum profits. But simply looking to generate the highest revenues at the least cost may lead to serious risks for consumers and irreparable environmental degradation. This is where the role of states comes in: they enact regulations that protect consumers and the environment from the potentially unsafe consequences of business activity. Importantly, however, states differ in what they define as consumer rights and which they deem worthy of protection. They also disagree on the appropriate level of environmental regulation. In the end, consumer and environment policies, imposed as restrictions on firms' free pursuit of profit, depend on historically institutionalized understandings of state–economy relations and the relative power of interest groups and parties.

6

Development: The State's Role in Advancing Economic Prosperity

What does it mean to speak of economic development? Put simply, there are some countries in the world that are wealthy, such as Norway, Singapore, and the US, where the inhabitants enjoy a high standard of living. Based on these economic characteristics, we usually refer to these countries as developed countries. However, there are also countries whose populations have low standards of living and are faced with rampant poverty and general economic underdevelopment, such as Zimbabwe, Congo, and Liberia. Consider again map 1.1 (p. 7), showing GDP per capita levels around the world, and compare it with figure 6.1, which shows levels of poverty across a handful of nations. The cross-country variations are significant and warrant an explanation. How do countries improve the standard of living of their people? That is a key question, but it doesn't have one single answer. In this chapter we review several different approaches to economic development and note how they implicate economy–state relations. We pay special attention to the concept of developmental states and the role of ideas in shaping the course of different developmental trajectories.

Paying attention to the social and economic change induced by industrialization, the classical sociologists Marx, Durkheim, and Weber could be seen as concerned with economic development. Still, it was only after World War II, at a time of economic reconstruction, the emancipation of colonies, and the beginning of the Cold War, that development became an ideologically explicit

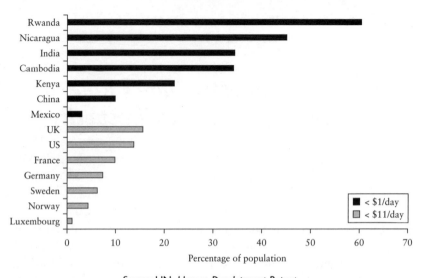

Source: UN, *Human Development Report.*

Figure 6.1   People living in poverty across countries, 2007–8

project and a systematic study of its causes started to flourish (McMichael 2000). One of the most important changes in the post-World War II period was the decolonization movement, through which former colonies became independent countries. At this time, people began to compare the economic conditions in different states, observing the stark contrasts that existed between former colonies in Africa and Latin America and the long-industrialized countries of the United States and Western Europe. Development became prioritized as a national ideal. At first, this "development project" was essentially aimed at universalizing Western development around the world in order to generate economic growth, which would in turn contribute to broader human development. This was modernization theory's understanding of development. However, modernization is not the only way to approach or understand how countries grow economically. Dependency theory, world-systems analysis, neoclassical economic theory, comparative institutionalism, and the late industrialization perspective are among other approaches. We review each of these in turn and pay special attention to what role they envision – or not – for the state in the economic development process.

Modernization Theory

After World War II, scholars and policy-makers focused on development as a means to reconstruct national economies devastated by the war and to build up the economies of newly independent ex-colonial states. **Modernization theory** was one of the pioneering attempts to identify the causes of and means by which development could be achieved around the world. Scholars identify the birth of modernization theory with the publication of W. W. Rostow's *The Stages of Economic Growth* (1960). This book discussed development as a phenomenon made up of stages through which all countries could progress, provided that the necessary inputs for each stage were present. Rostow's idea of development is essentially a linear one that describes a road down which all economies can travel to reach the end stage of development. This perspective can be illustrated by imagining an airplane going to one specific destination. All flights begin with the plane on the ground and must progress through a certain sequence of steps that lead up to a successful flight. Modernization theory sees development in a similar manner. Rostow identified five stages of development, which differ in terms of productive capacities, technological development, and value orientations. Each stage serves as a requirement for a society to move on to the next one, as the new institutions and social arrangements in each stage build on the previous stage.

The first stage is a traditional society that has limited productive functions and is marked by underdeveloped and out-of-date knowledge of science and technology. Though traditional societies might achieve modest gains over time, there is essentially a ceiling on their productive output stemming from the lack of modern technology and the devotion of substantial resources toward agricultural production. Traditional societies also exhibit what Rostow calls "long-run fatalism," where individuals think that the opportunities and life chances their children would experience would be about the same as their own. Rostow groups a range of societies into this category, including Chinese dynasties and medieval Europe. In spite of their many differences, what unifies them as traditional societies is the ceiling that exists on the productivity of their economic techniques and the inability of individuals to manipulate the environment to produce economic gain.

The second stage of development is called "preconditions for takeoff." This is a transitional period where societies are moving away from the traditional form and learning how to harness new technologies and productive techniques for their benefit and economic growth. Crucial to this process is a change in attitudes and values away from "long-run fatalism" toward viewing economic progress as something that is both possible and desirable. This attitudinal shift engenders changes in institutions, such as the educational system, which evolve to meet the needs of the modern economy. Here modernization theory highlights a role for the state and private investors in mobilizing capital for entrepreneurial endeavors and in taking risks to develop new technologies and techniques of production. In spite of the emergence of modern economic forms, production in this society is still slowed by the remaining vestiges of the traditional society.

Next is the "takeoff" phase of development, where the impediments to economic growth and progress are reduced and surmounted. Economic progress becomes a dominant force in society and is built into both its value system and its institutional structure. Though the initial economic takeoff is a result largely of the expansion and increased productivity in a selection of sectors, societies eventually move into the "maturity" stage of development, where the economy becomes diversified based on expanded and increasingly modern technology that can be used to process a variety of resources into just about anything. Finally, societies will arrive in the stage of "high mass-consumption," where real incomes rise and economic production proceeds into the arena of consumer goods. A key change in this state is that the dominance of technology can give way to the provision of social benefits and services to society. This indicates a move away from technological maturity as the ultimate goal of society toward the provision of goods and services for a largely urban population.

In modernization theory, forward-thinking actors, both private economic agents and bureaucratic state elites, play key roles in overcoming the traditionalism that impedes economic growth (McMichael 2000). Though Rostow and other modernization theorists provide evidence that the state can assist the movement of an economy through the stages of development (Kerr et al. 1960; Rostow 1960), they do not highlight the state as a central actor in this process, aside from its provision of a stable environment for the development of technology and enterprise.

After reading this, you might be questioning modernization theory's assertion that development is a process that is universally available to any state willing to follow the recipe of stages set forth by Rostow and others. Is it possible for one single recipe for development to achieve success in a variety of different national contexts? In fact, one of the main criticisms levied against modernization theory has concerned its bias toward Western-style development as the normative standard toward which all countries could and should strive (So 1990). Further, scholars have shown that the actual mechanisms that underlie the progression of a society through these stages are left unspecified, and, as such, modernization theory is more of a classification of the historical processes of the development of Western societies than it is a model for future growth around the world (Frank 1969; Wallerstein 1974b). Other critiques of this theory emphasize that it views development essentially as a national, within-country, process in spite of the possibly crucial influence of international economic patterns and external relationships among countries (Frank 1967). By locating the causes of underdevelopment within the affected societies themselves, this perspective has also been alleged to "blame the victims" – in this case, the underdeveloped societies – for their own economic problems (Bradshaw and Wallace 1996).

Dependency Theory

In reaction to modernization theory's proposition that the causes of underdevelopment were located *within* a country and could be overcome through a linear path of development, dependency theorists emphasized the role of complex *interrelationships* between developed and underdeveloped countries. In his critique of the sociology of development, André Gunder Frank (1969) argued that development and underdevelopment were influenced by more things than just the internal development and values of a society, and his writing is thought to have inspired the **dependency theory**.

Frank claimed that development and underdevelopment are essentially two sides of the same coin. This means that the methods Western countries used to achieve developmental goals correspondingly engendered the underdevelopment of other countries. Think of the colonial relationships that existed at the time of industrialization among Western countries. Dependency theorists argue that it was precisely the development of Western countries, which extracted raw materials, labor, and other inputs from colonial countries, that placed colonies in a state of dependency on their colonial masters. On account of this exploitative relationship, colonial countries did not see returns, in terms of profit and economic growth, from the resources and labor they provided to the ruling countries. For these reasons, former colonial relationships are one important set of factors that structure the dependence of underdeveloped on developed countries for access to technology, capital, and markets, all of which are seen as beneficial to economic growth (Frank 1969).

Dependency theorists also see the unequal relationship between developed and underdeveloped countries as one that persists into more modern forms of economic activity. International trade, for instance, is thought to work for developed countries while disadvantaging underdeveloped countries (Prebisch 1950; Frank 1967; Furtado 1970; Bruton 1998). Similarly, less developed states serve as attractive sites for multinational corporations, largely operating out of developed countries, which further increases the exploitative ties between developed and underdeveloped countries

(Haggard 1990), a point to which we return in chapter 7. In this way, dependency theorists think that inequality and exploitation are characteristic of many contemporary relations between developed and underdeveloped countries.

In view of these asymmetrical relationships between countries, how can developmental outcomes be achieved? Dependency theorists emphasize a key role for the state. An autonomous state bureaucracy with the capacity to formulate and enforce policies of import-substitution industrialization (ISI) was thought to provide an alternative to exploitative trading and other exchanges between states (Frank 1967; Bruton 1998). Dependency scholars noted that underdeveloped countries typically exported goods whose prices decreased over time while the goods they imported were becoming increasingly more expensive (Prebisch 1950). ISI policies aimed to reduce a country's foreign dependency on expensive imports through the local production of industrialized products. Government subsidies to spur domestic industrialization and protect infant industries were concrete actions that would help produce more goods domestically and exemplified a role that the state could take to improve the economic growth and development of a country (Gibson 1971; Hirschman 1958, 1968). The emphasis on state-led development through import substitution stands in stark contrast to the view of development proposed by modernization theorists. Dependency theorists suggested that, rather than being a natural progression through the same set of stages in each country, development could in fact be sparked by particular policy interventions emerging out of an understanding of the relations of dependent development. ISI was adopted in many Latin American countries from the 1930s until the late 1980s, and in some Asian and African countries from the 1950s onward. It achieved some success in countries, such as Brazil, where large populations could consume locally produced products but was less successful in smaller countries, such as Ecuador and Honduras. Ultimately, the greatest disadvantage of ISI was that countries needed to borrow money to promote their industrialization which, coupled with the oil crisis, led to massive debt and to a financial crisis – the Latin American Debt Crisis – in the early 1980s, when countries could no longer repay what they owed. The International Monetary Fund came to the rescue, but brought with it economic policies of neoliberalism (Blouet and Blouet 2009).

Dependency theory, and its vision of economic development, has also been criticized by scholars. Though it analyzes issues of power and domination between countries, scholars have asserted that it does not attend to issues of power relations within particular societies, which can reinforce traditional values and prevent widespread economic development (So 1990; Cardoso 1977). Others have noted that, even though dependency theory does in fact offer a theory of development and underdevelopment, its premises and suggestions have not been extensively subjected to empirical testing, and thus we do not know whether or not its prescriptions actually bring about the intended results in the "real world" (Hogan and Patterson 2004). In fact, there are scholars who have provided empirical evidence indicating that trade and foreign capital produce economic growth rather than, as dependency theorists thought, underdevelopment (Amsden 1979). In general, critics of dependency theory question the reliance on imperialism and domination as the sole explanatory factors in developmental analyses and call for an inclusion of internal social and productive relations.

The World-Systems Perspective

Like dependency theory, the **world-systems perspective** attributes importance to international connections between countries as key factors that help explain development and underdevelopment. Rather than focusing on the country as the unit of analysis, world-systems scholars view the world economy as the unit most relevant for studies of development (Wallerstein 1974b; Chase-Dunn and Rubinson 1977; Wallerstein 2004). Hence, world-systems researchers focus their analysis of economic development not within the context of any one state, but instead on the structural position that states occupy in the world-system and the relationships that exist between different structural positions.

Development

What explanation do world-systems theorists offer for the existence of underdevelopment in the world-system at large? The answer is that a state's peripheral position and incomplete integration in the world capitalist system explain why some are underdeveloped (Wallerstein 1974b). That is, some countries in the world-system are at the "core"; they are wealthy, central, and well integrated in the world economy, while those on the "periphery" are poor and less integrated. Countries on the "semi-periphery" lie somewhere in between the two (Wallerstein 2004). You might be wondering what prospects for development the world-systems perspective offers to countries. In fact, it is the states that have remained outside of this world-system, such as China during Mao's socialism, for instance, that will have the easiest time developing because they will not be plagued by relationships of exploitation and disadvantage that cut across the system at large (Ragin and Chirot 1984), a proposition that is in line with China's growth over the past couple of decades (see figure 6.2).

In the world-systems perspective, underdevelopment is not a stage to be passed through but, rather, is a relational position that is the result of a country's peripheral status in the world economy.

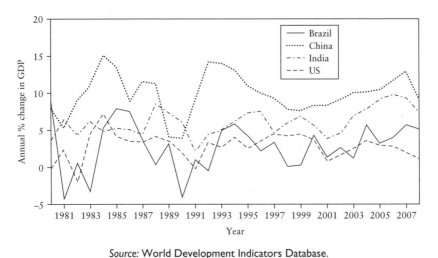

Source: World Development Indicators Database.

Figure 6.2   China's economic growth in comparative perspective

145

Still, we know little about which factor world-systems analysts consider the main cause of differential levels of development. Chase-Dunn and Rubinson (1977) suggested that the main culprit was a division of labor across countries, where some states engage in productive activities with high returns while others provide raw materials or other goods that receive lower returns. This geographical division of labor is akin to the class division of labor that Karl Marx scrutinized, as both have their foundations in the material bases of productive relations. The most valuable and central economic activities tend to be concentrated in core countries, while the less valuable or less central economic activities tend to exist in peripheral countries. This process is termed "unequal exchange" because it ensures that the surplus of the periphery is actually accumulated at the core. This constant outflow of surplus value from peripheral to core countries also impacts the possibilities for future development, which requires capital, investment, and the development of new technologies, but it also paints a very bleak picture of potential development for any country that is "stuck" in a peripheral position.

What is the role of the state in the capitalist world-system? States set the rules for the economic activity that occurs within their territory, including regulations on the mobility of labor, capital, and commodities across borders, employment regulations, and taxation and monopoly laws. Hence, as the preeminent world-systems theorist Immanuel Wallerstein (2004) argues, states set the rules by which the expansion of world capitalism can occur. Admittedly, the autonomy of states to implement their desired policy preferences is certainly not equal among all states, and some may be more or less able to enact protection policies that would obstruct the accumulation of capital by economic actors.

Like other theories of development, the world-systems perspective has been criticized on many grounds. Other Marxist scholars have argued that the focus on the core–periphery axis of exploitation fails to attend to the importance of class struggle between the proletariat and the bourgeoisie in its formulation of social change. Others have stated that world-systems theory downplays the autonomy of the state as an independent actor and consider it simply an arena of the world economy that has little power of its own (Skocpol 1977; Zolberg 1981). Such state-centric criticisms emphasize that the state is an autonomous actor and that international market pressures are not the only forces that shape its policy preferences. Still others have posited that the world-systems perspective is too economically reductionist in that it disregards the importance of culture and credits the economic realm as the predominant force shaping social reality (Aronowitz 1981).

The Neoclassical Approach to Economic Development

Dependency and world-systems theories are perspectives developed by sociologists and political economists. We want to contrast them with a **neoclassical economic approach,** following the classical doctrines of laissez-faire economics introduced by Adam Smith and others, which saw a resurgence among development policy-makers in the early 1980s and became labeled "neoliberalism." We discuss neoliberalism in more detail in chapter 7 but want to present the core arguments of the economic theory that underlies it here.

The neoclassical approach sees the state's role as an intervention in the economy that has detrimental consequences because it obscures the workings of the market and prevents the "invisible hand" from doing its job. Neoclassical economists eschew the gradual transition process described by modernization theory in favor of the sudden and far-reaching implementation of market policies for less developed economies. Key elements of a neoclassical policy program designed to spur development would include foreign trade, direct investment, deregulation, fiscal discipline, privatization, and liberalization. Such policies would set the stage for long-term, sustainable economic growth precisely because they are designed to keep the state out of the economy and let the market do its work. Regardless of the timing of industrialization among countries, neoclassical economists think that state intervention in

Development

the economy is a hindrance to development. States should enforce clear private property rights but aside from that let markets function in their own right. In countries where states do intervene in the economy, own productive assets, and impose protection, the neoclassical perspective calls for deregulation, privatization, and liberalization as the way to promote development (Guillén 2001b). This is powerfully illustrated by the shock therapy reform recommendations that many Central and Eastern European and former Soviet countries received, and more or less extensively embraced, upon the collapse of communism, as we discussed in chapter 2. It was also the case with the policy prescriptions advocated for Latin America and sub-Saharan Africa in the early 1990s, which we mention again in chapter 7.

Criticism of the neoclassical economic perspective has been launched by a wide variety of scholars and other social actors, emphasizing that the proposed roll-back of the state does not suit developing economies, which often lack the institutional structures and other factors necessary to support market operations (North 1990). Similarly, the single version of policy prescriptions available to developing countries is at odds with world-systems, dependency, and late industrialization theories, all of which emphasize that the particular situation of developing economies requires different policies from those of industrialized nations. The repeated state intervention in response to market failures in industrialized countries, such as the Keynesian responses of the US and Western European countries to the Great Depression, runs against the free-market policies advocated by neoclassical economics. Finally, some have brought empirical evidence to bear on this theory, questioning the improvements that free-market policies allegedly bring. As Rodrik (2006) reported for the case of Latin America, economic growth in countries that underwent neoliberal reforms never achieved the desired heights, and often resulted in crises and additional hardship. Similarly, Borocz (1999) questioned the impact that free-market reforms have had on the quality of life among Eastern and Central European states, noting marked decreases in the health and welfare for many social groups.

The Comparative Institutional Approach

All of the perspectives we have presented so far are united in their modernist orientation, which drives them to look for the "one best way" to solve social and economic problems among states. Modernization, dependency, world-system, and neoclassical economic theories all see development as a process that requires economies to overcome some particular obstacles via a specific set of policy prescriptions that are created and enforced, to varying degrees, by the modern state. However, the **comparative institutional approach** offers a theory of economic development that sees firms and states as using their particular advantages to find a unique place in the world economy (Bendix 1956; Dore 1989; Geertz 1963), leading to a variety of capitalism as we discussed in chapter 2. In this way, economic development is a process that highlights diversity and renewal rather than one bringing about convergence (Guillén 2001b).

One difference between this and other theories of development is that the particular social organization of a country is not seen as an obstacle that needs to be overcome but is instead cast as a foundational resource to be harnessed by a nation in its quest for economic development. Viewing a country's organization as an advantage rather than a disadvantage provides a different answer to the question of why some countries are less developed than others. A comparative institutionalist answer would point to the inattention to a country's individual sources of strength and advantage in the policy-making process. Such a perspective sees nothing "backward" or deviant about less developed countries. Successful economic development comes not from a particular, one-size-fits-all set of policies, but from matching the logics of social organization with the opportunities presented by the global economy (Orru, Hamilton, and Biggart 1997).

Organizing logics, which are the product of particular historical trajectories entrenched in a country's social and cultural organization, are particularly important to achieving development (Biggart and Guillén 1999). Different social settings provide various frameworks for appropriate action. It is perfectly suitable in some places, for instance, to raise capital through familial or other personal ties, but in other locations this is avoided in favor of accumulating money from banks or foreign investors. This is one example of the ways in which economic policies will differ among states in relation to their social, economic, and political organization. The strategies for capital accumulation or any other economic policy that succeed in one country may not be a good fit with the pre-existing organization of another country. As such, the course of development and the policies that enable it should build on the native strengths of a particular location.

Comparative institutionalists do see a role for the state in economic development, but they do not consider it to be the single most important actor. Instead it is but one of many actors, in conjunction with multinational corporations, banks, state-owned enterprises, business groups, small firms, individuals, and families, involved in the processes of industrial growth and development. A variety of actors and the diverse relationships between them are the important elements in the explanation of how countries develop and insert themselves into the global economy. Ideologies, organizing logics, state structures, and cultural norms are also highlighted as important factors that can steer a country's developmental path in a particular direction. Essentially, the comparative institutional perspective sees the economy as emerging from a social and institutional base that is different in each situation.

There are several important criticisms of this perspective. Neoclassical economists and others raise the point that it is difficult to pin down the policy recommendations of the comparative institutional approach, since they vary on a case-by-case basis. Some might further emphasize the deep understanding of a country and its organizing logics that would be required to direct a comparative institutional development program, as well as its inherent complexity because multiple social actors would need to be involved. It is unlikely that social actors would be this aware and capable of matching the opportunities presented by the global economy with the indigenous sources of strength present in any particular state, and to do so in a coordinated way. Indeed, analyses of comparative institutional development are rarely applied to explaining trajectories of underdeveloped countries that lack basic institutional capabilities and resources. Further, still, a world-systems or dependency analyst might argue that the comparative institutional perspective ignores the exploitative nature of the historical and contemporary ties between nations. Nevertheless, this perspective does overcome some shortcomings of unilateral views of development by asserting that configurations of different conditions can yield developmental outcomes, a point we raised in the discussion of the varieties of capitalism in chapter 2.

Late Industrialization and Developmental States

The last development perspective that we will highlight reserves a very important role for the state in this process. The **"late industrialization" perspective** sees globalization and development as convergent processes, and less developed countries are thought to need help and guidance to catch up with the more industrialized ones. The principal actor in this process is the **developmental state**. Countries that began to industrialize at relatively later times would need to be more developmental than others.

One of the earliest expositions of the late industrialization perspective was Alexander Gerschenkron's *Economic Backwardness in Historical Perspective* (1962), where the author argued that strong state involvement helped late industrializers such as Germany and Russia overcome initial economic backwardness. In contrast to common, modernist understandings that industrialization is a uniform, linear process that happens similarly in all countries, roughly following the English example, Gerschenkron argues that the involvement of the state can spur industrial growth in relatively unindustrialized, "backward" countries. In fact, the state's role in the economy seemed greatest in the countries that were most "backward" in terms of industrial development. In the case of Germany, the state helped to speed up industrialization through the formation of banks that secured access to capital for industrial expansion. In Russia, state planning of the economy achieved this goal. Though classical economists would recommend laissez-faire markets as the cure-all for economic hardship, "late industrialization" theorists disagree that unobstructed markets bring prosperity. Instead, development laggards should take active steps to protect local industry and to set prices on key goods to support economic development. By using subsidies to distort prices and enacting protectionist policies, developmental states could guide economic development, encouraging local firms to increase production and export levels, ultimately leading to the development of large industries similar to those in industrialized countries.

The late industrialization perspective became quite popular in the analysis of the successful postwar economic development of East Asian states. Rather than adopting free-market, competitive economic policies, these states have, in a variety of ways, been actively involved in their economies. This resulted in spectacular growth, as illustrated in figure 6.3, attributed to the actions of East Asian developmental states, which forged an alliance with domestic capital in order to improve their ability to compete globally. Through policies such as the selective and strategic use of protectionism, the provision of industrial subsidies and programs tied to performance, and the creation of close ties between financial capital, industrial capital, and the state, countries such as Japan, Korea, and Taiwan were able to industrialize rapidly and achieve remarkable economic growth (Johnson 1982; Amsden 1989; Wade 1990; Haggard 1990; Appelbaum and Henderson 1992; Evans 1995; Woo-Cumings 1999).

The type of economic intervention varied among East Asian states. In Taiwan, the state actively intervened in the economy through the ownership of key enterprises, tax incentive programs, labor training programs, infrastructure modernization, economic planning, and the control of inflation (Gold 2000). The Taiwanese state effectively gathered and deployed resources as well as creating an environment that was convincingly seen as conducive to private business. Similarly, in Japan and other East Asian countries, industry-specific regulation has been used as a tool to manage competition, regulate output, and improve the condition of troubled industries (Uriu 1996; Wade 1990). Legislation developed by

Development

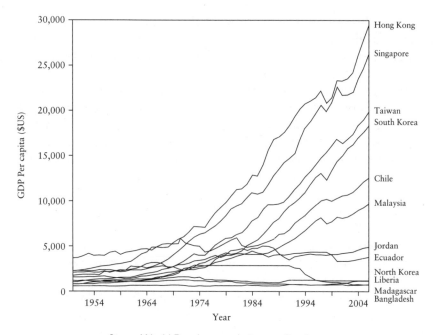

Source: World Development Indicators Database.

Figure 6.3 Economic development of East Asian Tigers in comparative perspective

the Ministry of International Trade and Industry (MITI) in Japan reflected the desires of actors in specific industries to manage competition through the formation of cartels. Japan and South Korea both embarked on a strategy of protecting domestic industries to allow their own "national champions" to grow in strength so that they could one day be formidable global competitors. In Hong Kong and Singapore, investment in human capital, subsidized housing, and other forms of social spending, among many other policies, underwrote business and allowed enterprises to flourish (Clark and Chan 1998). Through a variety of direct and indirect ways, East Asian states managed and directed the growth of their economies through means ranging from state ownership of industry, to managed competition and tax incentives, to investment in society to provide skilled labor to domestic corporations.

It is in the analysis of the role of MITI in the "Japanese miracle" that a political economist, Chalmers Johnson (1982), coined the term "developmental state." He did so to pinpoint the differing normative orientations of states toward private economic activities that result in different kinds of business–government relationships. In Johnson's words, "The United States is a good example of a state in which the regulatory orientation predominates, whereas Japan is a good example of a state in which the developmental orientation predominates." The **regulatory state** creates and sanctions regulatory agencies to govern the economy, in contrast to the more direct economic involvement of the developmental state (Johnson 1982; Moran 2002). Examples in the US include the Securities and Exchange Commission (SEC), which was created in the 1930s and provides supervision and governance to stock exchanges, accounting, bankruptcies, corporate reporting, and other important economic transactions, and the Occupational Health and Safety Administration (OSHA), which creates and enforces workplace safety regulations. Rather than concentrating its efforts on regulatory functions, a developmental state intervenes more directly in the economy through a variety of means to promote economic growth, by direct subsidies to nascent industries and support of high technology initiatives, for instance.

What makes a state a developmental state? Johnson's distinction between different "orientations of states" suggests that there is an *ideational* aspect to the definition. A developmental state is one that openly favors state involvement in the economy and makes state-led development an explicit goal in its economic policy. This is in stark contrast to states that uphold liberal market principles as the "right" way of development and, consequently, institute policies that grant it a minimal role in economic affairs.

There is also a *structural* aspect to the developmental state definition, which is espoused most forcefully by Peter Evans in his landmark book *Embedded Autonomy* (1995). As the title of the book suggests, Evans argues that the crucial feature of developmental states is "**embedded autonomy**," which occurs when an autonomous and capable state establishes collaborative relationships with business actors in society (box 6.1). States are

Box 6.1 Embedded autonomy

What role has the state played in advancing economic growth in newly industrializing countries? This question has preoccupied sociologists and other researchers, notably Peter Evans, who proposed the concept of embedded autonomy as part of the answer.

Since the 1970s, the global nature of economic development has become increasingly salient. Key relationships exist between local contexts of production and the global industrial networks that dominate the world economy. In fact, one of the main strategies for economic growth pursued by the East Asian and other newly industrializing countries was to encourage strong domestic industries that could eventually be major players in the world economy. These countries surprised many observers with the level of economic growth they were able to achieve through these strategies, sparking a lively debate that attempted to determine how this had been possible, especially in contrast to other developing nations that experienced different outcomes.

Evans introduced the term "embedded autonomy" to help explain the economic growth of developmental states in recent decades. At its core, embedded autonomy refers to a particular aspect of the relationship between a state and society. On the one hand, such states are autonomous in the sense that they have well-established bureaucracies and strong governments that can effectively act to determine and enforce policies and regulations. On the other hand, these states are also embedded in society: they are closely tied to society and rely on negotiations and exchanges with social actors to determine the course of policy and national goals. Thus, embedded autonomy is a quality of developmental states that refers to their independence and coherence as actors – *autonomy* – as well as their close ties and consultative exchanges with social groups to determine what policies to follow – *embeddedness*. You might be thinking that these two aspects of developmental states are somewhat at odds.

How can a state be autonomous and yet simultaneously embedded in social relations? Certainly, these do seem to be contrasting characteristics. But it is precisely the existence of these contradictory attributes that makes the developmental state especially effective in promoting economic growth.

Consider the development of the local information technology industry in Korea, Brazil, and India. In these cases, states designed policies to promote experimentation and research and development among local entrepreneurs whom they initially protected from international competition. In doing so, the state created the space in this field for the emergence of strong domestic actors who were eventually successful enough to compete on the global market. The role of the state in this process is twofold. First, it must be a coherent actor that can develop and enforce economic policies, such as those encouraging and protecting particular kinds of innovation. Second, it must be tied closely enough to society to facilitate the development of local industries and manage their connections to global markets. What is unique about developmental states and enables them to encourage economic growth is their capacity to act in ways negotiated with society.

embedded in local capital through the close social ties between state bureaucrats and domestic business owners and managers. However, states retain their *autonomy* because of the presence of a classic Weberian bureaucracy, based on meritocratic recruitment and promotion and norms of objective procedural rationality. In contrast, a **predatory state** ruthlessly extracts from society and provides nothing of value in return. Here, the preoccupation of the ruling class is rent-seeking, using the state apparatus to amass personal fortunes. In Zaire under Mobutu, for instance, the state apparatus was run by those who were personally tied to the president and whose principal concern was to increase their own wealth and privilege. Not only did the state frequently lash out with repressive violence against its people, but everything also came with a monetary price, meaning that citizens had frequently to make direct, personal payments to state officials in order to get things done, even things that we might consider common-place functions of bureaucracy, such as the filing of paperwork and other legal matters. In quite a contrast to developmental states, predatory states are characterized by low rational bureau-cratization, the prevalence of patrimonialism, and the absence of embeddedness in civil society.

Recent work by Vivek Chibber (2006) on the case of India also points to the *political* character of developmental state projects. Chibber argues that their success will depend largely on support from domestic capitalist interests, such as industrial actors. In spite of India's postcolonial attempt to launch state-led develop-ment, industrialists and other domestic agents rose up against this proposed project. This case stands in clear contrast to that of the East Asian countries, where coalitions between the developmental state and domestic capital were key to the success of development policies.

As with all other development theories, the "late industrializa-tion" and developmental state perspective has not been immune to criticism. Neoclassical economists, for example, have argued that this kind of state intervention in the economy serves only to distort the workings of pure markets and gets in the way of sustainable economic growth (Balassa et al. 1986). Rather than endorsing the protection of local industries and the use of subsidies to spur economic growth, economists have extolled the virtues of priva-tization, liberalization, and deregulation as a few among many neoliberal policies that underlie economic growth. The "late industrialization" perspective has also been criticized for its asso-ciation with the newly emerging economies in East Asia (Loriaux 1999). We cannot know, this critique goes, how the developmen-tal process would have occurred without the developmental state, and therefore we simply do not know if it is as crucial as this per-spective contends.

Nevertheless, the notion of a developmental state seems attrac-tive to scholars who have applied this label to different country experiences when trying to explain significant economic growth or lack thereof. One such debate concerns China. Since the 1970s,

Chinese industrial policy has focused on implementing significant tariffs as well as non-tariff barriers such as prices for technology transfers, preferential loans, state selection of partners for international joint ventures, and government procurement policies. These policies resulted in the relative success of Chinese industries, increased productivity, and the introduction of new technologies. Is China then a developmental state? According to Margaret Pearson (2005), the answer is not really. Though the Chinese state acts in some ways that are consistent with the developmental state model, such as trying to develop national champions and attempting to limit competition in some industries, it also functions partly as a regulatory state that is involved less directly in developmental aims than in producing the regulatory framework for industries. China's complicated institutional and normative patterns of the economy–state relationship, in Pearson's analysis, provide evidence supporting images of both the developmental and the regulatory state.

Ideas and Economic Development

In light of different approaches to economic development, one wonders how it is that states decide, for instance, to support infant industries, provide subsidies to innovative firms, or leave companies to their own devices. Economists argue that state policy-making is a matter of efficiency concerns. Because universal laws of supply and demand structure social systems, all action evolves toward solutions that maximize utility. Thus, in the case of policy-making, action aims at the maximization of "the common good." Nation-states, according to economists, make choices about economic affairs with the goal of ultimate efficiency – that is, deciding on a course of action that will maximize gains and minimize costs.

Sociologists have argued against this perspective, pointing to the role of political, institutional, and cultural factors in structuring economic policy-making. While it may not be surprising that political struggles and interest groups influence policy outcomes, it may be less obvious that ideas are also crucial. This is because policy-makers hold taken-for-granted world views, or cognitive paradigms, which limit the range of choices they are likely to consider when formulating economic policy. They carry with them conceptions of cause and effect relationships between certain strategies and their outcomes that shape the kinds of policy alternatives they are likely to perceive as plausible and/or useful. These ideas reflect national political cultures and thus vary across nations and over time (Hall 1989, 1993; Dobbin 1994; Block 1996, 1990; Heilbroner and Milberg 1995; Berman 1998; McNamara 1998; Hay 2001).

Ideas consolidated in policies also have path-dependent effects for future economic action (Steinmo, Thelen, and Longstreth 1992; Thelen 1999). This means that, once institutionalized, they constrain the range of alternatives from which actors choose, locking actors into certain courses of action which may be difficult to reverse (North 1990). This argument builds on a famous article by Paul David (1985) entitled "Clio and the Economics of QWERTY," where David tries to explain the standardization of a peculiar organization of letters on a keyboard even when more efficient alternatives were available.

Much scholarship provides empirical evidence for the role of ideas in economic development. For instance, in *The Great Transformation* (1944), Polanyi not only emphasized the concrete actions of the British state to help commodify land and labor, such as passing enclosure acts and new poor laws, but also wrote about the important role of the "liberal creed" in institutionalizing free markets in nineteenth-century England. Over time, ideas of economic liberalism, free trade, and unregulated production became entrenched in the "liberal creed," which Polanyi states was the relevant organizing principle. He writes that the liberal creed attained such power that it "evolved into a veritable faith in man's secular salvation through a self-regulating market" (1944: 135). Such convictions were behind support for anti-regulatory laws passed by the British state in the 1830s and 1840s and the repealing of harmful restrictions and other actions that allowed for free production, competition, and trade. Ultimately, so argues Polanyi,

Development

the emergence of the free-market system in England was a social project undertaken by adherents of the liberal creed.

Discussing more recent efforts of deregulation and privatization, Kogut and Macpherson (2007) make a case that the process of privatization should be understood as an economic policy idea that diffused across national borders as part and parcel of the world society culture. The rapid and widespread adoption of privatization has a lot to do with the number of US-trained economists in a country of adoption. Though many factors, such as the orientation of the political party in power, the legal traditions of an economy, and concerns over international institutions, have been shown to influence the amount of privatization that a state will undertake, there remains a larger question about why privatization policy "boomed" between the 1980s and the 1990s. Factors listed previously perhaps explain why certain countries chose to privatize at certain times, but such variables cannot explain the sudden and widespread emergence of privatization policies around the world in recent decades. Rather, it seems likely that a pre-existing community was present to manage the articulation of the policy as well as the practical knowledge of how to implement it. This pre-existing community was comprised of US-trained economists, particularly from the University of Chicago, who were essential to the articulation of privatization as a global economic policy that has become entrenched in world society.

Indeed, what is the influence of economic knowledge on economic policy-making? Sarah Babb's (2001) investigation of the economic development in Mexico highlights how economic knowledge led that country from nationalist to neoliberal development policies. According to Babb, one important factor for understanding the policy-making process is national social science expertise, including the stock of economic knowledge residing within economics as a discipline. As economies have become more globally linked, the corresponding globalization of economic expertise has contributed to the growing presence in Mexico of a technocracy of economists trained at the leading US universities. For Babb, this group's presence is crucial in explaining the country's economic policy transition to neoliberalism.

Though scholars have long emphasized that economic policy in developing nations is influenced by developed nations, they have focused on the role of international institutions and international advisors. Promoting a more direct kind of influence of the global North over the global South, the globalization of economic expertise serves to create domestic actors who get immersed in economic policies and ideas that originate in the West. Essentially, states no longer need to invite foreign experts to fly in to give them advice; there are plenty of individuals espousing this advice right at home.

Still, we should not be too quick to generalize that the West promotes only one kind of economics. Marion Fourcade's (2009) work on the construction of economic knowledge in three developed countries, the US, France, and the UK, is also insightful about the difference in the kind of economic policies favored by economists in different nations. Conducting a historical comparative analysis, Fourcade finds that, in England, the discipline of economics developed out of a political culture that valued small, cohesive societies that exerted much influence over the genesis of national policy. In France, economics was shaped by the administrative exercise of public power. In the US, it was the dominance of market institutions and the success of economists in influencing society and policy that shaped the particular contours of its economic development. This is in line with Fred Block's (1996) argument that economists, in particular those advocating for the power of free markets, have been quite strong in the US, resulting in a general tendency to portray the state as a negative influence on the economy.

Conclusion

Differences in economic development are some of the most salient distinctions among countries. The fact that some countries remain underdeveloped is also the source of the most pressing contemporary social problems, such as global inequality, dire poverty, and health crises. Trying to understand how countries can advance the standard of living for their people and prosper economically is nothing if not a key question for our times.

We have distinguished between several approaches to development: modernization, dependency, world-systems, neoclassical economics, comparative institutionalism and late industrialization. The modernization perspective sees development as a staged progression accompanied by a change in values from traditional to modern, a process fostered by modernizing elites and large-scale enterprises built on bureaucratic structures. The dependency approach, reacting to how the Third World countries have become dependent on advanced industrial ones, stipulated that an autonomous state bureaucracy capable of import-substitution industrialization would aid development in these countries. Policies were consciously designed to discourage imports and promote local production. The world-systems perspective sees underdevelopment as a consequence of countries' unequal positions of power. In particular foreign capital penetration from the core to peripheral countries is seen as detrimental to their development, especially in the long term. The neoclassical approach takes after classical economics pioneered by Adam Smith and identifies state intervention as an obstacle to development. The solution is less regulation and more in the way of free markets, which is expected to produce efficient enterprises. The comparative institutional approach focuses on matching the national logics of social organization with opportunities in the economy at large, contributing to a variety of capitalist organization. Last but not least, the late industrialization approach provides a crucial role for the developmental state, which is capable of remaining autonomous while acting in negotiated ways with society, encouraging protection of fledging domestic industries and support for high technology initiatives – all in all, promoting economic growth.

We highlighted the ideational, structural, and political dimensions of the developmental state concept. The ideational dimension refers to a state's own orientation toward government's role in economy, making state-led development an explicit goal of its economic policy. The structural dimension refers to the presence of embedded autonomy, whereby states maintain close ties to domestic capital and civil society but nevertheless uphold classic Weberian bureaucratic structures, based on meritocratic careers and procedural rationality. The political dimension emphasizes that ties between state bureaucrats and domestic capital must work to align political interests in common support for the developmental state projects, or else state efforts risk failure. It is crucial to distinguish between the different kinds of state–society relations, however, since some kinds of embedded ties, in particular patrimonial, nepotistic, or crony, lead quickly to corrupt relations and, if such relations are used by heads of state to extract from society for personal gain rather than country development, to predatory states.

Finally, we have also demonstrated the importance of ideas in shaping how it is that states decide to enact particular forms of involvement (or lack of it) in the economy to manage development. Though economists maintain that state policy-making is guided by the overarching principle of maximizing efficiency, sociologists have argued against this perspective, showing that political and cultural factors are important influences on economic policy. The image of politicians on the different sides of the political spectrum fighting to have their interests prevail makes it easy to envision that such struggles determine what ends up instituted in economic policy and law. However, the kind of ideas that policy-makers hold about which problems are more pressing and what are more or less appropriate ways to solve these problems are equally key. After all, it is precisely such ideas that affect the interests that people have and how they pursue them. Let us not forget that economic theories that professional economists learn and policy-makers use are such collections of ideas.

7

International and Global Economy: The State's Role in Managing the Territorial Boundaries of Economic Transactions

You may have heard of Marco Polo, a thirteenth-century trader and explorer from the Venetian Republic who was one of the first Westerners to travel the Silk Road to China (but did not bring back spaghetti, as it is often mistakenly believed). The Silk Road was an extensive network of trade routes connecting Asia with the Mediterranean world, including both North Africa and Europe. Alexander the Great is believed to have opened this route between West and East in around 300 BC. It was used to transport not only silk but also slaves, fine fabrics, perfumes, jewels, spices, and opiates. Silk Road routes provided venues for one of the first cross-territory economic connections. Trade has continued to have immense importance for economies and nation-states in modern times.

Taking a voyage to a much more recent history than that of the Silk Road, this chapter examines the role of states in managing economic exchanges that cross their borders and constitute the contemporary international and global economy that has intensified since World War II – most noticeably between the late 1980s and 2008. For instance, the value of total world exports in 1985 was $US 1.9 trillion. In 2000, this figure was at $6.3 trillion. Likewise, world foreign direct investment flows increased more than twentyfold between 1980 and 2000, and were valued at $1.4 trillion in the latter year (UNCTAD 2002). The spectacular growth in international trade and investment from the late 1980s to 2008 has been attributed to a move away from the protectionist policies of individual states to a neoliberal idea of a global free market. What is the role of nation-states in such conditions? Are nation-states relevant in managing economic affairs in times when many multinational corporations register higher revenues than the GDP of many individual states? These are the questions that motivate this chapter.

International Trade and its Regulation

International trade is the exchange of capital, goods, and services across international borders. It is the activity that assures that you can drink coffee from grains imported from African and Arab countries, among others, and that people all over the world get to watch Hollywood movies. (The entertainment industry is actually the top exporter in the US.) In this section we ask what role modern states have played historically in regulating trade and how global and regional trade governance institutions may be taking their place in the contemporary era.

Trade protectionism

Though trade exchange has been going on for millennia, our primary focus is on the role that nation-states have played in international trade, and because of this we will begin our inquiry in the early modern period, from the sixteenth to the eighteenth century. During this period, European economies followed **mercantilism**, a system that extolled the protection of domestic industry from foreign competition by imposing tariffs and other barriers to imports and encouraging exports. Some scholars believe that mercantilism was simply the best strategy that economic theory of early modernity was able to produce without the sophisticated analytical tools that we have today (Viner 1952). For others, it was less of an overarching economic strategy and more a product of strong state management of monopoly rights in favor of rent-seeking politically influential economic actors. In their examination of England, France, and Spain during this period, Ekelund and Tollison (1997) argue that mercantilism grew stronger and persisted for longer in countries, such as France, with strong, centralized states that could effectively monopolize the economy, and gave way earlier to free trade in Britain, where rising political competition and the state's inability to enforce monopoly regulations prevented its further development.

Indeed, it was in Britain in the late nineteenth century that the support for mercantilism began to diminish first. It was also during this time that Adam Smith published *The Wealth of Nations*, in which he railed against the protectionist mercantilist system, and argued that the principles of free trade, competition, and self-interest would spur economic development. Consistent with these ideas, Britain adopted a relatively unrestricted trade policy during the first half of the nineteenth century, in contrast to the protectionist policies of Germany, Japan, and the United States. (Recall our discussion in chapter 1 of Alexander Hamilton and Georg Friedrich List, who voiced their strong support for imposing tariffs, among other protectionist measures, during this time in the US and Germany, respectively.) In a more recent history, the import-substitution industrialization in Latin American countries discussed in chapter 6 is a form of trade protectionism.

An effort toward trade protectionism in the US was the adoption in the 1930s of the Smoot–Hawley Tariff Act. After World War I, the US tried hard to increase output and income, which were slowed down further with the weakening of labor markets in 1927 and 1928. In this economic context, Senator Reed Smoot of Utah, chairman of the Senate Finance Committee, and Representative Willis Hawley of Oregon proposed the Tariff Act of 1930. Labeled by Richard Cooper, an undersecretary of state for economic affairs during the Carter administration, as "the most disastrous single mistake" in international relations, the Smoot–Hawley Tariff Act was intended to protect American business and farming by raising tariffs on import-sensitive products, in some cases up to 60 percent, which was four times larger than previously (Cooper 1987: 38; Eckes 1995: 101).

Interpretations of the consequences of the Smoot–Hawley Act vary. Some have alleged that it caused foreign retaliation and ruinous trade wars during a time when there was considerable economic strain and that it was single-handedly responsible for the consequent 40 percent decline in levels of US imports (Cooper 1987; Meltzer 1976), or that "the single most important by-product of this policy initiative [was] the stock market boom and crash of 1928–1929" (Beaudreau 2005: 78). Others have questioned, at least the extent of, the disastrous effects often attributed to the Act. Irwin (1998a, 1998b) provides evidence that it was not exclusively responsible for declining levels of US imports, but rather that it worked together with deflationary economic pressures to reduce US trade substantially in the early 1930s. Eichengreen (1986: 63) observes that "the direct macroeconomic effects of the Smoot–Hawley tariff . . . were small relative to the Great Depression." The peculiar economic context of the Great Depression is likely to blame for the difficulty of empirically evaluating the different interpretations of the consequences of the Act. The impression that has seemed to persist, however, is that it is a powerful political legend invoked in trade policy debates warning against the evils of protectionism while serving to uphold visions of international cooperation and free trade (Eckes 1995). This may be partly on account of efforts after World War II to promote a multilateral trading agreement, which culminated in the signing of the Bretton Woods Agreement in 1944, the creation of the IMF and what is known today as the World Bank, and the establishment in 1947 of the General Agreement on Tariffs and Trade (GATT), devoted to the reduction of global trade tariffs. We turn to the discussion of the multilateral trade governance institutions, such as GATT, next.

Regional and global trade governance institutions

Prevailing attitudes and state policies in the twentieth century have largely moved away from protectionism toward principles of free liberalized trade and multilateralism. This does not mean that corporations freely trade with each other without any institutional regulation. In fact, regional agreements and the international trade governance body, the World Trade Organization, exist as institutional arrangements or governance institutions to support free trade. (This is yet another instance of how free-market behavior actually has to be institutionally supported in order to function, as Karl Polanyi argued.)

Numerous regional agreements are currently in place to govern trade across national borders. These include NAFTA, the North American Free Trade Agreement between Canada, the US, and Mexico, which entered into force on January 1, 1994. The European Union promotes free trade among the current twenty-seven Western and Eastern European member states. Mercosur is a trade agreement among Argentina, Brazil, Paraguay, and Uruguay, founded in 1991, and ASEAN is the Association of Southeast Asian Nations, founded in August 1967. Regional trading blocs promote free trade for member countries and serve as protectionist organizations restricting trade with non-member countries. Therefore, as Gibb and Michalak (1994) remark, economic regionalism is, in a sense, a move back toward the protectionist economic policies.

What characterizes regional trade agreements? Francesco Duina (2005) contends that these institutions are far from uniform, noting that the EU, Mercosur, and NAFTA are all successful regional trade agreements that specify differently the rights of labor, working women, and standardized products. Contrary to popular wisdom, joining these organizations does not mean that individual states lose all their power regarding their national trade policy. The multilateral system embodies a bargaining procedure in which a single small country can still make its voice heard. Each state is in fact a powerful influence on the regional trade agreements to which it belongs: national legal traditions and powerful actors within a state importantly shape regional trade agreements.

Beyond regional trade agreements, the World Trade Organization is the preeminent international governance institution for trade, which grew out of the multilateral General Agreement on Tariffs and Trade (GATT). Spearheaded by the United States and signed in 1947 by most of the world's powers at that time, GATT was established to commit its participants to lowering trade barriers and was renamed the World Trade Organization in 1995. In 2009, the WTO had 153 member countries, representing 97 percent of world trade (WTO 2010). The principal difference between GATT and the WTO is that the latter is a single undertaking, and any member country is bound by all its principles. This is in contrast to GATT, which allowed signatory countries to pick and choose which stipulations they would accept (Hoekman and Mavroidis 2007). The WTO, with its overarching goal of supervising and liberalizing international trade, is founded upon four main elements – non-discrimination, reciprocity, market access, and fair competition – all of which attempt to encourage free trade between nations. As such, some argue that the WTO restricts the ability of national governments to use certain trade-policy instruments that may be in their interest, limiting nation-state power in the global economy. While, in principle, the WTO gives each member state an equal vote, in practice the decisions are made by consensus, allowing an informal oligarchy of rich countries (led by the United States) to shape the agenda (Block and Evans 2005). However, Nitsan Chorev (2005) provides some evidence that the strength of the US within the organization is not so straightforward. She argues that the institutionalization of the WTO has both strengthened and threatened US hegemony. Though the WTO provided both a legitimate international basis and means of enforcement for US-favored liberalized trade rules, it also strengthened dispute resolution provisions, which limit the extent to which the US can autonomously pursue its own interests without consequences.

The WTO provides a forum for negotiations of trade agreements and dispute-resolution processes which, as in GATT, happen in rounds of negotiations, which are highly contentious. For instance, in 1999, the third conference in Seattle, Washington, was met with massive anti-globalization demonstrations requiring police and National Guard crowd-control efforts. In November 2001, the WTO launched the Doha Development Agenda, named after Doha, Qatar, in which the fourth ministerial conference that spearheaded this round of negotiations took place. The Doha agenda was very ambitious in its goals to respond to the growing disparities between the global North and South and to make globalization more inclusive, in particular by strengthening assistance to developing countries. The Doha negotiations have been largely unsuccessful, with disagreements over several issues and a North–South divide on the topic of developed countries' agricultural subsidies. As of 2010, no agreement has been reached.

In the shadow of the WTO, a different kind of global trade governance organization has become increasingly prominent – the alternative trading organization (ATO). ATOs are non-governmental organizations aligned with the Fair Trade social movement that aim to promote sustainability and alleviate poverty in developing countries by helping producers in these regions to gain access to markets in developed countries. Part of the ATO network consists of organizations that provide product and organization certifications to indicate that goods are produced under favorable labor, economic, and environmental conditions (Murray, Reynolds, and Taylor 2003). Between 2000 and 2007 the retail value of Fair Trade certified goods increased more than ten times, to $2.38 billion. The rise of ATOs can be seen as a response to the promotion of the neoliberal free-market model. As with Polanyi's concept of a "double movement" (see box 2.1, p. 34–5), except on a global scale, increasing market deregulation and liberalization are met with calls from groups in society to create programs that focus on reducing global economic inequality and encouraging environmental sustainability.

The State's Role in Foreign Direct Investment

Globalization – the intensification of cross-national flows of goods, services, people, technology, and capital that creates the compression of time and space – is distinctly marked by the recent unprecedented rise in foreign direct investment (FDI), as figure 7.1 clearly shows. Foreign direct investment refers to the efforts of firms in one country (the investor) to establish new companies or acquire existing ones in foreign (host) countries. Usually an investment of 10 percent or more is counted as FDI, while smaller stakes are considered portfolio investment. The companies that engage in FDI are called multinational corporations (MNCs).

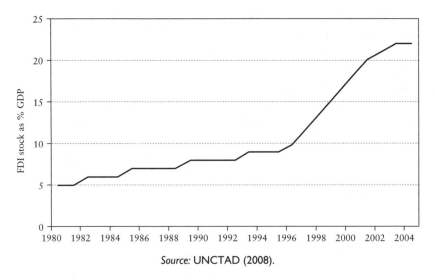

Source: UNCTAD (2008).

Figure 7.1   Rise in world FDI

The rise of multinational corporations and their consequences

Although recent decades saw the biggest surge in FDI ever, foreign investment is not a new phenomenon. American-based firms investing in other developed countries started to make a significant impact on the international economy as early as the 1950s (Gereffi 2005: 164). A couple of initial studies of MNCs examined these trends, highlighting the benefits of American investment for host economies (Dunning 1958; Safarian 1966). Among the earliest attempts to study MNCs extensively was the Multinational Enterprise Project, started in 1965 by Raymond Vernon, an economist at the Harvard Graduate School of Public Administration, who focused on the strategies of MNCs, highlighting the role of the product cycle in determining foreign investment decisions (Vernon 1971). Whether interested in macro-international capital flows or behavior at the firm level, these first studies of MNCs were all grounded in neoclassical economic theory, analyzing corporate strategies as examples of rational profit maximization and transnational investment as beneficial to global welfare

(Kindleberger 1970; Stopford and Wells 1972; Knickerbocker 1973; Hymer 1976).

New research approaches emerged in the 1970s, primarily among sociologists, who questioned the proclaimed positive spillovers of MNC activities and emphasized the uneven power relations between Western core nations that provided the source of FDI and underdeveloped peripheral countries that were the destinations. Concerned with how worldwide expansion of capitalism leads to dependent development in Third World countries, the dependency school argued that MNCs, as instantiations of the uneven link between developed and underdeveloped countries, create dependencies because they impede the ability of the Third World countries to build domestic industries controlled by locally owned firms (Cardoso and Faletto 1979; Gereffi 1978, 1983; Evans 1979).

With a similar focus on the political economy of FDI, world-systems theorists have argued that foreign investment serves primarily the investors from developed core states and thus retards the development of poor countries on the periphery (Wallerstein 1974a; Chase-Dunn 1975; Bornschier and Chase-Dunn 1985). Listing several negative effects for receiving countries of foreign capital penetration, including the fostering of low-wage, unskilled labor at the expense of building human capital and bureaucratic skills and increasing regional disparities and sectoral inequalities, scholars have also argued that, to attract foreign investment, countries implement policies that lower the bargaining power of labor, eliminate provisions that encourage full employment and wage enhancement (such as job training and local purchasing requirements), and thus remove institutional constraints on rising income inequality (McMichael 1996; De Martino 1998; Ranney 1998; Beer and Boswell 2002).

Nonetheless, arguments about the positive effects of liberalization and foreign investment re-emerged in the 1980s as part of the "Washington Consensus," which we discuss in more detail later (see also box 7.1). Suffice it to say that, for the Washington Consensus advocates, the principles of stabilization, liberalization, privatization, and deregulation are closely related to the neoclassical economic tenet that growth in the stock of capital is the primary driver of economic expansion. (See the discussion of neoclassical theory in chapter 6.) According to this view, for underdeveloped countries lacking domestic capital, the inflow of foreign investment increases the stock of capital and stimulates domestic economic growth (Balasubramanyam, Salisu, and Sapsford 1999). In addition to propelling capital accumulation, investment by MNCs is expected to have positive spillover effects, including job creation, skill upgrading, and the transfer of technological and managerial know-how to domestic firms (Markusen and Venables 1999). We want to note, however, that empirical research does not necessarily find these positive externalities of MNCs (Aitken and Harrison 1999; Singh 2007).

The "race to the bottom"

Foreign investment seems to be an activity between multinational corporations and firms that is established and acquired in different countries. Is there any role that states play in this process? Indeed, many believe that states in today's globalizing world actually play an important role because they are engaged in the "race to the bottom," where competition between nations over investment capital leads to a progressive lowering of regulatory standards (in particular the loosening of environmental protection and the relaxing of labor standards) to facilitate the unhindered profit-making of MNCs. As some argue, to provide workers with health insurance, higher wages, or other protection functions as a "tax" on employment, something that makes business enterprises more expensive. As the cost of labor rises, a global economy makes it possible for employers to consider moving production to lower-wage countries. At this point, workers have either to accept lower standards or face potential job losses to workers in a lower wage country.

Among skeptics, prominent economist Jagdish Bhagwati (2003: 58) has countered that "we have little evidence that governments actually play the race (choosing to attract investment) by offering to cut [labor and environment] standards or that multinational corporations actually are attracted by such concessions and thus are competing in such a race." However, he added that the "race to the bottom occurs in tax concession offered by governments to attract multinationals" (ibid.: 59). In one of the more recent studies, political scientist Nathan Jensen tested how tax policy affects FDI and found little support that governments "must slash spending and taxation in a race for the neoliberal bottom" (2006: 55). Instead, he emphasized that FDI flows to those countries offer political stability and hence lower political risks to investors. John Campbell also reports that convergence on relatively low tax rates has not happened. In fact, between 1965 and 1995, business taxes in the Scandinavian social democracies rose most dramatically, from about 4 to about 10 percent of GDP, while in the more neo-liberal states such as the US and the UK this figure was from about 5 to 6 percent (2003: 241).

Layna Mosley (2003), too, finds mixed empirical evidence to substantiate the "race to the bottom" viewpoint. Though economic globalization has curtailed the autonomy of national governments in some areas, states still have some control over their policies in the face of ever expanding capital markets. Autonomy, however, is differentially distributed among states. While developed countries are able to enforce more extensive regulation and social protection if they so wish, this is not as likely for lesser developed countries.

A different strand of research on the role of states in cross-border investment focuses less on "race to the bottom" policies than on the role of the state in institutionalizing and legitimizing FDI as an appropriate and desirable economic strategy. In her study of Central and Eastern Europe after the fall of communism, Bandelj (2009) finds that what really matters in determining levels of FDI in particular postsocialist countries is not formal state policies (such as those privileged in the "race to the bottom" arguments) but informal norms and practices. For instance, states commit resources to create FDI promotion agencies and engage in prominent deals that set precedents for other domestic and inter-national actors to emulate. Curiously, investors are not the only ones who need to be interested in doing business across borders; hosts have to be willing to accept and perpetuate this behavior as well. Both potential investors and hosts need to be socialized into global market roles, and, according to Bandelj, states play a crucial role in facilitating this socializing process, and therefore help constitute global markets.

The Financialization of the Global Economy

Besides significant increases in trade and foreign direct investment, research demonstrates that the global economy has become increasingly dependent since the 1970s on financial flows and services rather than production, leading to the financialization of the global economy. Admittedly, this is not the first period of financialization that has existed in the history of the world. Indeed, the existence, importance, and expansion of financial capital have been demonstrated to be recurrent characteristics of the global economy from its very beginnings in the late thirteenth and early fourteenth centuries. Since then, Giovanni Arrighi (2002) has traced four "long centuries" in the history of capitalism, each with its own expansion of the financial sector and dominated by a particular leading actor: the Italian city-state of Genoa, the Netherlands, Britain, and, in its current version, the United States.

In each cycle, the expansion of financial exchanges over trade in commodities is a key process in the decline of the old power and the rise of the new one. For instance, British hegemony was initiated by a period of financial expansion that coincided with the decline of the Dutch era, and the rise of the US to global dominance occurred during the same period of financial expansion that signaled the waning of British influence. In this analysis, periods of financial expansion, such as the one the US has been experiencing since the 1970s, are an indicator that a hegemonic power is on the decline and that a new one might be emerging. On account of their impressive economic growth in recent decades, the East Asian countries have been identified by many as a potential site of the world power that could follow the US.

Though the financialization of the global economy is not a new phenomenon, there are some distinctive aspects of its current form that are worth our attention. Scholars have remarked on the investment patterns of the global economy since the 1970s and emphasized the new geography of international transactions. In the 1950s and 1960s, international flows were composed primarily of raw materials, agricultural materials, or other goods coming principally from Africa, Latin America, and the Caribbean. However, international flows today are composed mainly of finance and specialized services that are concentrated in a relatively small cluster of countries. Thus, it can be said that the geography of the global economy is narrowing. Most financial flows and foreign direct investment occur in developed countries. Four countries in particular – the United States, Germany, France, and the United Kingdom – are the major recipients and exporters of capital and together make up over 50 percent of the inflows and outflows of foreign capital in the global system. While financial flows tend to be concentrated in a small range of places, it is important to note that the overall volume and value of transactions has increased. This means that developing countries are also receiving more capital and transactions than before, even if they do not capture the largest shares overall. The geography of financial institutions, such as major banks, illustrates the same patterns of concentration among developed countries (Arrighi 2002; Sassen 2006).

The global nature of financialization poses particular challenges for individual countries as well as the overall world-system. The more that global financial flows dominate a domestic economy, the more such an economy depends on them. This means that crisis or trouble anywhere within the global financial system could have vast consequences on the overall health of domestic economies. Further, financial trouble in one location could have a contagious effect. This is exemplified in the global economic crisis that began in 2008, with the failure of many large financial institutions based in the US that spread to other firms, governments, and stock markets around the world. This crisis caused questions of the appropriate level of state intervention in the economy to re-emerge with new vigor, as policy-makers debated corporate takeovers and massive amounts of economic assistance to troubled industries. It also raised questions about the appropriate levels of regulation, rather than liberalization, of financial flows. This has been a priority among world leaders as they try to resolve the current economic situation. In April of 2009, the Group of 20 (G20) countries met to discuss strategies to handle the economic meltdown and to determine a way forward that would prioritize sustainable economic growth. They put forth plans to strengthen financial regulation at the global level, through increased transparency of financial organizations, limits to executive pay and risk-taking, and more stringent rules for lending agencies. Essentially, the G20 leaders agreed that states' domestic efforts need to be bolstered by regulation and oversight from above the state in order to limit the extent of the current crisis and prevent future turmoil from occurring.

Neoliberalism and the Washington Consensus

So far we have discussed international trade, foreign investment, and international financial capital flows, which are all indicators of increased economic integration across the globe. However, it is important to keep in mind that globalization also has cultural manifestations which shape economic outcomes. Increases in cross-border exchanges of financial capital, goods, and people are accompanied by a diffusion of ideas about appropriate economic strategies. Many scholars have claimed that the last two decades of the twentieth century saw a rise in market deregulation and economic liberalization on a global scale (Campbell and Pedersen 2001). While most economists welcome these developments as evidence that the market has finally been freed to select out the most efficient policies, sociologists prefer to consider these changes as a result of a political project – **neoliberalism** – promoted by international organizations and domestic political forces, such as the Reagan and Thatcher governments, in favor of reducing the role of the state in the economy and unleashing the unrestrained functioning of markets. In fact, neoliberalism has recently been described as "an ideological system that holds the 'market' sacred" (Mudge 2008: 706).

Where did these neoliberal ideas originate? Most explanations trace them back to the oil shocks of the 1970s, a turning point for advanced nations whose postwar industrialization and economic growth had been founded largely on plentiful and free-flowing oil. As Prasad (2005) explains, the oil crisis was a seminal moment that shaped the relationship between the state and the economy in advanced industrial nations, such as the US, Britain, Germany, and France, which were hit hard by the decision of the Organization of Petroleum Exporting Countries (OPEC) to restrict oil output. They suffered rising costs for goods, inflation and economic stagnation. It is important to remember that the time after World War II up until the economic crises of the 1970s was a period of peace and economic prosperity, a time when Keynesian economic policies reigned and states played an active role in planning for economic growth and providing for the well-being of their citizens. Until the 1970s, all major industrialized states had accepted and implemented a version of capitalism that allowed a central role for the state in planning and directing economic growth, along with conscious sanctions to ameliorate the most brutal aspects of capitalist production for the working classes. Though the oil shocks posed common crises, the paths that the US, Germany, Britain, and France took to deal with them diverged. According to Prasad, both the US and Britain took neoliberal policy pathways that dramatically cut the Keynesian policies of higher taxes and government spending levels as well as substantially limiting the role that the state could play in the economy. These measures have been long-lasting and were reflected in the neoliberal policies that the Reagan and the Thatcher governments were keen on implementing. After all, the economic crises of the 1970s combined with an adversarial power structure allowed neoliberal reforms to present an alternative policy platform to voters who were dissatisfied with the ruling regimes and the economic hardship they experienced.

But neoliberal policies spread beyond the US and Britain. As Sarah Babb (2009) contends, this was because the US congressional debates over the funding for multilateral development banks, such as the World Bank and the IMF, have influenced these agencies to adopt US-style reform policies in order to get funding.

According to Babb, Washington exerts a kind of "shareholder" pressure over the institutions that it funds, which causes them to act in ways that please the US. This suggests that Washington politics influenced the spread of neoliberalism both through direct policy prescriptions and through more indirect means of shareholder-type pressures on the international financial institutions. Not surprisingly, then, the codification of the neoliberal agenda explicitly aimed at developing countries came to be known as the "*Washington* Consensus" (Williamson 1990: xiii). This consensus advocated the liberalization of trade and foreign direct investment regimes as well as the privatization of state enterprises as vehicles to prosperity in developing countries. According to Charles Gore (2000: 789), the Washington Consensus involved a shift from state-led to market-led policies but also a shift in the way in which development policies were justified. According to the economist who coined the term, John Williamson, it constituted "the common core of wisdom embraced by all serious economists" (1993: 1334). Political scientist Dani Rodrik concisely summarized the essential tenets of the Washington Consensus as they were communicated to developing countries: "Get your macro balances in order, take the state out of business, give markets free rein" (2006: 973).

The Washington Consensus prescriptions emerged most succinctly in the early 1990s in debates over Latin American economic reforms following the Latin American Debt Crises, but also for sub-Saharan Africa and the countries of Central and Eastern Europe and the former Soviet Union after the collapse of state socialism. These countries have seen state-led development efforts of import-substitution industrialization in Latin America and state socialism in the former Soviet world end in giant foreign debt and economic crises. Thus, it is not surprising that new development policy prescriptions would go against the role of the state in economy. Indeed, the neoliberal agenda emphasized deregulation and cuts to social services, as well as the expansion of private economic action through privatization and the introduction of competitive markets through liberalization policies.

However, the Washington Consensus was controversial from

its inception (see box 7.1). Though some reformers in Latin America and elsewhere undertook consensus-style reforms gladly and believed in their efficacy, others felt forced by powerful international organizations, such as the World Bank and the IMF, to accept these policy prescriptions, which often required them to implement such policies as prerequisites for getting loans and international aid (Williamson 2003). Moreover, the empirical results of Washington Consensus reforms in Latin America have been much less successful than many hoped. Economic growth never achieved the desired heights, and the crises experienced during the transition to privatization and liberalization were much greater and more sustained than imagined. Likewise, in sub-Saharan Africa, economic growth and success were limited, and pro-market reforms hardly seem capable of addressing the growing public health issues that span the region (Rodrik 2006). In Mexico, for instance, after the implemention of IMF-conditioned neoliberal policies in 1995, GDP growth was a negative 6 percent, "its worst since the Great Depression" (Carruthers and Babb 2000: 207).

Despite some early acknowledgments of the inadequacy of neoliberal development policies, it seems that the ideas about the power of the free market spread quickly and widely across the global economy, carried by international organizations such as the IMF and the World Bank (Gore 2000). However, as Fourcade-Gourinchas and Babb (2002) argue, neoliberalism actually didn't take hold in all countries equally strongly. Its adoption, more or less, depended on institutionalized patterns of state–society relations and was somewhat irrespective of the level of economic development. The authors compare and contrast the developments in Chile, Britain, Mexico, and France to illuminate these processes. Though globalization played a key role in the diffusion and legitimacy of neoliberal economic policies around the world, local conditions shaped understandings of the necessity and function of neoliberalism as well as the paths through which ideas could influence the policy-making process. In Britain and Chile, failed economic policies, social conflict, and inflation turned many social actors, including both capital and labor, against the existing state. Those who proposed alternative

Box 7.1 The failure of the Washington Consensus

Critics of the Washington Consensus argued that it was simply a formal cover for an attempt to force the neoliberal ideologies and pro-market policies consistent with American hegemony on developing countries (Rodrik 2006: 974). The lack of clear economic success in countries that utilized Washington Consensus-style policies further strengthens the claims of such critics and illustrates that a single, standard set of economic policies does not work for all countries.

Economist John Williamson, who initially coined the term "Washington Consensus" in 1989 to reflect the agreement on a "standard reform package" for crisis-wrought developing countries among institutions such as the World Bank, the International Monetary Fund, and the US Treasury Department based in Washington, DC, responded to the critics in 2003. He argued that it may not have been the policy instruments themselves that led to the lack of economic success, but rather the pace at which such changes were implemented. He further wrote that the Washington Consensus did not reflect some of his own important recommendations for development, such as the equity of income distribution, which he feels are crucial to sustainable growth (Williamson 2003: 1476). Finally, he responded to those who blame the Washington Consensus for failed economic growth by noting that he intended his policies to be generally applicable to Latin American countries but not necessarily to other regions of the world.

Not particularly appeased by Williamson's reconsiderations, critics have been vocal. Intellectuals such as Noam Chomsky and Naomi Klein argued that Washington Consensus policies lead to further exploitation of the poor countries by the rich ones. Moreover, a host of mid-1990s financial crises – including those in Mexico (1994), Asia (1997), Russia (1998), and Brazil (1999) – posed a shock to the consensus surrounding neoliberal development prescriptions (Florio 2002). Thus, those institutions that initially conceded to these practices, such as the World

Bank, have moved away from advocating a single blueprint and instead call for policy experimentation and diversification (World Bank 2005). Hence a "post-Washington Consensus" is focusing less on all-encompassing economic reform packages and more on case-specific policies tailor-made for each country. Of course, such suggestions are not new. Development scholars have been arguing for country-specific policy development since before the Washington Consensus took off. As discussed in chapter 6, the comparative institutional approach to development revolves centrally around this point.

Dani Rodrik, a Harvard political scientist, wrote in 2006: "While the lessons drawn by proponents and skeptics differ, it is fair to say that nobody really believes in the Washington Consensus anymore. The question now is not whether the Washington Consensus is dead or alive; it is what will replace it." In light both of the rise of socialists in Latin American countries – well-known critics of neoliberalism – and of the economic crises of 2008 that painfully exposed the limits of financial deregulation, Rodrik's words were more than prescient. The message of the G20 after their 2009 London summit was that the Washington Consensus is over. It is time to try something different. Time will tell what that will be.

policies garnered support and eventually gained control over the state, opening up the policy-making process to these alternative ideas. The Thatcher administration and the Pinochet dictatorship are examples of this. In these two countries, the ability (or lack thereof) of the government to mediate distributional conflicts impacted the neoliberal transition. In Mexico and France, however, the process occurred differently, much later and in a less radical way. Economic difficulties as well as deliberate political commitments to international organizations on the part of technocrats were the key factors that led Mexico and France down the path of neoliberal reforms as part of their modernization mission. In spite of the convergence of outcomes around the neoliberal policy agendas, important differences exist in the ways in which this occurred in different countries. Each country's understanding of its own economic challenges as well as the benefits of neoliberal policies are important in explaining the differences in the timing and means of reform.

Researchers have also noted that states can block pressures of neoliberalism for long periods of time. Campbell (2003) reports that the Scandinavian governments, for instance, have maintained high levels of taxation and government spending in the face of global pressures for fiscal austerity and other neoliberal policy items. Similarly, labor unions and leftist politics have also aided the resistance of some states to global pressures. However, as world-systems research warns, not all states are in an equal position of power to resist international pressures. What may be possible for Scandinavia may be less so for the developing countries in Central and Eastern Europe, for instance, where postcommunist elites largely embraced neoliberal reforms (Bockman and Eyal 2002). Still, the question remains as to the successful implementation of reforms, if these are largely externally imposed onto domestic contexts. It is likely that formally adopted free-market policies may be decoupled from practice (Bandelj 2003). On account of all these reasons, it may well be that "[g]lobalization does not consist of an inevitable march to a neoliberal order but is a politically contested process in which different state–market models of interaction come into conflict locally, nationally, and transnationally" (O Riain 2000: 188).

Finally, we should ask whether states that adopt the neoliberal doctrine completely relinquish their power over the economy to the market. The answer is, not really. Greta Krippner describes states as victims of two contradictory imperatives of the "neoliberal dilemma" since the 1970s. On the one hand, worsening economic conditions and stagnating growth make politicians and governments eager to avoid being associated with economic ills – hence, the general roll-back of the state's action in the economy and a shift in "the focus of policy makers . . . from *claiming credit* for the economy to *avoiding the blame*" (2007: 479). On the other hand, these states still have market economies, which require state guidance to function. To negotiate these conflicting trends, states remove themselves from the developmental to a regulatory role. This solution allows states, governments, and policy-makers to maintain some distance from the economy, and thus to avoid being associated with hard times and economic deprivation, while still providing the necessary market guidance and governance. Clearly, the state still manages the economy in the era of neoliberal globalization, but the way in which it does so substantively changes. Still, there are many who doubt that nation-states remain relevant actors in times when most economic exchanges are global. We take up this issue in the final part of this chapter.

Nation-States' Role in the Global Era

As long as economic exchanges were conducted primarily within national boundaries, states could exert control over them. They could easily lower interest rates to stimulate production investment or raise taxes on corporations to finance social spending (Carruthers and Babb 1996). What happens when economic exchanges are global? Lowering interest rates means that investors participating in the global financial market will look for countries offering higher interest rates for their investments. Raising taxes means that corporations will move their production to countries with lower tax rates. Although research shows that these kinds of cause and effect relationships are not as straightforward as they may seem, it is worthwhile considering important arguments about the possible obsolescence of the nation-state in the era of globalization.

Whither the state on the global stage?

One of the key reasons for doubting the importance of nation-states is to claim that global processes seem controlled more by multinational corporations than by national governments, which are losing their regulatory power (Vernon 1971; Kennedy 1993; Cox 1996). Indeed, table 7.1 shows that, among the top economies in 2002, almost fifty were multinational corporations rather

Table 7.1 Power of multinational corporations: 100 largest economies by GDP or sales

1	US	38	**Toyota Motor Corporation**	74	**ConocoPhillips**
2	Japan			75	**Hewlett-Packard**
3	Germany	39	Thailand		
4	UK	40	Portugal	76	Peru
5	France	41	Ireland	77	Algeria
6	China	42	**Mitsubishi Corporation**	78	**Vivendi Universal**
7	Italy			79	**Fiat SpA**
8	Canada	43	**Mitsui & Co. Ltd**	80	**Merck & Co.**
9	Spain	44	Iran	81	**Metro AG**
10	Mexico	45	South Africa	82	**Samsung Electronics**
11	India	46	Israel		
12	South Korea	47	Argentina	83	Bangladesh
13	Brazil	48	**Chevron Texaco Corporation**	84	**Unilever**
14	Netherlands			85	Romania
15	Australia	49	**Total Fina Elf**	86	**Électricité de France**
16	Russian Federation	50	Malaysia		
17	Switzerland	51	Venezuela	87	**ENI Group**
18	Belgium	52	Egypt	88	**RWE Group**
19	**Wal-Mart**	53	Singapore	89	**France Télécom**
20	Sweden	54	**Volkswagen Group**		
21	Austria	55	**IBM**	90	**Suez Group**
22	**ExxonMobil**	56	Colombia	91	Nigeria
23	Norway	57	**Philip Morris Co.**	92	**Proctor & Gamble**
24	Poland	58	Philippines		
25	Saudi Arabia	59	**Siemens AG**	93	**Vodafone Group plc**
26	**General Motors**	60	UAE		
27	Turkey	61	Czech Republic	94	Ukraine
28	**British Petroleum**	62	**Verizon**	95	**AOL Time Warner Inc.**
29	**Royal Dutch/Shell**	63	**Hitachi Ltd**		
30	Denmark	64	Hungary	96	**BMW AG**
31	Indonesia	65	**Honda Motor Co. Ltd**	97	**Motorola Inc.**
32	**Ford Motor Corporation**	66	**Carrefour SA**	98	**Deutsche Post WorldNet**
33	Hong Kong, China	67	Chile	99	**British American Tobacco**
34	**DaimlerChrysler AG**	68	**Sony Corporation**		
35	Greece	69	**Matsuhita Electric**	100	**Johnson & Johnson**
36	**General Electric**	70	**Royal Ahold NV**		
37	Finland	71	Pakistan		
		72	New Zealand		
		73	**Nestlé**		

Source: Brakman et al. (2006).

than nation-states. Wal-Mart, Royal Dutch/Shell, and the Toyota Motor Corporation had sales greater than the GDP of Finland, Greece, Ireland, Israel, or Argentina, not to mention all African countries. In 1971, arguably an early stage in the contemporary form of globalization, Raymond Vernon presciently observed many of the tensions that continue to exist around the increasing presence and power of multinational corporations. Existing in multiple jurisdictions, such companies seem to defy the scope of national economic regulation and are often implicated as key agents in the diminution of state sovereignty (Cox 1996). Moreover, as another strand of research emphasizes, it is global cities, such as London, New York, and Tokyo, that have become the loci of economic power, providing headquarters of sorts to the dispersed productive networks (Sassen 1996).

Those arguing that states have lost their power also emphasize the importance of international agreements over national decisions (Robinson 1995), which we discussed at the beginning of this chapter. Moreover, neoliberalism makes "statelessness . . . [a] dominant global ideology and potential institutional reality" (Evans 1997: 64). If we accept the view that states are becoming more and more irrelevant as globalization progresses, then any attempts to bolster state capacity to act will be rebuffed as useless or a waste of time and resources.

From all of the above reasons, the power in the global economy may be moving from states to markets. Susan Strange argued this when saying that "the impersonal forces of world markets, integrated over the postwar period more by private enterprise in finance, industry and trade than by the cooperative decisions governments, are now more powerful than the states to whom ultimate political authority over society and economy is supposed to belong" (1996: 3). Though states once directed the functioning of markets, the situation has now been reversed: markets are increasingly directing the functioning of states. In this view, the challenges posed by the global economy have compromised the extent to which states are authoritative and capable actors at this historical juncture (Mishra 1999; Huber and Stephens 2001).

States still matter a great deal

In stark contrast to the argument about "statelessness" in the global era, a Stanford group of sociologists led by John Meyer wrote that "globalization certainly poses new problems for states, but it also strengthens the world-cultural principle that nation-states are the primary actors charged with identifying and managing those problems on behalf of their societies" (Meyer et al. 1997: 157). For Meyer and colleagues, the international system has increasingly become made up of states that strive to demonstrate conformity with existing models of statehood, nationality, and sovereignty. These world cultural models of sovereign identity specify appropriate modes of organization, function, and policy governance. Since World War II, global culture has prized the existence of strong yet tamed national states and has valued and prescribed the particular form that nation-states take as well as a host of policy choices in which they engage.

Not only is the "nation-state" as a model of governance globally diffused, states are also maintaining their relevance because global pressures provoke responses from them to engage in regionalization and protectionism. The liberal, international postwar economy has undergone significant transformations in that Bretton Woods-style multilateralism has given way to a variety of regionalist and protectionist policies (Gilpin 1987). Citing the variety of regional trade agreements as examples, Gilpin demonstrates the emergence of regionalism in spite of the rhetoric of liberalized political economy in the age of globalization. Governments have paradoxically responded to economic interdependence by enhancing their control over some economic activities.

Finally, critics of the obsolescence of the nation-state in the global era maintain that we cannot expect that freer international markets will reduce the necessity of regulation at the domestic level. For instance, Steven Vogel, in his book *Freer Markets, More Rules* (1996), shows that the process of increasing the international exposure of national industries such as telecommunications and banking actually involves more elaborate rules that are ultimately enforced by national regulatory institutions.

Telecommunications and financial services are two highly globalized industries; however, even here, globalization has not produced a singular deregulatory response from governments around the world. Studying these industries leads Vogel to offer three observations about globalization. First, it is more about *reregulation* than deregulation. Though the "big bang" in the United Kingdom in 1986 made radical changes to the commission and ownership structures of the Stock Exchange, it also led to the passing of a new, more complicated Financial Services Act. This is an example of how we have seen the emergence of freer markets on the one hand and more regulation on the other. Second, global pressures have not produced a uniform set of policy responses among countries. While the US and the UK embraced the logic of liberalization, France, Germany, and Japan have, in different ways, tried to retain control over industry and to coordinate the reform process. Third, states continue to have important functions in the global era, as they, rather than interest group forces, have been behind the reregulation process, such as in the case of the Thatcher administration, and not capital interest groups, as may have been expected, driving the privatization of the telecommunications industry.

Not whether but how states matter in the global economy

How to make sense of the diverging perspectives on the role of states in the global economy? A poignant way to characterize states in the era of globalization is not as defenseless and passive but rather "adapting, whether out of necessity or desire" (O Riain 2000: 205). The active role that they have played as architects of the global system emphasizes that globalization may not work simply against the state. Though globalization may threaten them in some ways, states have helped shape the content and form of the globalization that currently exists and will likely continue to do so. For instance, Sean O Riain discusses how the post-World War II US legal innovations have reached global prominence in Anglo-American corporate and trade law. Also, the particular rules that are enforced or ignored within the European Union have been shaped

International and Global Economy

by the desires of individual member states. Thus, it is too simplistic
to imagine that states are withering away or being made powerless
by globalization. Still, it is quite likely that state actions have been
substantially transformed. The "local" and the "global" continue
to be connected through the national, but they do so in new and
different ways. Regional supranational political organizations, such
as the European Union, that reflect the social democratic natures of
many member states provide one such example. Accounting for the
increasing role of transnational civil society and global social movements in the future economy–state relationship is another issue, and
one deserving of more scholarly attention. The relevant question
in the study of states and economic globalization is, therefore, not
whether states matter but how they matter.

Still, we should not forget that the hierarchies in power across
individual states have not lessened with global integration. There
is very little mobility in the world-system and structural inequalities persist (Mahutga 2006). Consider table 7.2, which shows
the top ten receiving and sending countries in trade and foreign
investment. While hypothetically these could be forty different
countries, they are in fact only fourteen of what we may consider
the world's most economically powerful nations. On this list,
only three – China, Hong Kong, and Russia – are not Western
core nations. This list makes it hard to believe that the core states
could be losing their power on the global stage. It is quite possible, however, that the power of peripheral states is diminishing.
Hence, questions about how states matter in globalization should
be cognizant of the persistent power inequalities across nations.

Nevertheless, the fact that there is an increasing level of interdependence among different levels of governance – local, national,
regional, and transnational – has potential, as Block and Evans
(2005: 521) hope, for "a virtuous cycle of multilevel institutional
innovation." This means that:

Changes in global governance could open up space for institutional
innovations at the national level that could accelerate the development
in poor countries and encourage new welfare state initiatives in rich
ones. These changes at the national level that deepen democracy and

189

Table 7.2 Distribution of FDI and trade ($US millions)

Rank	Top 10 receivers of FDI	Top 10 senders of FDI	Top 10 importers	Top 10 exporters
1	US (232,839)	US (313,787)	US (2,190,000)	Germany (1,530,000)
2	UK (223,966)	UK (265,791)	Germany (1,202,000)	China (1,465,000)
3	France (157,970)	France (224,650)	China (1,156,000)	US (1,377,000)
4	Canada (108,655)	Germany (167,431)	France (833,000)	Japan (776,800)
5	Netherlands (99,438)	Spain (119,605)	Japan (696,200)	France (761,000)
6	China (83,521)	Italy (90,781)	UK (645,700)	Italy (566,100)
7	Hong Kong (59,899)	Japan (73,549)	Italy (566,800)	Netherlands (537,500)
8	Spain (53,385)	Canada (53,818)	Netherlands (485,300)	Russia (476,000)
9	Russian Fed (52,475)	Hong Kong (53,187)	Spain (444,900)	UK (468,700)
10	Germany (50,925)	Luxembourg (51,649)	Canada (436,700)	Canada (461,800)

Source: Data for 2007 FDI inflows is from UNCTAD's "Inward FDI flows, by host region and economy 1970–2007"; Data for 2007 FDI outflows is from UNCTAD's "Outward FDI flows, by host region and economy 1970–2007"; 2008 Import and Export data taken from the CIA World Factbook Country Comparisons.

economic vitality would in turn expand the local roots of transnational constituencies working toward further institutional renewal at the global level. (Ibid.)

Conclusion

What is the role of states in constraining or facilitating economic exchange across national borders? Although trade has been going on for centuries, in early modern history most economies followed

190

a system that favored the protection of domestic industry by imposing import tariffs. Since the beginning of the twentieth century the
outlook has changed. Free trade is privileged and valued, and
international organizations such as the WTO play an important
role in supporting this development. In addition to international
trade institutions, we also have numerous regional trade agreements, which promote free exchange among the member countries
but restrict it among non-members. There is also a growing trend
in alternative trade governance that aims to address persistent
inequalities between the global North and South and strives for
social justice and environmental sustainability.

We also discussed two other aspects of economic globalization that have seen most spectacular intensity in the recent years:
the rise in foreign direct investment and participation in global
financial markets. In explaining these phenomena, scholars realize
that liberal ideas about governmental deregulation and market
freedom, which were institutionalized in neoliberal "Washington
consensus" policies, have had an important role in driving investment and finance behavior. However, in light of some devastating
economic outcomes in developing countries that followed austere
neoliberal reforms and the global economic crisis of 2008, the
agreement on the benefits of the Washington Consensus has been
lost, and the time is ripe for a different understanding of how to
approach the global economy.

What kind of a role should states play in this? Hasn't globalization undermined the role of the state in economy? We provided
arguments in favor and against this claim. We also tried to consider this question in a longer historical purview. Indeed, since the
establishment of modern nation-states, there have been periods
when these questions take center stage in public and scholarly
debates: What about the state? Is state power withering away? We
find that Paul, Ikenberry, and Hall (2003) answer pointedly when
they write: "As in the past, state capacities continue to evolve,
declining in some areas and rising in others. [Yet] there are no rival
political formations – local, regional, transnational, or global –
that have the full multidimensional capacities of the state."

8

Conclusion

Economic sociologists view the production, distribution, consumption, and exchange of goods and services – the economy – as embedded in social forces: social networks, cultural understandings, and political forces. Focusing on network embeddedness, much economic sociology research strives to uncover how connections between individuals and firms influence a range of their behaviors. Inquiries into inter-firm strategic alliances and interlocking directorates effectively reveal the importance of social networks for the behavior of firms. Likewise, examining how social networks facilitate getting a job (Granovetter 1974) shows how the web of social relations determines individuals' economic lives. Networks have also been considered important for the establishment of new organizations. Literature on entrepreneurship shows that social networks help nascent entrepreneurs start businesses (Aldrich 2005). Moreover, the types of social links between firms and their suppliers or clients, in particular the positioning of firms as the link between two unconnected parties, as Ronald Burt (1992) argued, matters for the size of profits. Brian Uzzi (1996, 1997) advanced our understanding of the relationship between network ties and efficiency. In his work on the New York garment industry, he found that firms employ both "embedded" and "arm's length" ties, and that relying on a mix of both kinds gives a firm the best probability of survival. Thus, Uzzi pointed to "the paradox of embeddedness," suggesting an inverse-U curvilinear relationship between a firm's performance and its reliance on embedded ties, where embeddedness has positive effects on performance up to a certain threshold but over-embeddedness has its downsides.

Economic sociologists have also emphasized that social relations between economic actors cannot be well understood if the meaning that parties attribute to the economic exchange between them is not taken into consideration. Max Weber ([1922] 1978) emphasized that, for an economic exchange between social actors to happen, all parties involved must make sense of the transaction, the economic strategies and goals, the transaction partners, and the media of exchange. The attention to meaning has been central to cultural economic sociology. Scholars have examined issues such as valuation in auctions (Smith 1990), cultural differences in systems of worker remuneration (Biernacki 1995), and the culture of hyper-rationality on Wall Street (Abolafia 1996). They have also been concerned with how people started pricing life to allow for the rise of life insurance (Zelizer 1978), and what meaning prices convey to art collectors and gallery owners on the contemporary art scene (Velthuis 2005).

The third strand of research in economic sociology pays attention to issues of power and how they shape economic life. It is in this broad line of inquiry that much of the work on the role of the state in the economy is situated. The state is the principal political entity. Decision-making about economic laws and policies is undertaken by the government. State agencies oversee compliance with laws and policies. State-mandated enforcement bodies, such as the courts and police, exercise state jurisdiction and punishment if laws are broken.

In chapter 1 we reviewed the classical perspective on economy and state which sees these spheres as two relatively distinct realms of operation, and therefore understands any state action as an intervention into the autonomous economic field. Such a perspective rests on the view of the market as a self-regulating price-setting mechanism emerging, almost magically, from the intersection of demand for and supply of goods and services. Self-regulating free markets are at the core of the classical economic theory that dates back to Adam Smith. We want to underscore that, when we conceive of markets as self-regulating, then it is perfectly reasonable that we prefer to avoid any state involvement, which could do more harm than good by throwing markets out of balance. But is this self-regulating view of markets realistic?

In fact, what markets are and how they operate has been largely assumed by economists (Barber 1977). Sociologists have done more empirical research on markets and have reached a consensus that departs sharply from the self-regulating view. From the sociological standpoint, markets are social structures – repeated patterns of social interaction – that are socially defined and have institutional foundations. This constructivist view of markets makes clear that they are not natural but need to be put in place through social intervention. As Karl Polanyi has shown in the case of nineteenth-century England, the rise of a market society was facilitated by concrete state actions, such as the English Enclosure Acts, which promoted the commercialization of land, and the New Poor Law of 1834, which reduced and stigmatized social protection for dispossessed people, so that they were practically forced to sell their labor to industrialists in the burgeoning cities. However, neither land nor labor is a genuine commodity by its nature. Land is a limited resource that cannot be expanded in response to increased market demand. Attempts to extract more and more labor power from any single worker, well motivated by the profit-making imperative of capitalists, would eventually result in labor annihilation. Therefore, it is imperative that some modicum of state regulation be put in place to protect the complete exhaustion of natural and labor resources. The fact that states are responsible for commodifying land and labor sufficiently to *facilitate* the working of markets, but at the same time need to protect these commodities from complete commodification and thus *constrain* pure market forces, characterizes the embedded nature of economy–state relations. For economic sociologists, the management of the fictitious commodities of land and labor, but also money, represents the central logic of state involvement in the market economy. It elucidates that economy and state are not separate spheres but tightly connected worlds. As Peter Evans (1995: 3) succinctly puts it, "without the state, markets cannot function."

Conclusion

From the economy–state embeddedness perspective, on which we elaborated in the first chapter of this book, states always play some role in economic affairs. However, *what kind* of a role states play, and *to what effect* for different economic outcomes, is far from obvious. What are the different types of state involvement in the economy? How do they vary across time and space?

What combination of conditions produces predatory states that parasitically feed on the economy? What combination promotes economic growth as a result of developmental state actions? What combination helps ameliorate inequality on account of welfare provision? Moreover, what is the role of ideas, politics, and institutions in shaping economic policy-making and thus the course of economic development, domestically and globally?

We hope that the preceding chapters have provided plenty of empirical illustration to address these questions. We approached them by considering the two central economic objects, property and money, two major economic subjects, labor and firms, and two consequential economic processes, development and globalization.

We began with the most basic function of states in defining systems of economic organization, which is the definition of property rights. Since the early 1990s, most of the economies in the world have been capitalist. This was not always the case, as for several decades after World War II almost one-third of the world's population lived under socialism. As expected, the state in a capitalist economy has less direct power over the economy than does the state in a socialist one. Because under socialism property is collectivized, production is controlled, and economic gains are redistributed through universal education, healthcare, full employment, and guaranteed pensions, the state seems omnipresent, hence the name *state* socialism. In capitalism, the state sets the rules through the enforcement of property rights, rules of market exchange, and governance structures. It channels resources by taking a portion from individual economic subjects, citizens and firms, via taxation, to support functions such as education, the military, healthcare, social protection, research and development, and public goods which benefit all the citizens.

Conclusion

Classical sociological writers did not focus on the efficiency of markets as price-setting mechanisms but on the economy as a social system, influenced by social relations, power distribution, and the meanings that people attach to economic actions. Max Weber's ideas about bureaucracy have particular salience in contemporary research about the role of the state in the economy. Aspects of organization, in particular meritocratic recruitment and the provision of predictable and rewarding career ladders, help states advance economic growth, and they are essential for carrying out developmentally oriented policies.

Weber's focus on bureaucracies has continued to occupy a prominent place in contemporary research on the state. For example, scholars focusing on the East Asian developmental states indicate that their ability to promote economic growth depended largely upon their capacity to act coherently when creating and enforcing policies. With this understanding, the key question then becomes one of how states can increase their capacity to function effectively as coherent actors. It is here that we return to Weber's notion of bureaucracies as a key element of the capacity of developmental states to achieve economic growth. The existence of bureaucracies and bureaucratic rationality in the state apparatus is one of the most important parts of state capacity, but it is also imperative that the different parts of this bureaucracy function together cooperatively rather than in a competitive manner. The mission and desires of particular parts of the state bureaucracy could, at times, conflict with overarching developmentalist goals. In such cases, a large, competitively oriented bureaucracy can in fact be a hindrance to economic development. Bureaucracies are essential to carry out developmentally oriented policies, but the power relations between their different branches must be organized in a way that also supports coherent state action (Chibber 2002).

Weber's influence over contemporary understandings of state–economy relations is matched by the ideas of Karl Polanyi, whose analysis of the transformation of the British economy into a free-market one is considered a classic on the social construction of markets. In *The Great Transformation*, Polanyi argued that

Conclusion

laissez-faire markets do not emerge spontaneously but are created and enforced by states. He also used the notion of embeddedness, arguing that "economic activity is embedded and enmeshed in institutions, economic and non-economic." Both the state-led construction of markets and ideas about embeddedness have been used by scholars to understand the dramatic transformations that occurred in Central and Eastern Europe and the former Soviet Union following the collapse of communist rule. This transformation of the centrally planned socialist economies into market-driven ones was really another historic instance of the creation of markets by (postsocialist) states, much as in nineteenth-century England, when, for the first time in history, society became dominated by market exchange as a core principle of economic organization.

When property was privatized and the state no longer guaranteed full employment, workers in the former socialist world were left to the mercy of the market. They had to compete with others and sell their labor. Indeed, as Marx forcefully stated, the main consequence of instituting private property is that society bifurcates into the propertied and the property-less classes – the capitalists who own the means of production and the workers who sell their labor power on the market. Labor becomes a commodity like any other. Should the state do something to mediate this labor commodification process? If so, what kinds of social protection should the state be responsible for? As we discussed in chapter 4, this is a perennial political and economic question. T. H. Marshall claimed that people have a right to social protection (social rights), just as they have a right to vote (political rights). Not everyone agrees. Despite these controversies, it is clear that all states need to guarantee some form of social protection in order to manage the use of the fictitious commodity of labor. Which states are more generous than others depends on their welfare regimes. We have little evidence to claim that larger welfare states either impede or promote economic growth. Research does substantiate, however, that all types of welfare provision generally ameliorate inequalities and deprivation, although not all kinds of social provision are similarly effective.

The money that is spent on social welfare policies comes from state funds. One of the state's central economic functions is its fiscal role: government spending, borrowing, and taxation. For economists, taxation, like any other economic transaction, is mostly a cost–benefit calculation. Fiscal sociology, however, sees taxation policy as a set of codes that reveal a lot about society, such as the balance of power between interest groups, the institutionalized values that a country holds, and its more or less egalitarian orientation. An important explanation also holds that taxation was necessary for state-building: resource extraction from people within a territory could assure centralization of power, just as the development of national currencies played a significant role in the creation of national markets. Only since the nineteenth century have territorial, national currencies been the dominant medium of payment. Such images as the major historical figures or monuments portrayed on dollar or peso bills, for instance, reveal that these pieces of paper do not only represent value but also symbolize nationhood. As we discussed in chapter 3, issuing money, controlling its availability in the economy, and influencing its costs for borrowers are all monetary functions of the state. To be sure, not all agree that states should actually influence the supply of money. Skeptics believe that, left to their own devices, market forces are well able to set the price for money, just as for any other good. Still, almost every single country has a central bank, and they all have monetary policy roles. However, these roles differ over time. While since World War II countries have routinely manipulated interest rates as a way to influence economic investment or saving, since the 1970s these actions have been much fewer and more subtle. This is consistent with a more general trend in economic deregulation that followed the stock market crash in 1973–4 and the oil crises of the mid-1970s.

In the early 1980s, the Thatcher and Reagan governments, in the UK and the US respectively, adopted a laissez-faire stance to the economy (laissez faire in French literally means, "let do"). President Reagan deregulated the economy and implemented substantial tax cuts in 1981. This was a period when global economic connections began to intensify in increased flows of cross-border foreign direct investment and world financial markets took off.

Conclusion

Although trading between countries has been an economic activity going on for millennia, this most recent phase of globalization is distinguished by its intensity. The contemporary "compression of time and space" is also aided by the diffusion of internet and other transportation and communication technologies.

In chapter 7, we argued that the global economy has also been propelled by a particular set of ideas about the most appropriate and desirable strategy of economic development, which had origins in the classical, Smithian, ideals about markets. In their neoliberal reincarnation, these ideas, also called market fundamentalism, have privileged liberalization, deregulation, and privatization as the best means to economic development. Neoliberal policies didn't often work as planned, particularly where the economic development of non-Western nations is concerned.

Strikingly, those countries that have been able to achieve marked economic growth since the late 1970s have relied on an active role in the economy by the state (chapter 6). One such success is China, where the state, run by the Communist Party, keeps a firm hand over the economy, even if markets are an increasingly common form of economic organization. The other cases are the East Asian Tigers: South Korea, Singapore, Hong Kong, and Taiwan. Scholars have called these countries developmental states, in contrast to regulatory states, such as the US, for instance. Peter Evans argued that the key characteristic of developmental states is embedded autonomy. Embeddedness here refers to the close social ties between state bureaucrats, domestic business owners and managers, and other civil society groups. However, this doesn't lead to informality and corruption because the state remains autonomous in a classic Weberian bureaucracy sense. It retains the norms of procedural rationality and maintains meritocratic recruitment and promotion. This is conducive to economic development.

Organizational features of bureaucracy are also characteristic of large corporations. In chapter 5 we considered how states matter for firms, which, like labor, are central economic actors. In fact, states had a major role in facilitating the rise of large bureaucratic corporations. Unlike economistic explanations, which privilege economic efficiency rationales (because economies of scale are greater in larger firms), those of sociologists contend that legal regulation was responsible for the rise of corporations. Particularly consequential was competition law, known in the US as antitrust law, which prohibited the colluding behavior of firms and repressed cartels (also known as "trusts" – hence the name "antitrust").

More generally, in addition to a whole slew of other things, controlling monopolistic tendencies, restricting the formation of business groups, and prohibiting interlocking directorates are some of the corporate governance issues that regulatory states set to accomplish, while other kinds of states may be more permissive of strategic coordination among firms and may also engage in active industrial policies or research and development aimed at fostering economic growth. While protection for and subsidies to industry have been found to work toward developmental goals when states exhibit features of embedded autonomy and Weberian bureaucracy, researchers caution that, as regards R&D and innovation policy, states need to remain flexible in providing enough support to firms but not too much regulation. Because the balancing act of trying simultaneously to enable and constrain the use of natural, human, and monetary resources as market commodities lies at the heart of the state's role in economy, the idea of providing enough support but not over-regulation likely yields productive synergies in economy–state interactions for other substantive issues as well.

Although the focus of this book has been on production and employment, consumption is another important sphere of the economy, and we devoted some attention to it in the second half of chapter 5. Although it is certainly not as drastic as the Florentine ruler Savonarola's decree to burn all the luxuries in order to maintain a prudent lifestyle, the state's role in consumption today is very important. After all, if firms were left to maximize profits no matter what, then many unsafe practices would ultimately impact the welfare of consumers. While we may be aware that what we consume and how reveals much about who we are, we often forget that what is available for consumption and its quality is a result

Conclusion

of governmental regulation on the businesses that provide us with
goods and services, and that what is not available for (legal) consumption is decreed by state regulations and differs significantly
across time and space.

Overall, the state's broad preoccupation with the economy is to
facilitate growth, while at the same time balancing at least some
of the social inequalities that instituting property rights and free
pursuit of profit-making inevitably fosters. The economic recession of 2008 has placed questions about (renewed) economic
growth front and center. We discussed the financialization of the
economy as the cause of this crisis and a shift away from neoliberal economic policy as a consequence of it. What kinds of roles
crisis-stricken states assume and with what consequences will
remain uncertain for years to come. But what we can gather from
history and the current actions of governments worldwide is that
the paths considered will depend not only on economic but also,
we dare say, mostly on political and ideational factors, on the
political struggles of interest groups and what they deem as valuable priorities.

What is the future of the state's role in the economy? Can we
even speak about the importance of states in the era of globalization? In the last pages of chapter 7 we addressed this hotly debated
issue. We reviewed arguments in favor and against, concluding
that, as time goes by, the capacities of the state evolve, declining
in some areas and rising in others. Such is the case also in contemporary globalization. It is true that the global stage is larger than
the local one, and it needs to accommodate more players. States
are not the most important actors on the global stage, as they are,
by default, on the national one. However, as long as they remain
the preeminent political entities with multidimensional capacities,
states will continue to play one of the leading roles. We remain
hopeful that an increasing degree of interdependence among
different levels of governance – local, national, regional, and transnational – will foster institutional innovation, and possibly new
strategies for development of poor countries, new welfare initiatives in the developed ones, and new capacities of transnational
actors to shape global markets (Block and Evans 2005).

The debate about the relevance of states in the global economy also reminds us that, since the establishment of modern nation-states, there are periods when this question rises to prominence in public and scholarly debates, and there are periods when other issues seem more pressing. In reality, the state is not somehow more important or involved when it is in the public eye, and less otherwise. Our focus on the embedded nature of economies should have made that clear. We also hope that the embeddedness perspective on economy–state relations has helped the reader understand that variations across different forms of economic organization, such as socialism and capitalism, result from the different kinds of institutions that states put in place. There are in addition a variety of developmental strategies adopted across countries and over time, with varied consequences. This is because there is no one right mix of economic institutions that have been proven to be most effective, and also because different developmental goals – economic growth, increased employment, a reduction in social inequality, the elimination of poverty – may not be achieved simultaneously. But it is only when we let go of the assumption about the natural-ness of a self-regulating market that magically functions without state involvement that we can identify meaningful possibilities for change and envision potential influences over different kinds of economic outcomes – employment, productivity, social welfare, knowledge – whatever we set as our priority.

Therefore, in lieu of predicting the future of economy–state relations, we use someone else's words. These words are not of a sociologist, but they are very sociological. They are about a particular moment in history, but still quite timeless:

> The question we ask today is not whether our government is too big or too small, but whether it works – whether it helps families find jobs at a decent wage, care they can afford, a retirement that is digni-fied. Where the answer is yes, we intend to move forward. Where the answer is no, programs will end. And those of us who manage the public's dollars will be held to account – to spend wisely, reform bad habits, and do our business in the light of day – because only then can we restore the vital trust between a people and their government . . . Nor is the question before us whether the market is a force for good

or ill. Its power to generate wealth and expand freedom is unmatched, but this crisis has reminded us that, without a watchful eye, the market can spin out of control – the nation cannot prosper long when it favors only the prosperous. The success of our economy has always depended not just on the size of our Gross Domestic Product, but on the reach of our prosperity; on the ability to extend opportunity to every willing heart – not out of charity, but because it is the surest route to our common good. (Barack Obama, presidential inauguration speech, January 20, 2009)

Glossary

Antitrust Legislation regulating competition among firms, involving the prohibition of market dominance, the restriction of cartels, and the limiting of mergers, which had major repercussions for the organization of the American economy, including facilitating the emergence of large corporations.

Bureaucracy As defined by Max Weber, administrative organizations with specific structural features which include a focus on rules, defined roles in the division of labor, records, and meritocratic rewards.

Capitalism An economic system in which the means of production are mostly privately owned and operated for profit, and where the principal economic organization is free-market competition.

Comparative institutional approach A perspective suggesting that development can occur by firms and states using their particular advantages to find a unique place in the world economy.

Competition Free contest between firms and other actors on the market which is often protected by states through antitrust laws.

Corporate governance The set of procedures, policies, and laws affecting the way a corporation is directed, administered, or controlled.

Glossary

Corporations Large firms that, in the sociological view, did not arise as a matter of simple market efficiency but instead were created by specific acts of legislation that favored large firms over small ones.

Corporatist bargaining One way in which labor can resist commodification, corporatist bargaining generally includes tripartite bargaining between the state and centralized representative organizations of labor and capital.

Decommodification The protection of workers from the labor market. Labor is decommodified when welfare state benefits allow individuals to maintain their standard of living even when separated from the labor market as a result of old age, disability, or illness.

Dependency theory A theory which sees development as influenced by more than just the internal development and values of a society, recognizing that complex interrelationships exist between developed and underdeveloped countries that influence the levels of development among states.

Developmental state A term used to explain the spectacular growth in East Asia in the late twentieth century, where states forged an alliance with domestic capital in order to improve their economic performance through policies such as selective protectionism, industrial subsidies and incentives, and the creation of close ties between financial capital, industrial capital, and the state.

Economy The complex of activities involving the production, distribution, exchange, and consumption of goods and services, including paid activities in the formal sector and unpaid, informal, and illegal economic activities.

Economy–state dualism A classical perspective on state–economy relations that sees the state and the economy as two distinct, opposing entities with different logics of orientation – the state is about governance while the economy is about the management of resources. The key question of this perspective is about the degree to which the state should intervene in the economy.

Economy–state embeddedness An alternative perspective on state–economy relations that sees states and economies as intimately connected rather than as two separate entities – states are constitutive of economy, continually shaping and managing economic activity. The key question of this perspective is about the different ways in which states are involved in the economy and their varied consequences.

Embedded autonomy A quality of developmental states that refers to the simultaneous presence of independent and coherent state actors (autonomy) and these actors' close ties and consultative exchanges with society to determine economic policies (embeddedness).

Fictitious commodities Land, labor, and money are not commodities like other things that firms produce for market sale because they are not generated primarily to be sold on the market and their demand has to be regulated to prevent exhaustion to the point of annihilation. On account of both reasons, states need continually to manage these economic objects to make markets sustainable.

Financialization A term describing how the manipulation of money and credit, or investments in financial instruments and lending and borrowing, have became ever more important sources of profit.

Fiscal policy Government actions of borrowing, spending, and taxation in order to ensure economic prosperity. John Maynard Keynes advocated an active fiscal policy to stimulate the economy.

Illegal economy Activities that, though illegal, are part of the economy because they involve the production, distribution, and consumption of illicit goods and services – such as the drug trade.

Glossary

Informal economy Economic activities that happen outside of the purview of the state, such as by street vendors, housecleaners, day laborers, and "off the books" employees. Though often considered as opposed to the formal economy, many informal economic activities play a part or support formal industries and economic activity.

Interlocking directorates The linkages among corporations created by individuals who sit on two or more corporate boards, allowing for information sharing and the diffusion of corporate practices.

Interventionist state In the economy–state dualism perspective, a state which actively intervenes in the economy by imposing rules or regulations on it is seen as an interventionist state engaged in market manipulation.

Invisible hand A key concept of Adam Smith's economic theory that sees the economy as naturally self-regulated by an "invisible hand" that works to the mutual benefit of buyers and sellers. Attempts by the government to regulate economic affairs would prevent a market from reaching equilibrium.

Labor unions One way in which labor can resist the commodification process is through labor unions, or the collective organization of workers in an effort to achieve goals in the workplace, such as improved conditions, expanded benefits, or increased wages.

"Late industrialization" perspective A perspective which sees development as a convergent process and suggests that less developed countries need to utilize developmental state activities to catch up with more industrialized countries.

Market exchange The primary principle of economic organization where buyers and sellers, whether individuals or firms, exchange goods and services on the market.

Glossary

Market fundamentalism Conventional economic wisdom dictating that firms should be left alone to weather market forces without governmental involvement.

Mercantilism A political economic system that promotes exports while protecting domestic industry through tariffs and other barriers to imports.

Modernization theory One of the pioneering attempts to identify how development could be achieved around the world, which saw development as a phenomenon made up of stages for all countries. Modernization theory is typified in W. W. Rostow's *Stages of Economic Growth* (1960).

Monetary policy The process by which the monetary authority of a country controls both how much money circulates in the economy (monetary supply) and how much it costs (interest rates).

Neoclassical approach to economic development A perspective that maintains that development for less developed economies is best achieved via far-reaching implementation of market policies, such as free trade, foreign direct investment, deregulation, fiscal discipline, privatization, and liberalization.

Neo-institutionalism A sociological theory explaining how and why institutional structures and functions have become more similar over time, focusing on normative, mimetic, and coercive isomorphism to explain the similarity of institutional forms.

Neoliberalism Economic policies advocating a reduced role for the state and unrestrained markets, promoted by international organizations and domestic political interests such as the Reagan and Thatcher governments.

Predatory state A state that ruthlessly extracts from society and provides nothing of value in return, where the ruling class uses the state for personal gain. Predatory states are contrasted to states with embedded autonomy.

Private property Private property includes the right to exclusive control over the use of a resource, the right to exclusive access of the services of the resource, and the right to sell, give, or rent any part of the resource. These rights are legally protected social relationships that allow actors to exclude others from the opportunity to use some resource.

Protectionist state A type of interventionist state where intervention in the economy occurs through protectionism, as seen in mercantilist states of the sixteenth to eighteenth centuries. A key device used by such states was tariffs on international trade to encourage national economic development.

Public goods state A type of interventionist state whereby the intervention of states in the economy is justified to provide public goods, commodities, and services that markets cannot produce by themselves, such as defense or basic infrastructure.

Redistribution An alternative form of economic organization to market exchange, characterized by the distribution of goods to a population by a central authority.

Regulatory state A state that creates and sanctions regulatory agencies to govern the economy, in contrast to the more direct economic involvement of the developmental state.

Socialist state A type of interventionist state which can be seen as an extreme example of the social rights and protectionist states. Socialism is the intermediary stage on the way to communism, where the state is necessary to alleviate the inequality and human alienation that stem from capitalism.

Stabilization state An interventionist state that controls economic growth and manages economic downturns to prevent serious crises. Actions by stabilization states range from controlling the monetary supply to more extensive Keynesian types of intervention.

Transaction costs The costs of engaging in market transactions other than money, i.e. the time spent searching or gathering information on what is of value, bargaining to set the terms of exchange, and enforcing the exchange. Institutional economics views firms as useful because they lower market transaction costs.

Welfare state A state that sets limits to market forces and institutionalizes different kinds of guarantees regarding the social rights of its citizens, including the provision of a minimum income, assistance to those who cannot work, and other social services. Most industrialized nations today are considered welfare states.

World-systems perspective A perspective that sees economic development not within the context of any one state, but as the result of the structural position that states occupy in the world-system (i.e. core, periphery, and semi-periphery). Underdevelopment results from a state's peripheral position and incomplete integration in the world capitalist system.

References

Abolafia, Mitchel (1996) *Making Markets: Opportunism and Restraint on Wall Street*. Cambridge, MA: Harvard University Press.

Abolafia, Mitchel (2004) "Framing Moves: Interpretive Politics at the Federal Reserve," *Journal of Public Administration Research and Theory* 14(3): 349–70.

Abolafia, Mitchel (2005) "Interpretive Politics at the Federal Reserve," in Karen Knorr Cetina and Alex Preda (eds), *The Sociology of Financial Markets*. Chicago: University of Chicago Press.

Aguilera, Ruth, and Gregory Jackson (2003) "The Cross-National Diversity of Corporate Governance: Dimensions and Determinants," *Academy of Management Review* 28(3): 447–65.

Aitken, Brian, and Ann Harrison (1999) "Do Domestic Firms Benefit from Direct Foreign Investment? Evidence from Venezuela," *American Economic Review* 89(3): 605–18.

Akard, Patrick J. (1992) "Corporate Mobilization and US Economic Policy in the 1970s," *American Sociological Review* 57: 597–615.

Aldrich, Howard (2005) "Entrepreneurship," pp. 451–77 in Neil J. Smelser and Richard Swedberg (eds), *The Handbook of Economic Sociology*. 2nd edn, Princeton, NJ: Princeton University Press; New York: Russell Sage Foundation.

Amenta, Edwin (1998) *Bold Relief: Institutional Politics and the Origins of Modern American Social Policy*. Princeton, NJ: Princeton University Press.

Amsden, Alice (1979) "Taiwan's Economic History: A Case of Etatisme and a Challenge to Dependency Theory," *Modern China* 5: 341–80.

Amsden, Alice H. (1989) *Asia's Next Giant*. New York: Oxford University Press.

Appelbaum, Richard P., and Jeffrey Henderson (eds) (1992) *States and Development in the Asian Pacific Rim*. Newbury Park, CA: Sage.

Ardant, Gabriel (1975) "Financial Policy and Economic Infrastructure of Modern States and Nations," pp. 164–242 in Charles Tilly (ed.), *The Formation of Nation-States in Western Europe*. Princeton, NJ: Princeton University Press.

References

Aronowitz, Stanley (1981) "A Metatheoretical Critique of Immanuel Wallerstein's *The Modern World-System*," *Theory and Society* 10: 503–20.

Arrighi, Giovanni (2002) *The Long Twentieth Century*. New York: Verso.

Atkinson, Richard, and William Blanpied (2008) "Research Universities: Core of the US Science and Technology System," *Technology in Society* 30: 30–48.

Babb, Sarah (2001) *Managing Mexico: Economists from Nationalism to Neoliberalism*. Princeton, NJ: Princeton University Press.

Babb, Sarah (2009) *Behind the Development Banks: Washington Politics, World Poverty, and the Wealth of Nations*. Chicago: University of Chicago Press.

Backhaus, Jurgen (2002) "Fiscal Sociology: What For?" *American Journal of Economics and Sociology* 61(1): 55–77.

Balassa, Bela, Gerado M. Bueno, Pedo-Pablo Kuczynski, and Mario Henrique Simonsen (1986) *Toward Renewed Economic Growth in Latin America*. Washington, DC: Institute for International Economics.

Balasubramanyam, V. N., M. Salisu, and D. Sapsford (1999) "Foreign Direct Investment and Growth in EP and IS Countries," *Economic Journal* 106: 92–105.

Bandelj, Nina (2003) "Particularizing the Global: Reception of Foreign Direct Investment in Slovenia," *Current Sociology* 51(3–4): 377–94.

Bandelj, Nina (2008) *From Communists to Foreign Capitalists: The Social Foundations of Foreign Direct Investment in Postsocialist Europe*. Princeton, NJ: Princeton University Press.

Bandelj, Nina (2009) "The Global Economy as Instituted Process: The Case of Central and Eastern Europe," *American Sociological Review* 74: 128–49.

Bandelj, Nina, and Matthew C. Mahutga (2010) "How Socio-Economic Change Shapes Income Inequality in Postsocialist Central and Eastern Europe," *Social Forces* 89 (July).

Barber, Bernard (1977) "The Absolutization of the Market: Some Notes on How We Got from There to Here," pp. 15–31 in G. Dworkin, G. Bermant, and P. Brown (eds), *Markets and Morals*. Washington, DC: Hemisphere.

Baron, James N., Frank Dobbin, and P. Deveraux Jennings (1986) "War and Peace: The Evolution of Modern Personnel Administration in US Industry," *American Journal of Sociology* 92: 350–83.

Baturo, Alexander, and Julia Gray (2009) "Flatliners: Ideology and Rational Learning in the Adoption of the Flat Tax," *European Journal of Political Research* 48(1): 130–59.

Bean, Frank D., and Gillian Stevens (2003) *America's Newcomers and the Dynamics of Diversity*. New York: Russell Sage Foundation.

Beaudreau, Bernard C. (2005) *How the Republicans Caused the Stock Market Crash of 1929: GPT's, Failed Transitions, and Commercial Policy*. New York: iUniverse.

Beckert, Jens (2008) *Inherited Wealth*. Princeton, NJ: Princeton University Press.

Beer, Linda, and Terry Boswell (2002) "The Resilience of Dependency Effects

References

in Explaining Income Inequality in the Global Economy: A Cross-National Analysis, 1975–1995," *Journal of World-System Research* 7(1): 30–59.

Bendix, Reinhard (1956) *Work and Authority in Industry: Ideologies of Management in the Course of Industrialization.* Berkeley and Los Angeles: University of California Press.

Bensel, Richard F. (1990) *Yankee Leviathan: The Origins of Central State Authority in America, 1859–1877.* Cambridge and New York: Cambridge University Press.

Benton, Lauren A. (1989) "Industrial Subcontracting and the Informal Sector: The Politics of Restructuring in the Madrid Electronics Industry," pp. 228–44 in Alejandro Portes, Manuel Castells, and Lauren A. Benton (eds), *The Informal Economy: Studies in Advanced and Less Developed Countries.* Baltimore: Johns Hopkins University Press.

Berman, Sheri (1998) *The Social Democratic Moment.* Cambridge, MA: Harvard University Press.

Bernanke, Ben (2004) Remarks by Governor Ben S. Bernanke at the meetings of the Eastern Economic Association, Washington, DC, 20 February. Available at: www.federalreserve.gov/boarddocs/speeches/2004/20040220/default.htm.

Bhagwati, Jagdish N. (2003) *Free Trade Today.* Princeton, NJ: Princeton University Press.

Biernacki, Richard (1995) *The Fabrication of Labor: Germany and Britain, 1640–1941.* Berkeley and Los Angeles: University of California Press.

Biggart, Nicole, and Mauro Guillén (1999) "Developing Difference: Social Organization and the Rise of the Auto Industries of South Korea, Taiwan, Spain, and Argentina," *American Sociological Review* 64(5): 722–47.

Blanchfield, J. Ralph (ed.) (2000) *Food Labelling.* Cambridge: Woodhead.

Block, Fred (1990) *Postindustrial Possibilities: A Critique of Economic Discourse.* Berkeley: University of California Press.

Block, Fred (1994) "The Roles of the State in the Economy," pp. 691–710 in Neil J. Smelser and Richard Swedberg (eds), *The Handbook of Economic Sociology.* Princeton, NJ: Princeton University Press.

Block, Fred (1996) *The Vampire State and Other Myths and Fallacies about the US Economy.* New York: New Press.

Block, Fred (2008) "Swimming against the Current: The Rise of a Hidden Developmental State in the United States," *Politics and Society* 36(2): 169–206.

Block, Fred, and Peter Evans (2005) "State and Economy," pp. 505–26 in Neil J. Smelser and Richard Swedberg (eds), *The Handbook of Economic Sociology.* 2nd edn, Princeton, NJ: Princeton University Press.

Blouet, Brian W., and Olwyn M. Blouet (2009) *Latin America and the Caribbean: A Systematic and Regional Survey.* 6th edn, Hoboken, NJ: Wiley.

Bockman, Johanna, and Gil Eyal (2002) "Eastern Europe as a Laboratory for Economic Knowledge: The Transnational Roots of Neoliberalism," *American Journal of Sociology* 108: 310–52.

References

Bolzendahl, Catherine (2009) "Making the Implicit Explicit: Gender Influences on Social Spending in Twelve Industrialized Democracies, 1980–99," *Social Politics: International Studies in Gender, State & Society* 16(1): 40–81.

Bonacich, Edna, and Richard P. Appelbaum (2000) *Behind the Label: Inequality in the Los Angeles Apparel Industry*. Berkeley and Los Angeles: University of California Press.

Boorstin, Daniel (1974) *The Americans: The Democratic Experience*. New York: Vintage.

Booth Thomas, Cathy (2006) "The Enron Effect," *Time Magazine*, 28 May. Available at: www.time.com/time/magazine/article/0,9171,1198917,00.html?iid= sphere-inline-sidebar.

Bornschier, Volker, and Christopher Chase-Dunn (1985) *Transnational Corporations and Underdevelopment*. New York: Praeger.

Borocz, Josef (1999) "From Comprador State to Auctioneer State: Property Change, Realignment, and Peripheralization in Post-State-Socialist Central and Eastern Europe," pp. 193–209 in David A. Smith, Dorothy J. Solinger, and Steven C. Topik (eds), *States and Sovereignty in the Global Economy*. London and New York: Routledge.

Boycko, Maxim, Andrei Shleifer, and Robert Vishny (1996) "A Theory of Privatisation," *Economic Journal* 106: 309–19.

Bradshaw, York, and Michael Wallace (1996) *Global Inequalities*. Thousand Oaks, CA: Pine Forge Press.

Brady, David (2005) "The Welfare State and Relative Poverty in Rich Western Democracies, 1967–1997," *Social Forces* 83: 1329–64.

Brady, David, Jason Beckfield, and Martin Seeleib-Kaiser (2005) "Economic Globalization and the Welfare State in Affluent Democracies, 1975–2001," *American Sociological Review* 70: 921–48.

Brakman, Steven, Harry Garretsen, Charles Van Marrewijk, and Arjen Van Witteloostuijn (2006) *Nations and Firms in the Global Economy*. Cambridge: Cambridge University Press.

Briggs, Asa (1961) "The Welfare State in Historical Perspective," *Archives Européennes de Sociologie* 2(2): 221–59.

Brooks, Clem, and Jeff Manza (2006) "Social Policy Responsiveness in Developed Democracies," *American Sociological Review* 71: 474–94.

Browning, Edgar K. (2008) *Stealing from Each Other: How the Welfare State Robs Americans of Money and Spirit*. New York: Praeger.

Bruton, Henry J. (1998) "A Reconsideration of Import Substitution," *Journal of Economic Literature* 36: 903–36.

Bumiller, Elizabeth (2002) "Bush Signs Bill Aimed at Fraud in Corporations," *New York Times*, 31 July, section A1.

Burawoy, Michael (1996) "The State and Economic Involution: Russia through a Chinese Lens," *World Development* 24(6): 1105–17.

Bureau of Economic Analysis (2009) "Gross Domestic Product: Fourth Quarter

References

2009 (Second Estimate)." Available at: www.bea.gov/newsreleases/national/gdp/2010/pdf/gdp4q09_2nd.pdf.

Bureau of Engraving and Printing (2009) "FAQs Library: U.S. Currency." Available at: www.bep.treas.gov/faqlibrary.html.

Burt, Ronald (1992) *Structural Holes*. Cambridge, MA: Harvard University Press.

Camp, Roderik (1989) *Entrepreneurs and Politics in Twentieth Century Mexico*. Oxford: Oxford University Press.

Campbell, John (1993) "The State and Fiscal Sociology," *Annual Review of Sociology* 19: 163–85.

Campbell, John L. (2003) "States, Politics, and Globalization: Why Institutions Still Matter," pp. 234–59 in T. V. Paul, G. John Ikenberry, and John A. Hall (eds), *The Nation-State in Question*. Princeton, NJ: Princeton University Press.

Campbell, John L., and Leon Lindberg (1990) "Property Rights and the Organization of Economic Activity by the State," *American Sociological Review* 55: 634–47.

Campbell, John L., and Ove K. Pedersen (eds) (2001) *The Rise of Neoliberalism and Institutional Analysis*. Princeton, NJ: Princeton University Press.

Cardoso, Fernando H. (1977) "The Consumption of Dependency Theory in the United States," *Latin American Research Review* 12: 7–24.

Cardoso, Fernando Henrique, and Enzo Faletto (1979) *Dependency and Development in Latin America*, trans. Marjory Mattingly Urquidi. Berkeley and Los Angeles: University of California Press.

Carruthers, Bruce (2005) "The Sociology of Money and Credit," pp. 355–78 in Neil J. Smelser and Richard Swedberg (eds), *The Handbook of Economic Sociology*. 2nd edn, Princeton, NJ: Princeton University Press.

Carruthers, Bruce, and Sarah Babb (1996) "The Color of Money and the Nature of Value: Greenbacks and Gold in Postbellum America," *American Journal of Sociology* 101(6): 1556–91.

Carruthers, Bruce, and Sarah Babb (2000) *Economy/Society: Markets, Meanings, and Social Structure*. Thousand Oaks, CA: Pine Forge Press.

Chandler, Alfred J. (1977) *The Visible Hand*. Cambridge, MA: Harvard University Press.

Chase-Dunn, Christopher (1975) "The Effects of International Economic Dependence and Inequality: A Cross-National Study," *American Sociological Review* 40: 720–38.

Chase-Dunn, Christopher, and Richard Rubinson (1977) "Toward a Structural Perspective on the World-System," *Politics and Society* 7(4): 453–76.

Chernow, Ron (2004) *Alexander Hamilton*. New York: Penguin.

Chibber, Vivek (2002) "Bureaucratic Rationality and the Developmental State," *American Journal of Sociology*, 107(4): 951–89.

Chibber, Vivek (2006) *Locked in Place: State-Building and Late Industrialization in India*. Princeton, NJ: Princeton University Press.

References

Chomsky, Aviva (2007) *"They Take Our Jobs!" and 20 Other Myths about Immigration*. Boston: Beacon Press.

Chorev, Nitsan (2005) "The Institutional Project of Neo-Liberal Globalism: The Case of the WTO," *Theory and Society* 34(3): 317–55.

Clark, Cal, and Steve Chan (1998) "Market, State, and Society in Asian Development," pp. 25–37 in Steve Chan, Cal Clark, and Danny Lam (eds), *Beyond the Developmental State*. New York: St Martin's Press.

Coase, Ronald H. (1974) "The Lighthouse in Economics," *Journal of Law and Economics* 17(2): 357–76.

Cohen, Benjamin J. (1998) *The Geography of Money*. Ithaca, NY: Cornell University Press.

Coleman, David (2006) "Population Ageing: An Unavoidable Future," in Christopher Pierson and Francis G. Castles (eds), *The Welfare State Reader*. 2nd edn, Cambridge: Polity.

Cooper, Richard N. (1987) "Trade Policy as Foreign Policy," in Robert M. Stern (ed.), *US Trade Policies in a Changing World Economy*. Cambridge, MA: MIT Press.

Cox, Robert W. (1996) "A Perspective on Globalization," pp. 21–30 in James H. Mittelman (ed.), *Globalization: Critical Reflections*. Boulder, CO: Lynne Rienner.

David, Paul (1985) "Clio and Economics of QWERTY," *American Economic Review* 75: 332–7.

De Martino, George (1998) *Foreign Direct Investment*. Washington, DC: Foreign Policy in Focus, 1 May.

DiMaggio, Paul, and Walter Powell (1983) "The Iron Cage Revisited: Institutional Isomorphism and Collective Rationality in Organizational Fields," *American Sociological Review* 48: 147–60.

Dobbin, Frank (1994) *Forging Industrial Policy*. Cambridge: Cambridge University Press.

Dobbin, Frank, and Timothy Dowd (2000) "The Market that Antitrust Built: Public Policy, Private Coercion, and Railroad Acquisition, 1825–1922," *American Sociological Review* 65: 631–57.

Dobbin, Frank, and John Sutton (1998) "The Strength of a Weak State: The Employment Rights Revolution and the Rise of Human Resources Management Divisions," *American Journal of Sociology* 104: 441–76.

Domhoff, William (2006) *Who Rules America? Power and Politics*. New York: McGraw-Hill.

Dore, Ronald (1973) *British Factory – Japanese Factory: The Origins of National Diversity in Industrial Relations*. Berkeley: University of California Press.

Dorsi, Giovanni, Luigi Orsenigo, and Mauro Sylos Labini (2005) "Technology and the Economy," pp. 678–702 in Neil J. Smelser and Richard Swedberg (eds), *The Handbook of Economic Sociology*. 2nd edn, Princeton, NJ: Princeton University Press.

References

Dreier, Peter (2007) "The United States in Comparative Perspective," *Contexts* 6(3): 38–46.

Duina, Francesco (2005) *The Social Construction of Free Trade: The European Union, NAFTA, and Mercosur.* Princeton, NJ: Princeton University Press.

Dunning, John H. (1958) *American Investment in British Manufacturing Industry.* London: Allen & Unwin.

Eckes, Alfred (1995) *Opening America's Market: US Foreign Trade Policy since 1776.* Chapel Hill: University of North Carolina Press.

ECLAC (Economic Commission for Latin America and the Caribbean) (2000) *Social Panorama of Latin America, 1999–2000: Annual Report.* Santiago: ECLAC.

Edelman, Lauren N. (1992) "Legal Ambiguity and Symbolic Structures: Organizational Mediation of Civil Rights Law," *American Journal of Sociology* 97: 1531–76.

Eichengreen, Barry (1986) "The Political Economy of the Smoot–Hawley Tariff," *NBER Working Paper* no. 2001. Available at: www.nber.org/papers/ w2001.pdf.

Ekelund, Robert, and Robert Tollison (1997) *Politicized Economies: Monarchy, Monopoly, and Mercantilism.* College Station: Texas A&M University Press.

Esping-Andersen, Gøsta (1990) *The Three Worlds of Welfare Capitalism.* Princeton, NJ: Princeton University Press.

Evans, Peter (1979) *Dependent Development: The Alliance of Multinational, State and Local Capital in Brazil.* Princeton, NJ: Princeton University Press.

Evans, Peter (1995) *Embedded Autonomy: States and Industrial Transformation.* Princeton, NJ: Princeton University Press.

Evans, Peter (1997) "The Eclipse of the State?" *World Politics* 50: 62–87.

Evans, Peter, and James Rauch (1999) "Bureaucracy and Growth: A Cross-National Analysis of the Effects of 'Weberian' State Structures on Economic Growth," *American Sociological Review* 64: 748–65.

Evans, Peter, Dietrich Rueschemeyer, and Theda Skocpol (1985) *Bringing the State Back In.* New York: Cambridge University Press.

Ezra, Marni, and Melissa Deckman (1996) "Balancing Work and Family Responsibilities: Flextime and Child Care in the Federal Government," *Public Administration Review* 56(2): 174–9.

Fligstein, Neil (1990) *The Transformation of Corporate Control.* Cambridge, MA: Harvard University Press.

Fligstein, Neil (1996) "Markets as Politics: A Political-Cultural Approach to Market Institutions," *American Sociological Review* 61(4): 656–73.

Fligstein, Neil (2001) *The Architecture of Markets: An Economic Sociology of Twenty-First-Century Capitalist Societies.* Princeton, NJ: Princeton University Press.

Florio, Massimo (2002) "Economists, Privatization in Russia, and the Waning

References

of the 'Washington Consensus,'" *Review of International Political Economy* 9(2): 359–400.

Fourcade, Marion (2009) *Economists and Societies: Discipline and Profession in the United States, Britain, and France, 1890s–1990s*. Princeton, NJ: Princeton University Press.

Fourcade-Gourinchas, Marion, and Sarah L. Babb (2002) "The Rebirth of the Liberal Creed: Paths to Neoliberalism in Four Countries," *American Journal of Sociology* 108(3): 533–79.

Frank, André Gunder (1967) *Capitalism and Underdevelopment in Latin America: Historical Studies of Chile and Brazil*. New York: Monthly Review Press

Frank, André Gunder (1969) "The Sociology of Development and the Underdevelopment of Sociology," *Catalyst* 3: 20–73.

Friedman, Milton (1962) *Capitalism and Freedom*. Chicago: University of Chicago Press.

Friedman, Milton, and Anna Jacobson Schwartz (1963) *A Monetary History of the United States, 1867–1960*. Princeton, NJ: Princeton University Press.

Froud, Julie, Sukhdev Johal, Adam Leaver, and Karel Williams (2006) *Financialization and Strategy: Narrative and Numbers*. London: Routledge.

Furtado, Celso (1970) *Obstacles to Development in Latin America*. Garden City, NY: Doubleday.

Gallagher, Mary E. (2005) "China in 2004: Stability Above All," *Asian Survey* 45(1): 21–32.

Gao, Bai (1997) *Economic Ideology and Japanese Industrial Policy: Developmentalism from 1931 to 1965*. New York: Cambridge University Press.

Geertz, Clifford (1963) *Peddlers and Princes: Social Development and Economic Change in Two Indonesian Towns*. Chicago: University of Chicago Press.

Geiger, Roger (1992) "Science, Universities, and National Defense, 1945–1970," *Osiris* 7: 26–48.

Gereffi, Gary (1978) "Drug Firms and Dependency in Mexico: The Case of the Steroid Hormone Industry," *International Organization* 32(1): 237–86.

Gereffi, Gary (1983) *The Pharmaceutical Industry and Dependency in the Third World*. Princeton, NJ: Princeton University Press.

Gereffi, Gary (2005) "The Global Economy: Organization, Governance, and Development," pp. 160–82 in Neil J. Smelser and Richard Swedberg (eds), *The Handbook of Economic Sociology*. 2nd edn, Princeton, NJ: Princeton University Press.

Gerlach, Michael (1992) *Alliance Capitalism: The Social Organization of Japanese Business*. Berkeley: University of California Press.

Gerschenkron, Alexander (1962) *Economic Backwardness in Historical Perspective: A Book of Essays*. Cambridge, MA: Belknap Press.

Gibb, Richard, and Wieslaw Michalak (1994) *Continental Trading Blocs: The Growth of Regionalism in the World Economy*. Chichester: Wiley.

References

Gibson, Charles R. (1971) *Foreign Trade in the Economic Development of Small Nations: The Case of Ecuador.* New York: Praeger.

Gilpin, Robert (1987) *The Political Economy of International Relations.* Princeton, NJ: Princeton University Press.

Gold, Thomas B. (2000) "The Waning of the Kuomintang State on Taiwan," pp. 84–113 in Kjeld Erik Brodsgaard and Susan Young (eds), *State Capacity in East Asia.* Oxford: Oxford University Press.

Goldstone, Jack A. (1991) *Revolution and Rebellion in the Early Modern World.* Berkeley: University of California Press.

Gore, Charles (2000) "The Rise and Fall of the Washington Consensus as a Paradigm for Developing Countries," *World Development* 28(5): 789–804.

Gouldner, Alvin (1980) *The Two Marxisms: Contradictions and Anomalies in the Development of Theory.* New York: Seabury Press.

Govindan, Parayil (2005) "From 'Silicon Island' to 'Biopolis of Asia': Innovation Policy and Shifting Competitive Strategy in Singapore," *California Management Review* 47(2): 50–73.

Granovetter, Mark (1974) *Getting a Job: A Study of Contacts and Careers.* Cambridge, MA: Harvard University Press.

Granovetter, Mark (1985) "Economic Action and Social Structure: The Problem of Embeddedness," *American Journal of Sociology* 91(3): 481–510.

Granovetter, Mark (2005) "Business Groups and Social Organization," pp. 429–50 in Neil J. Smelser and Richard Swedberg (eds), *The Handbook of Economic Sociology.* 2nd edn, Princeton, NJ: Princeton University Press.

Guillén, Mauro (2001) *The Limits of Convergence.* Princeton, NJ: Princeton University Press.

Guthrie, Doug, Richard Arum, Josipa Roksa, and Sarah Damaske (2007) "Giving to Local Schools: Corporate Philanthropy and the Receding Welfare State," *Social Science Research* 974: 1–18.

Hacker, Jacob (2002) *The Divided Welfare State: The Battle over Public and Private Social Benefits in the United States.* New York: Cambridge University Press.

Haggard, Stephan (1990) *Pathways from the Periphery: The Politics of Growth in the Newly Industrializing Countries.* Ithaca, NY: Cornell University Press.

Haggard, Stephan, and Robert R. Kaufman (2008) *Development, Democracy, and Welfare States: Latin America, East Asia, and Eastern Europe.* Princeton, NJ: Princeton University Press.

Hall, John A. (2003) "Nation-States in History," pp. 1–28 in T. V. Paul, G. John Ikenberry, and John Hall (eds), *The Nation-State in Question.* Princeton, NJ: Princeton University Press.

Hall, Peter (1989) *The Political Power of Economic Ideas: Keynesianism across Nations.* Princeton, NJ: Princeton University Press.

Hall, Peter (1993) "Ideas and the Social Sciences," pp. 31–56 in Judith Goldstein and Robert Keohane (eds), *Ideas and Foreign Policy.* Ithaca, NY: Cornell University Press.

References

Hall, Peter (2007) "Evolution of Varieties of Capitalism in Europe," in Bob Hancké, Martin Rhodes, and Mark Thatcher (eds), *Beyond Varieties of Capitalism: Conflict, Contradictions, and Complementarities in the European Economy.* Oxford: Oxford University Press.

Hall, Peter, and David Soskice (2001) *Varieties of Capitalism: The Institutional Foundations of Comparative Advantage.* Oxford: Oxford University Press.

Hansmann, Henry, and Reinier H. Kraakman (2000) "The Essential Role of Organizational Law," *Yale Law Journal* 110: 387–440.

Hay, Colin (2001) "The 'Crisis' of Keynesianism and the Rise of Neoliberalism in Britain," pp. 193–218 in John L. Campbell and Ove K. Pedersen (eds), *The Rise of Neoliberalism and Institutional Analysis.* Princeton, NJ: Princeton University Press.

Heilbroner, Robert L., and William Milberg (1995) *The Crisis of Vision in Modern Economic Thought.* New York: Cambridge University Press.

Helleiner, Eric (1996) *States and the Reemergence of Global Finance: From Bretton Woods to the 1990s.* Ithaca, NY: Cornell University Press.

Helleiner, Eric (2002) *The Making of National Money: Territorial Currencies in Historical Perspective.* Ithaca, NY: Cornell University Press.

Heyns, Barbara (2005) "Emerging Inequalities in Central and Eastern Europe," *Annual Review of Sociology* 31: 163–97.

Hicks, Alexander (1999) *Social Democracy and Welfare Capitalism.* Ithaca, NY: Cornell University Press.

Hicks, Alexander, and Lane Kenworthy (1998) "Cooperation and Political Economic Performance in Affluent Democratic Capitalism," *American Journal of Sociology* 103: 1631–72.

Hirschman, Albert O. (1958) *The Strategy of Economic Development.* New Haven, CT: Yale University Press.

Hirschman, Albert O. (1968) "The Political Economy of Import-Substituting Industrialization in Latin America," *Quarterly Journal of Economics* 82: 2–32.

Hoekman, Bernard M., and Petros C. Mavroidis (2007) *The World Trade Organization: Law, Economics, and Politics.* London and New York: Routledge.

Hogan, Michael J., and Thomas G. Patterson (2004) *Explaining the History of American Foreign Relations.* 2nd edn, Cambridge and New York: Cambridge University Press.

Holt, Michael (2008) *The Sarbanes–Oxley Act: Costs, Benefits, and Business Impacts.* Oxford, and Burlington, MA: CIMA.

Huber, Evelyne, and John D. Stephens (2001) *Development and Crisis of the Welfare State.* Chicago: University of Chicago Press.

Hymer, Stephen H. (1976) *The International Operations of National Firms: A Study of Foreign Direct Investment.* Cambridge, MA: MIT Press.

Ingram, Paul, and Hayagreeva Rao (2004) "Store Wars: The Enactment and

References

Repeal of Anti-Chain Legislation in the United States," *American Journal of Sociology* 110: 446–87.

Irwin, Douglas A. (1998a) "The Smoot–Hawley Tariff: A Quantitative Assessment," *Review of Economics and Statistics* 80(2): 326–34.

Irwin, Douglas A. (1998b) "From Smoot–Hawley to Reciprocal Trade Agreements: Changing the Course of US Trade Policy in the 1930s," pp. 325–52 in Michael D. Bordo, Claudia Goldin, and Eugene N. White (eds), *The Defining Moment: The Great Depression and the American Economy in the Twentieth Century*. Chicago: University of Chicago Press.

Jenkins, Craig, and Zeynep Benderlioglu (2005) "Mass Protest and the Democratic Transitions in Eastern Europe, 1984–1994," mimeo.

Jensen, Nathan (2006) *Nation-States and the Multinational Corporation: A Political Economy of Foreign Direct Investment*. Princeton, NJ: Princeton University Press.

Johnson, Chalmers (1982) *MITI and the Japanese Miracle*. Stanford, CA: Stanford University Press.

Johnson, Juliet (2000) *A Fistful of Rubles*. Ithaca, NY: Cornell University Press.

Keister, Lisa (2000) *Chinese Business Groups: The Structure and Impact of Interfirm Relations during Economic Development*. Oxford: Oxford University Press.

Keister, Lisa A., and Stephanie Moller (2000) "Wealth Inequality in the United States," *Annual Review of Sociology* 26: 63–81.

Kelly, Erin, and Frank Dobbin (1999) "Civil Rights Law at Work: Sex Discrimination and the Rise of Maternity Leave Policies," *American Journal of Sociology* 105: 455–92.

Kennedy, Paul (1993) *Preparing for the Twenty-First Century*. New York: Random House.

Kerr, Clark, Frederick H. Harbison, John T. Dunlop, and Charles A. Myers (1960) *Industrialism and Industrial Man: The Problems of Labor and Management in Economic Growth*. London: Heinemann.

Keynes, John Maynard (1924) "The Theory of Money and the Foreign Exchange," in *A Tract on Monetary Reform*. London: Macmillan.

Keynes, John Maynard (1936) *The General Theory of Employment, Interest and Money*. London: Macmillan.

Keynes, John Maynard (1937) "The General Theory of Employment," *Quarterly Journal of Economics* 51: 209–23.

Kim, Eun Mee (1997) *Big Business, Strong State: Collusion and Conflict in South Korean Development, 1960–1990*. Albany: State University of New York Press.

Kindleberger, Charles P. (1970) *The International Corporation*. Cambridge, MA: MIT Press.

King, Lawrence P., and Aleksandra Sznajder (2006) "The State Led Transition to Liberal Capitalism," *American Journal of Sociology* 112: 751–801.

221

References

Kiser, Edgar, and Audrey Sacks (2009) "Improving Tax Administration in Contemporary African States: Lessons from History," pp. 183–200 in I. W. Martin, A. K. Mehrotra, and M. Prasad (eds), *The New Fiscal Sociology: Taxation in Comparative and Historical Perspective*. New York: Cambridge University Press.

Knickerbocker, Frederick T. (1973) *Oligopolistic Reaction and the Multinational Enterprise*. Cambridge, MA: Harvard University Press.

Kogut, Bruce, and J. Muir Macpherson (2007) "The Decision to Privatize: Economists and the Construction of Ideas and Policies," pp. 104–40 in B. A. Simmons, F. Dobbin, and G. Garrett (eds), *The Global Diffusion of Markets and Democracy*. Cambridge and New York: Cambridge University Press.

Kornai, János (1980) *Economics of Shortage*. Amsterdam: North-Holland.

Kornai, János (1992) *Socialist System: Political Economy of Communism*. Princeton, NJ: Princeton University Press.

Korpi, Walter (1983) *The Democratic Class Struggle*. London: Routledge.

Krippner, Greta (2007) "The Making of US Monetary Policy: Central Bank Transparency and the Neoliberal Dilemma," *Theory and Society* 36: 477–513.

Krippner, Greta (2010) *Capitalizing on Crisis: Political Origins of the Rise of Finance*. Cambridge, MA: Harvard University Press.

Lazerson, Mark (1988) "Small Firm Growth: An Outcome of Markets and Hierarchies," *American Sociological Review* 53: 330–42.

Leader, Shelah G. (1983) "Fiscal Policy and Family Structure," pp. 139–47 in Irene Diamond (ed.), *Families, Politics, and Public Policy*. New York: Longman.

Leonhardt, David (2010) "The Perils of Pay Less, Get More," *New York Times*, 16 March. Available at: www.nytimes.com/2010/03/17/business/economy/17leonhardt.html?hp.

Light, Ivan (2005) "The Ethnic Economy," pp. 650–77 in Neil J. Smelser and Richard Swedberg (eds), *The Handbook of Economic Sociology*. 2nd edn, Princeton, NJ: Princeton University Press.

Lindberg, Leon N., and John L. Campbell (1991) "The State and the Organization of Economic Activity," pp. 356–95 in John. L. Campbell, Joseph R. Hollingsworth and Leon N. Lindberg (eds), *Governance of the American Economy*. New York: Cambridge University Press.

Liptak, Adam (2010) "Justices, 5–4, Reject Corporate Spending Limit," *New York Times*, 21 January. Available at: www.nytimes.com/2010/01/22/us/politics/22scotus.html.

Lomnitz, Larissa (1988) "Informal Exchange Networks in Formal Systems: A Theoretical Model," *American Anthropologist* 90: 42–55.

Loriaux, Michael (1999) "The French Developmental State as Myth and Moral Ambition," pp. 235–76 in Meredith Woo-Cummings (ed.), *The Developmental State*. Ithaca, NY: Cornell University Press.

Lopoo, Leonard M., and Bruce Western (2005) "Incarceration and the Formation

References

and Stability of Marital Unions," *Journal of Marriage and the Family* 67: 721–34.

Luo, Yadong (2007) *Global Dimensions of Corporate Governance*. Oxford: Blackwell.

MacDonald, R. (1994) "Fiddly Jobs, Undeclared Working, and the Something for Nothing Society," *Work, Employment, and Society* 8: 507–30.

Mahutga, Matthew (2006) "The Persistence of Structural Inequality: A Network Analysis of International Trade, 1965–2000," *Social Forces* 84(4): 1863–89.

Mann, Michael (1984) "The Autonomous Power of the State: Its Origins, Mechanisms and Results," *Archives Européennes de Sociologie*, 25(2): 185–213.

Mann, Michael (1988) "State and Society, 1130–1815: An Analysis of English State Finances," pp. 73–123 in Michael Mann (ed.), *States, War, and Capitalism*. Oxford: Blackwell.

Mares, Isabela (2001) "Firms and the Welfare State: When, Why and How does Social Policy Matter to Employers," pp. 184–212 in Peter Hall and David Soskice (eds), *Varieties of Capitalism: The National Foundations of Comparative Institutional Advantage*. Oxford: Oxford University Press.

Markham, Jerry (2002) *A Financial History of the United States*, Vol. 3. Armonk, NY: M. E. Sharpe.

Markowitz, Gerald, and David Rosner (1999) "Corporate Responsibility for Toxins," *Annals of the American Academy of Political and Social Science* 584: 159–74.

Markusen, James R., and Anthony J. Venables (1999) "Foreign Direct Investment as a Catalyst for Industrial Development," *European Economic Review* 43(2): 335–56.

Marshall, T. H. (1950) *Citizenship and Social Class and Other Essays*. Cambridge: Cambridge University Press.

Martin, Isaac W., Ajay K. Mehrotra, and Monica Prasad (2009) "The Thunder of History: The Origins and Development of the New Fiscal Sociology," pp. 1–28 in I. W. Martin, A. K. Mehrotra, and M. Prasad (eds), *The New Fiscal Sociology: Taxation in Comparative and Historical Perspective*. New York: Cambridge University Press.

Marx, Karl, and Friedrich Engels (1978) "The Communist Manifesto," pp. 469–500 in Robert C. Tucker (ed.), *The Marx–Engels Reader*. 2nd edn, New York: Norton.

Masten, Scott E. (1988) "A Legal Basis for the Firm," *Journal of Law, Economics, and Organization* 4: 181–98.

McCaffery, Edward (2009) "Where's the Sex in Fiscal Sociology? Taxation and Gender in Comparative Perspective," pp. 216–36 in I. W. Martin, A. K. Mehrotra, and M. Prasad (eds), *The New Fiscal Sociology: Taxation in Comparative and Historical Perspective*. New York: Cambridge University Press.

References

McConnell, Campbell R., and Stanley L. Brue (2004) *Microeconomics*. New York: McGraw-Hill.

McMichael, Phillip (1996) "Globalization: Myths and Realities," *Rural Sociology* 61(1): 25–55.

McMichael, Phillip (2000) *Development and Social Change: A Global Perspective*. 2nd edn, Thousand Oaks, CA: Pine Forge Press.

McNamara, Kathleen R (1998) *The Currency of Ideas: Monetary Politics in the European Union*. Ithaca, NY: Cornell University Press.

McNeil, Kenneth, John R. Nevin, David M. Trubek, and Richard E. Miller (1979) "Market Discrimination against the Poor and the Impact of Consumer Disclosure Laws: The Used Car Industry," *Law and Society Review* 13(3): 695–720.

Meissner, Doris, Deborah W. Meyers, Demetrios G. Papademetriou, and Michael Fix (2006) *Immigration and America's Future: A New Chapter*. Washington, DC: Migration Policy Institute.

Meltzer, Allan H. (1976) "Monetary and Other Explanations for the Start of the Great Depression," *Journal of Monetary Economics* 2: 455–72.

Meyer, John, John Boli, George M. Thomas, and Francisco Ramirez (1997) "World Society and the Nation-State," *American Journal of Sociology* 103: 144–81.

Mingione, Enzo (1990) "The Case of Greece," pp. 23–58 in P. Barthélemy, F. Miguelez Lobo, E. Mingione, R. Pahl, and A. Wenig (eds), *Underground Economy and Irregular Forms of Employment (travail au noir): Final Synthesis Report*. Luxembourg: Commission of the European Communities.

Mishel, Lawrence, Jared Bernstein, and Heidi Shierholz (2008) *The State of Working America 2008/2009*. Washington, DC: Economic Policy Institute.

Mishra, Ramesh (1999) *Globalization and the Welfare State*. Northampton, MA: Edward Elgar.

Mokyr, Joel (1990) *The Lever of Riches: Technological Creativity and Economic Progress*. Oxford: Oxford University Press.

Moran, Michael (2002) "Understanding the Regulatory State," *British Journal of Political Science* 32(2): 391–413.

Morgan, Kimberly, and Monica Prasad (2009) "The Origins of Tax Systems: A French–American Comparison," *American Journal of Sociology* 114(5): 1350–94.

Mosley, Layna (2003) *Global Capital and National Governments*. Cambridge: Cambridge University Press.

Mudge, Stephanie Lee (2008) "The State of the Art: What is Neoliberalism?" *Socio-Economic Review* 6: 703–31.

Murray, Charles A. (1984) *Losing Ground: American Social Policy, 1950–1980*. New York: Basic Books.

Murray, Douglas L., Laura T. Reynolds, and Peter Leigh Taylor (2003) *One Cup at a Time: Poverty Alleviation and Fair Trade Coffee in Latin America*. Fort Collins: Colorado State University, Fair Trade Research Group.

224

References

Naughton, Barry (1999) "China's Transition in Economic Perspective," pp. 30–44 in Merle Goldman and Roderick MacFarquhar (eds), *The Paradox of China's Post-Mao Reforms*. Cambridge, MA: Harvard University Press.

Neeson, Janet M. (1993) *Commoners: Common Right, Enclosure and Social Change in England, 1700–1820*. Cambridge: Cambridge University Press.

North, Douglass (1990) *Institutions, Institutional Change, and Economic Performance*. New York: Cambridge University Press.

North, Douglass, and Barry Weingast (1989) "Constitutions and Commitment: The Evolution of Institutions Governing Public Choice in Seventeenth-Century England," *Journal of Economic History* 49(4): 803–32.

Offe, Claus (1982) "Some Contradictions of the Modern Welfare State," *Critical Social Policy* 2(2): 7–14.

O Riain, Sean (2000) "States and Markets in an Era of Globalization," *Annual Review of Sociology* 26: 187–213.

O Riain, Sean (2004) *The Politics of High Tech Growth*. Cambridge: Cambridge University Press.

Orloff, Ann S. (1993) *The Politics of Pensions: A Comparative Analysis of Britain, Canada and the United States, 1880s–1940*. Madison: University of Wisconsin Press.

Orru, Marco (1991) "The Institutional Logic of Small-Firm Economies in Italy and Taiwan," *Studies in Comparative International Development* 26(1): 3–28.

Orru, Marco, Gary Hamilton, and Nicole Biggart (1997) *The Economic Organization of East Asian Capitalism*. Thousand Oaks, CA: Sage.

Pager, Devah (2003) "The Mark of a Criminal Record," *American Journal of Sociology* 108(5): 937–75.

Paine, Thomas ([1791] 2006) "The First Welfare State?" in Christopher Pierson and Francis G. Castles (eds), *The Welfare State Reader*. 2nd edn, Cambridge: Polity.

Paul, T. V., G. John Ikenberry, and John Hall (2003) *The Nation-State in Question*. Princeton, NJ: Princeton University Press.

Pearson, Margaret M. (2005) "The Business of Governing Business in China: Institutions and Norms of the Emerging Regulatory State," *World Politics* 57(4): 296–322.

Pennings, Johannes M. (1980) *Interlocking Directorates: Origins and Consequences of Connections among Organizations' Boards of Directors*. San Francisco: Jossey–Bass.

Perrow, Charles (2002) *Organizing America: Wealth, Power, and the Origins of Corporate Capitalism*. Princeton, NJ: Princeton University Press.

Poggi, Giovanni (1978) *The Development of the Modern State: A Sociological Introduction*. Stanford, CA: Stanford University Press.

Polanyi, Karl (1944) *The Great Transformation: The Economic and Social Origins of our Time*. Boston: Beacon Press.

Polanyi, Karl (1957) "The Economy as Instituted Process," pp. 243–70 in

References

K. Polanyi, C. M. Arensberg, and H. W. Pearson (eds), *Trade and Market in the Early Empires: Economies in History and Theory*. New York: Free Press.

Pontusson, Jonas (1992) *The Limits of Social Democracy*. Ithaca, NY: Cornell University Press.

Portes, Alejandro, and William Haller (2005) "The Informal Economy," pp. 403–25 in Neil J. Smelser and Richard Swedberg (eds), *The Handbook of Economic Sociology*. 2nd edn, Princeton, NJ: Princeton University Press.

Portes, Alejandro, and Ruben G. Rumbaut (2006) *Immigrant America: A Portrait*. Berkeley and Los Angeles: University of California Press.

Post, Diahanna L. (2005) "Standards and Regulatory Capitalism: The Diffusion of Food Safety Standards in Developing Countries," *Annals of the American Academy of Political and Social Sciences*, 598: 168–83.

Prasad, Monica (2005) "Why is France so French? Culture, Institutions, and Neoliberalism," *American Journal of Sociology*, 111(2): 357–407.

Prasad, Monica (2009) "Three Theories of the Crisis," *Accounts: ASA Economic Sociology Section Newsletter* 8(2): 1–4.

Prebisch, Raul (1950) *The Economic Development of Latin America and its Principal Problems*. New York: United Nations.

Przeworski, Adam (1991) *Democracy and the Market: Political and Economic Reforms in Eastern Europe and Latin America*. New York: Cambridge University Press.

Ragin, Charles, and Daniel Chirot (1984) "The World System of Immanuel Wallerstein: Sociology and Politics and History," pp. 276–312 in Theda Skocpol (ed.), *Vision and Method in Historical Sociology*. New York: Cambridge University Press.

Ranney, David (1998) *Investment Liberalization Agenda*. Washington, DC: Foreign Policy in Focus. Available at: www.fpif.org/briefs/vol3/v3n21trad.html.

Rao, Hayagreeva (1998) "Caveat Emptor: The Construction of Nonprofit Consumer Watchdog Organizations," *American Journal of Sociology* 103: 912–61.

Revkin, Andrew C. (2009) "Obama's Call to Create, Not Just Consume," *New York Times*, 27 April. Available at: http://dotearth.blogs.nytimes.com/2009/04/27/obamas-call-to-create-not-just-consume/?scp=2&sq=april%2027%20obama%20research%20and%20development&st=cse.

Ricardo, David ([1817] 1996) *Principles of Political Economy and Taxation*. Amherst, NY: Prometheus Books.

Robinson, Ian (1995) "The NAFTA Labour Accord in Canada: Experience, Prospects, and Alternatives," *Connecticut Journal of International Law* 10(2): 475–531.

Rodrik, Dani (2006) "Goodbye Washington Consensus, Hello Washington Confusion? A Review of the World Bank's 'Economic Growth in the 1990s: Learning from a Decade of Reform,'" *Journal of Economic Literature* 44(4): 973–87.

References

Roethlisberger, F. H., and William J. Dickson (1939) *Management and the Worker*. Cambridge, MA: Harvard University Press.

Róna-Tas, Ákos (1997) *The Great Surprise of the Small Transformation: The Demise of Communism and the Rise of the Private Sector in Hungary*. Ann Arbor: University of Michigan Press.

Rostow, Walt (1960) *The Stages of Economic Growth: A Non-Communist Manifesto*. Cambridge: Cambridge University Press.

Roy, Donald (1952) "Quota Restriction and Goldbricking in a Machine Shop," *American Sociological Review* 57(5): 427–42.

Roy, William G. (1997) *Socializing Capital: The Rise of the Large Industrial Corporation in America*. Princeton, NJ: Princeton University Press.

Sachs, Jeffrey (1993) *Poland's Jump to the Market Economy*. Cambridge, MA: MIT Press.

Safarian, A. Edward (1966) *Foreign Ownership of Canadian Industry*. Toronto: University of Toronto Press.

Sassen, Saskia (1996) *Losing Control? Sovereignty in an Age of Globalization*. New York: Columbia University Press.

Sassen, Saskia (2006) *Cities in a World Economy*. 3rd edn, Thousand Oaks, CA: Pine Forge Press.

Schnaiberg, Allan (2005) "The Environment and the Economy," pp. 703–26 in Neil J. Smelser and Richard Swedberg (eds), *The Handbook of Economic Sociology*. 2nd edn, Princeton, NJ: Princeton University Press.

Schumpeter, Joseph A. ([1918] 1991) "The Crisis of the Tax State," pp. 99–140 in R. Swedberg (ed.), *Joseph A. Schumpeter: The Economics and Sociology of Capitalism*. Princeton, NJ: Princeton University Press.

Scruggs, Lyle, and James P. Allan (2006) "The Material Consequences of Welfare States: Benefit Generosity and Absolute Poverty in 16 OECD Countries," *Comparative Political Studies* 39: 880–904.

Singh, Jasjit (2007) "Asymmetry of Knowledge Spillovers between MNCs and Host Country Firms," *Journal of International Business Studies* 38(5): 764–86.

Skocpol, Theda (1977) "Wallerstein's World Capitalist System: A Theoretical and Historical Critique," *American Journal of Sociology* 82(5): 1075–90.

Skocpol, Theda (1979) *States and Social Revolutions*. New York: Cambridge University Press.

Skocpol, Theda (1988) "The Limits of the New Deal System and the Roots of Contemporary Welfare Dilemmas," in Margaret Weir, Ann Shola Orloff, and Theda Skocpol (eds), *The Politics of Social Policy in the United States*. Princeton, NJ: Princeton University Press.

Slevin, Peter (2006) "US Prison Study Faults System and the Public," *Washington Post*, 8 June, p. A04.

Smith, Adam ([1776] 2000) *The Wealth of Nations*, intro. Robert Reich. New York: Modern Library.

References

Smith, Charles W. (1990) *Auctions: The Social Construction of Value*. Berkeley and Los Angeles: University of California Press.

So, Alvin Y. (1990) *Social Change and Development: Modernization, Dependency, and World-Systems Theories*. Newbury Park, CA: Sage.

Solinger, Dorothy J. (1993) *China's Transition from Socialism: Statist Legacies and Market Reforms, 1980–1990*. Armonk, NY: M. E. Sharpe.

Somers, Margaret R., and Fred Block (2005) "From Poverty to Perversity: Ideas, Markets, and Institutions over 200 Years of Welfare Debate," *American Sociological Review* 70(2): 260–87.

Soysal, Yasemin (1994) *Limits of Citizenship: Migrants and Postnational Citizenship in Europe*. Chicago: University of Chicago Press.

Stark, David (1992) "Path Dependence and Privatization Strategies in East Central Europe," *East European Societies and Politics* 6(1): 17–54.

Stark, David, and László Bruszt (1998) *Postsocialist Pathways: Transforming Politics and Property in East Central Europe*. Cambridge: Cambridge University Press.

Steinberg, Ronnie J., and Alice Cook (1988) "Politics Affecting Women's Employment in Industrial Countries," pp. 307–28 in Ann H. Stromberg and Shirley Harkess (eds), *Women Working: Theories and Facts in Perspective*. Mountain View, CA: Mayfield.

Steensland, Brian (2007) *The Failed Welfare Revolution: America's Struggle over Guaranteed Income Policy*. Princeton, NJ: Princeton University Press.

Steinmo, Sven, Kathleen Thelen, and Frank Longstreth (1992) *Structuring Politics: Historical Institutionalism in Comparative Analysis*. New York: Cambridge University Press.

Stopford, John M., and Louis T. Wells (1972) *Managing the Multinational Enterprise*. New York: Basic Books.

Strange, Susan (1996) *The Retreat of the State: The Diffusion of Power in the World Economy*. New York: Cambridge University Press.

Streeck, Wolfgang (1992) *Social Institutions and Economic Performance*. Beverly Hills, CA: Sage.

Stuber, Jennifer, and Karl Kronebusch (2004) "Stigma and Other Determinants of Participation in TANF and Medicaid," *Journal of Policy Analysis and Management* 23(3): 509–30.

Svallfors, Stefan (1997) "Worlds of Welfare and Attitudes to Redistribution: A Comparison of Eight Western Nations," *European Sociological Review* 13(3): 283–304.

Swank, Duane (2002) *Global Capital, Political Institutions, and Policy Change in Developed Welfare States*. New York: Cambridge University Press.

Swedberg, Richard (2003) *The Principles of Economic Sociology*. Princeton, NJ: Princeton University Press.

Swenson, Peter (1997) "Arranged Alliances: Business Interests in the New Deal," *Politics and Society* 25: 66–116.

References

Szelényi, Ivan, and Balazs Szelényi (1994) "Why Socialism Failed?" *Theory and Society* 23: 211–31.

Szelényi, Ivan, Katherine Beckett, and Lawrence P. King (1994) "The Socialist Economic System," pp. 234–51 in Neil J. Smelser and Richard Swedberg (eds), *The Handbook of Economic Sociology*. New York: Russell Sage Foundation.

Thelen, Kathleen (1999) "Historical Institutionalism in Comparative Politics," *Annual Review of Political Science* 2: 369–404.

Tilly, Charles (1978) *From Mobilization to Revolution*. Reading, MA: Addison-Wesley.

Tilly, Charles (1985) "War Making and State Making as Organized Crime," in Peter Evans, Dietrich Rueschemeyer, and Theda Skocpol (eds), *Bringing the State Back In*. Cambridge: Cambridge University Press.

Tolliday, Steven, and Jonathan Zeitlin (eds) (1987) *The Automobile Industry and its Workers: Between Fordism and Flexibility*. Cambridge: Polity.

Trabut, Loic, and Florence Weber (2009) "How to Make Care Work Visible? The Case of Dependence Policies in France," pp. 343–68 in Nina Bandelj (ed.), *Economic Sociology of Work*. Bingley: Emerald Group.

UNCTAD (United Nations Conference on Trade and Development) (2002) *World Investment Report 2002: Transnational Corporations and Export Competitiveness*. New York and Geneva: United Nations.

UNCTAD (United Nations Conference on Trade and Development) (2008) *World Investment Report: Transnational Corporations and the Infrastructure Challenge*. New York and Geneva: United Nations.

UNDP (United Nations Development Programme) (1999) *Human Development Report 1999*. Oxford and New York: Oxford University Press.

United Nations (2009) "United Nations Member States: Growth in United Nations Membership, 1945–Present." Available at: www.un.org/en/members/growth.shtml.

United Nations (2010) "Standard Country or Area Codes for Statistical Use." Available at: http://unstats.un.org/unsd/methods/m49/m49.htm.

Uriu, Robert M. (1996) *Troubled Industries: Confronting Economic Change in Japan*. Ithaca, NY: Cornell University Press.

US Bureau of the Census (1980) *Current Population Surveys*. Washington, DC: Government Printing Office.

US Bureau of the Census (2000a) *Current Population Surveys*. Washington, DC: Government Printing Office.

US Bureau of the Census (2000b) *Statistical Abstract of the United States*. 120th edn, Washington, DC: Government Printing Office.

Uzzi, Brian (1996) "The Sources and Consequences of Embeddedness for the Economic Performance of Organizations: The Network Effect," *American Sociological Review* 61(4): 674–98.

Uzzi, Brian (1997) "Social Structure and Competition in Interfirm Networks: The Paradox of Embeddedness," *Administrative Science Quarterly* 42(1): 35–67.

References

Velthuis, Olav (2005) *Talking Prices: Symbolic Meanings of Prices on the Market for Contemporary Art*. Princeton, NJ: Princeton University Press.

Vernon, Raymond (1971) *Sovereignty at Bay: The Multinational Spread of US Enterprises*. New York: Basic Books.

Viner, Jacob (1952) *International Trade and Economic Development*. Glencoe, IL: Free Press.

Visser, Jelle (2006) "Union Membership Statistics in 24 Countries," *Monthly Labor Review* 129(1): 38–49. Available at: www.bls.gov/opub/mlr/2006/01/art3abs.htm.

Vogel, Steven (1996) *Freer Markets, More Rules*. Ithaca, NY: Cornell University Press.

Wade, Robert (1990) *Governing the Market*. Princeton, NJ: Princeton University Press.

Waldinger, Roger (1985) "Immigration and Industrial Change in the New York City Apparel Industry," pp. 323–49 in George J. Borjas and Marta Tienda (eds), *Hispanics in the US Economy*. New York: Academic Press.

Wallerstein, Immanuel (1974a) *The Modern World System*. New York: Academic Press.

Wallerstein, Immanuel (1974b) "The Rise and Future Demise of the World Capitalist System: Concepts for Comparative Analysis," *Comparative Studies in Society and History* 16: 387–415.

Wallerstein, Immanuel (2004) *World-Systems Analysis: An Introduction*. Durham, NC: Duke University Press.

Wang, Hongying (2001) *Weak State, Strong Networks: The Institutional Dynamics of Foreign Direct Investment in China*. New York: Oxford University Press.

Weber, Max (1958) "Politics as a Vocation," pp. 77–129 in Hans Gerth and C. Wright Mills (eds), *From Max Weber: Essays in Sociology*. New York: Oxford University Press.

Weber, Max ([1922] 1978) *Economy and Society*. Berkeley and Los Angeles: University of California Press.

Western, Bruce (1997) *Between Class and Market: Postwar Unionization in the Capitalist Democracies*. Princeton, NJ: Princeton University Press.

Western, Bruce, and Katherine Beckett (1999) "How Unregulated is the US Labor Market? The Penal System as a Labor Market Institution," *American Journal of Sociology* 104: 1030–60.

Western, Bruce, Meredith Kleykamp, and Jake Rosenfeld (2006) "Did Falling Wages and Employment Increase US Imprisonment?" *Social Forces* 84: 2291–312.

Whitley, Richard (1992) *Business Systems in East Asia: Firms, Markets and Societies*. London: Sage.

Wilberforce, Richard, Alan Campbell, and Neil Elles (1966) *The Law of Restrictive Practices and Monopolies*. 2nd edn, London: Sweet & Maxwell.

References

Wilensky, Harold (1975) *The Welfare State and Equality*. Berkeley: University of California Press.

Wilensky, Harold (2002) *Rich Democracies: Political Economy, Public Policy, and Performance*. Berkeley: University of California Press.

Williamson, John (1990) "What Washington Means by Policy Reform," in J. Williamson (ed.), *Latin American Adjustment: How Much Has Happened*. Washington, DC: Institute for International Economics.

Williamson, John (1993) "Democracy and 'the Washington Consensus,'" *World Development* 21(8): 1329–36.

Williamson, John (2003) "The Washington Consensus and Beyond," *Economic and Political Weekly* 38(15): 1475–81.

Windolf, Paul (2002) *Corporate Networks in Europe and the United States*. Oxford: Oxford University Press.

Woo-Cumings, Meredith (1999) *The Developmental State*. Ithaca, NY: Cornell University Press.

World Bank (2005) *Economic Growth in the 1990s: Learning from a Decade of Reform*. Washington DC: World Bank.

WTO (World Trade Organization) (2010) "WTO in Brief." Available at: www. wto.org/english/res_e/doload_e/inbr_e.pdf.

Yang, Dennis Tao (2008) "China's Agricultural Crisis and Famine of 1959–1961: A Survey and Comparison to Soviet Famines," *Comparative Economic Studies* 50: 1–29.

Zatz, Noah D. (2009) "Prison Labor and the Paradox of Paid Nonmarket Work," pp. 369–98 in Nina Bandelj (ed.), *Economic Sociology of Work*. Bingley: Emerald Group.

Zelizer, Viviana A. (1978) "Human Values and the Market: The Case of Life Insurance and Death in 19th-Century America," *American Journal of Sociology* 84: 591–610.

Zelizer, Viviana (1999) "Official Standardization vs. Social Differentiation in Americans' Use of Money," in Emily Gilbert and Eric Helleiner (eds), *Nation-States and Money: The Past, Present, and Future of National Currencies*. London and New York: Routledge.

Zelizer, Viviana (2005) "Culture and Consumption," pp. 331–54 in Neil J. Smelser and Richard Swedberg (eds), *The Handbook of Economic Sociology*. 2nd edn, Princeton, NJ: Princeton University Press.

Zolberg, Aristide (1981) "Origins of the Modern World System: A Missing Link," *World Politics* 33(2): 253–81.

Index

Index

Index

Index

Index

Index

List, Georg Friedrich 17, 166
lobbying 72, 112, 124, 131–2
Los Alamos National Laboratory
127–8

Maastricht Treaty 10
Mann, Michael 8, 75
market exchange 20–1, 26, 31–3, 40,
54, 131, 195, 197, 207
market fundamentalism 118, 136,
199, 208
market liberalization 44, 47, 49, 55,
147–8, 157, 170, 172, 177–80,
188, 199
markets 135, 142, 206, 208, 209
capitalism and 26, 31–44, 53–4,
111
competition and 121–2
development and 156–63
financial markets 10, 59, 62, 64,
66, 101, 121, 174–5, 191, 198
free markets 13–14, 126, 148,
152, 179, 194, 199
globalization and 170, 186–9, 201
postsocialism and 46–9
social construction of 19–22,
196–7
Marshall, T. H. 15, 87, 131, 197
Marx, Karl 28–31, 40, 42, 44, 53,
137, 146, 197
maternity leave policies 103, 109,
117–19, 135
McCain–Feingold 110
mercantilism 17, 165–6, 208
Mercosur 168
Mexico 10, 50, 71, 92, 98, 108, 138,
168, 180, 182, 185
economic development in 160–1
financial crisis in 180–1
US trained economists in 161
Meyer, John 187
military 127
minimum wage 4

minimum wage legislation 35,
102, 109
MITI (Japanese Ministry of
International Trade and Industry)
18, 153–4
modernization theory 128, 139–41
criticisms of 141
role of the state in 140–1
monetarism 15
monetary policy 15, 60–6, 76, 78–9,
82, 198, 208
as contractionary/expansionary 60
failed 65
money 2, 6, 12, 15, 23–4, 56–83,
85, 143, 150, 197, 198, 208
coins 56
Confederate dollars 58
fiat money 57
as a fictitious commodity 20–1,
34, 56, 83, 194, 206
paper money 57
territorial currencies 58
Morgan, Kimberly 72
mortgage market collapse 11, 81
Mosley, Layna 174
multinational corporations 142, 150,
165, 170, 171–5, 184, 185–6
Multinational Enterprise Project 171
Murray, Charles 84

national debt 5, 6, 23
national economic logic 40
National Institutes of Health 127
National Science Foundation 127
Naughton, Barry 52
neoclassical economic theory 138,
147–9, 150, 157, 162, 171, 173,
208
criticism of 148
role of the state in 147
neo-institutionalism 115, 208
neoliberalism 144, 147, 177–184,
186, 208

Index

Index

neoliberalism and 177–8
recycling of solid waste in 134–5
as a regulatory state 23, 154,
 199–200, 209
taxes and 72, 76
US Bureau of Engraving and
 Printing 59
US Department of Agriculture 130
US Food and Drug Administration
 130
US Mint 59
US Treasury 59, 181
welfare benefits in 89, 90–1, 93,
 94, 100–1
welfare state in 89, 92–3
USSR (Union of Soviet Socialist
 Republics) 9, 41, 51
Uzzi, Brian 192

vacation 3–4, 102, 107
 compulsory vacation policies 102
varieties of capitalism 38–40, 54,
 151
 coordinated market economies
  (CMEs) 38–40
 liberal market economies (LMEs)
  38–40
 market competition and 38
 strategic coordination and 38
Vernon, Raymond 171, 184, 186
Vogel, Steven 112, 187–8
Volcker, Paul 15

Wal-Mart 114, 132, 185–6
Wall Street 193
Wall Street Journal 62
Wallerstein, Immanuel 141, 144–5,
 146, 172
War Manpower Board 116
War Production Board 116
warfare state 88
Washington Consensus 172, 177–84,
 191

controversy and 179–82
failure of 180, 181–2
post-Washington Consensus 182
The Wealth of Nations (Smith) 27,
 166
Weber, Max 8, 28–31, 33, 35, 53,
 137, 193, 196, 204
welfare regimes 89, 91, 197
welfare state 9, 15, 19, 79, 86,
 87–101, 109, 189, 197, 205,
 210
 consequences of 96–7
 culture and 94
 demographic forces and 93–7
 gender and 94–5
 industrialization and 93
 in Latin America, Eastern Europe,
  and East Asia 95–6
 power distribution and 93–4
 role of employers in 99–101
 state capacity, state structure, policy
  legacies, and 93
 welfare state expenditure 91–6
Williamson, John 111, 179–81
women
 labor markets and 95, 102–3, 117,
  168
 maternity leave policies 103, 109,
  117–19, 135
 representation in national
  legislatures 95
work 3, 4, 22, 39, 85–6, 90, 101–9,
 116, 117–18, 129, 173, 194
 informal work 4–5, 85, 104,
  107–8, 109, 207
 work weeks 3, 103
world culture 187
world-system 23, 138, 144–7, 210
 core in 145
 criticisms of 146–7
 periphery in 145
 role of the state in 146
 semi-periphery in 145